AF341326

MAD IN U.S.A.

MICHEL DESMURGET

MAD IN U.S.A.
The ravages of the "American model"

Max Milo

Max Milo Editions, Paris, 2023
www.maxmilo.com
ISBN : 978-2-31501-112-4

"Rather than being seduced and anesthetized by the myths of America, we must wake up to its realities."
M.R. Rank

(M.R. Rank, Professor of Sociology, Washington St. Louis University, quoted in One Nation Underprivileged: Why American Poverty Affects Us All, 2005, Oxford, Oxford University Press, p. 253)

Contents

Introduction

I lived in the United States for almost eight years. Since I returned to France in 2006, I have lost count of the number of generous testimonies of compassion: "It must be difficult to come back like this. It's hard here, it's not like in America, but hey, we don't always have a choice." The idea that one could, by simple aspiration, join the Hexagon and Europe seems, in essence, totally inaccessible to the majority of my compatriots. It must be said that the "New World" apparently looks like a splendid land of milk and honey to them: an unparalleled standard of living, remarkable fiscal parsimony, daring entrepreneurs, derisory unemployment, state-of-the-art hospitals, an exemplary educational system, relentless justice, flawless social mobility and the immutable assurance that wealth is given to work rather than to heredity. Of course, this idyllic picture only takes on its true meaning in negative terms, in comparison with the supposedly sclerotic world of our "Old Europe". Our fellow citizens would be crushed by taxes, our companies exhausted by charges, our young people sadly lazy, our unemployment endemic, our health systems decaying, our universities dilapidated, our schools tragic, our justice servile and our social model based on an iniquitous welfare by which the sweat of the productive would feed the laziness of a legion of leeches. "The traps of assistance[1]", "France assisted[2]", "The great anger of the middle classes: downgraded, stunned

1. *Marianne*, n° 513, February 17-23, 2007.
2. *Le Point*, n° 1804, April 12, 2007.

by taxes, disillusioned with growth[3]", could be read in recent months on the front page of several major French weeklies. "For 25 years, everything has been done to discourage work, penalize effort, and discourage merit (...). Those who work sometimes earn less than those who live on welfare," thundered Nicolas Sarkozy during the 2007 presidential campaign[4]. These ideas are so strongly anchored in our collective unconscious that a major car brand recently chose to make them the focus of its advertising campaign: "Entrepreneurs, the state is bleeding you, it is taking everything from you, leaving you with only your eyes to cry at the end of the month; luckily, Fiat is there to understand and help you with prices that are as modest as they are unbeatable[5].

Unfortunately, there is often a gap between myth and fact. The America we hear about all day long is, I fear, a media chimera devoid of substance. "Our" United States is a delusion. Through ignorance or design, we are fed false, not to say felonious, information. It is true that the current climate is not one of subtlety. For politicians and other journalists, the world seems to exist only in its elementary dimensions. There are the good guys and the bad guys, the winners and the losers, the active and the profiteers, the pragmatists and the utopians, the progressives and the nerds. In the heart of this bipolar space, there is no way out, you have to choose sides, perish or adapt. Sad reductionist straitjacket that dissolves reality and offers our consciousness to the heuristic nothingness of the great dichotomies. From philosophy, history and science, we should have learned that the reality of the world is rarely black or white. As Haffner has shown with regard to Nazism[6], it is in the details of individual fortunes that the essence of collective destinies inevitably lies. Nothing exists in the absolute. One cannot proclaim the universal relevance of a model without considering

---

3. *Le Point*, n° 1774, September 14, 2006.
4. French presidential campaign, 2007, campaign leaflet, "La valeur travail", available on the UMP website: http://www.sarkotheque.com/home/index.php
5. Heard on RMC Info at the end of August 2002.
6. Sebastian Haffner, *Histoire d'un Allemand*, Arles, Actes Sud, 2000.

the concrete effects of this model. One cannot elevate a socio-economic thought to the rank of sovereign paradigm without measuring the palpable fruits of this thought. One cannot penetrate the intimate reality of a country without appreciating the material conditions of its inhabitants. These Americans that we idealize to the point of intoxication, how do they live? What about their social system, their schools, their justice system? Is their unemployment as low as they claim? Are their hospitals the best and safest on the planet? Do we want the "American model" to rule our children's lives tomorrow? These are probably questions we should ask ourselves before proclaiming the archaism of our values and the modernity of contemporary America. We might be surprised at the answers we get, as the following few examples show. These examples and the conclusions they inspire will, of course, be amply substantiated in the chapters to come. My purpose here is only to offer the reader a brief taste of the myths that structure our vision of modern America.

Let's start with Nathan and the founding myth. Our man, a restaurant entrepreneur, is both a great adulator of Anglo-Saxon liberalism and an implacable critic of the "welfare state. According to Nathan, only the market can produce abundant and accessible wealth. The opulence of America and its middle class would demonstrate, beyond any doubt, the validity of this assertion. For the benefit of skeptics, Nathan likes to quote Reagan's famous harangue in his first address to the nation in 1981: "In the present crisis, government is not the solution to our problem. Government is the problem[7]." A nice idea, which unfortunately does not hold. The facts clearly show, as Michael Lind coolly summarizes, that "successive American middle classes have been artificially created by government-sponsored social engineering[8]." In other words, it is not the fabled market, but a collective will, instrumentalized by a vigorous state,

---

7. Ronald Reagan, "First Inaugural Address," January 20, 1981, available online: http://www. reaganfoundation.org/reagan/speeches/first.asp

8. Michael Lind, "Are We Still a Middle Class Nation?" in *The Real State of the Union*, T. Halstead (ed.) (New York: Basic Books, 2004), pp. 15-26, quote p. 17.

that is responsible for America's opulence and its middle class[9]. Since the state abandoned the reins of the economy to the sacrosanct "market," the indicators have largely gone awry. Despite Nathan's comments, it is no longer a tendency to become richer, but rather a trend towards the impoverishment of the middle and lower classes that has been measured over the past 30 years in the United States[10]. In 1970, a skilled worker's salary was enough to keep an American household in the middle class. Now it takes two incomes for an overwhelming majority of households to achieve the same result. And still; these two wages leave families (in constant dollars) with less discretionary income than the 1970 single wage[11]. Since 1997, the minimum wage has been frozen at $5.15/hr (~ 4 euros[12]) in the United States. Between 1979 and 2005, a poor male worker (30% of the lowest paid) saw his wage fall by an average of almost 10% in constant dollars. The punishment was "only" 5% for a median worker. The most advantaged workers (top 5% of earners) saw a 30% increase[13]. Europe and France are still far from such a panorama, there is no denying it. Nathan and the liberal zealots can rest assured, however, that the number of indigent workers is beginning to increase on the old continent[14] and

---

9. John Iceland, *Poverty in America: a handbook* (Berkeley: University of California Press, 2006), 2nd ed. at 118-126; Tamara Draut, *Strapped: Why America's 20 - and 30 - Somethings Can't Get Ahead* (New York: Doubleday, 2006), at 30-35.

10. M. Lind, "Are We Still a Middle Class Nation?" in *The Real State of the Union, op. cit.* (*supra*, n. 8); T. Draut, *Strapped...*, *op. cit.* (*supra*, n. 9); Mark Robert Rank, *One Nation Underprivileged: Why American Poverty Affects Us All* (Oxford: Oxford University Press, 2005), pp. 24-25; Beth Shulman, *The Betrayal of Work: How Low-Wage Jobs Fail 30 Million Americans* (New York: The New Press, 2003), p. 121; Elizabeth Warren & Amelia Warren Tyagi, *The Two Income Trap: Why Middle-Class Mothers and Fathers Are Going Broke* (New York: Basic Books, 2003)

11. Elizabeth Warren & Amelia Warren Tyagi, *The Two Income Trap, op. cit.* (*supra*, n. 10).

12. In this book, euro-dollar conversions are calculated on the basis of 1 euro to 1.3 dollars. This value corresponds approximately to the average rate over the last two years; the current rate (January 2008) is 1 euro for 1.47 dollar; data available: http://fr.finance.yahoo.com/q/bc?s=EURUSD=X&t=2y&l=off&z=m&q=b&c=

13. *The State of Working America 2006-2007*, Advanced Proofs, Economic Policy Institute, 2007, Ithaca (NY), Cornell University Press, table 3.5.

14. Jacques Cotta, *7 millions de travailleurs pauvres*, Paris, Fayard, 2006.

14

our middle classes are slowly sliding into poverty[15]. The market is finally penetrating our skies.

Margot doesn't like the State either. As an employee of a large airline company, she is tired of working to support a cohort of unproductive civil servants and welfare recipients. Like Ted Stanger[16], she thinks that, as in America, taxes and the number of government employees should be reduced. However, Margot seems to miss a few important points in her enthusiasm. First, to subscribe to the American model is to accept a system of taxation and tax benefits that outrageously favours the wealthiest at the expense of the poorest[17]. Second, it means agreeing to transfer the burden of public services from the collective sphere to the private domain. Everything that escapes taxation then necessarily falls to the individual. In practice, this means that individual prosperity becomes the main factor of access to certain essential "goods" such as health, justice or education. In the United States, millions of unfortunate people receive an undignified education, and "the denial of the 'means to compete' is perhaps the most consistent result of the education offered to poor children.[18]" Similarly, the extent of the sentences handed down by the courts depends largely on the financial means of the accused and his or her ability to afford private counsel for a given crime[19]. In Texas, for example, a poor person is three times more likely to be sentenced to the electric chair for a blood crime than a wealthy person[20]. In the area of health care, 100 million Americans

---

15. Louis Chauvel, *Les Classes moyennes à la dérive*, Paris, Le Seuil, 2006.

16. Ted Stanger, *Sacrés fonctionnaires*, Paris, Michalon, 2006.

17. Maya MacGuineas, "Radical Tax Reform," in *The Real State of the Union, op. cit.* (*supra*, n. 8) at 51-62.

18. J. Kozol, *Savage Inequalities* (New York: Harper Collins, 1992), p. 83.

19. Jeffrey Reiman, *The Rich Get Richer and the Poor Get Prison: Ideology, Class, and the Criminal Justice* (Boston: Allyn and Bacon, 2001); Ken Armstrong, Florangela Davila & Justin Mayo, "An Unequal Defense: the Failed Promise of Justice For the Poor," *Seattle Times*, 3-part report, April 4-6, 2004.

20. *David R. Dow, Executed On a Technicality: Lethal Injustice on America's Death Row (Boston: Beacon Press, 2005), p. 8.*

have inadequate coverage (1 in 3)[21]. For 47 million individuals, this deficiency actually signals a complete lack of coverage[22]. In the words of a major recently published research study, being without coverage means "unnecessary deaths, untreated illnesses, casual management of chronic conditions, medical debt and bankruptcy, and the need to use alcohol as a substitute for effective pain management[23]." In other words, millions of human beings are paying in their flesh and blood for the fiscal restraint of their rulers. Of all the OECD countries, America has the lowest life expectancy (22nd)[24] and the highest infant mortality rate (23rd)[25]. Twice as many newborns die in the United States as in France, Norway, Sweden, or Japan[26]. For those Americans fortunate enough to have access to care, the sacrosanct market translates into exploding costs and dramatically reduced efficiency[27]. These poor performances are not specific to the health sector. Attempts to privatize the education system have also revealed a strong tendency towards functional inefficiency and financial waste[28]. The

---

21. D.L. Barlett & J.B. Steele, *Critical Condition* (New York: Broadway Books, 2006); Susan S. Sered & Rushika Fernandopulle, *Uninsured in America: Life & Death in the Land of Opportunity* (Berkeley: University of California press, 2005).

22. Carmen DeNavas-Walt, Bernadette D. Proctor & Cheryl Hill Lee, *Income, Poverty, and Health Insurance Coverage in the United States*, Bureau of Census, Report P60-231, table C-1, 2005, available online: http://www.census.gov/prod/2006pubs/p60-231.pdf

23. S.S. Sered & R. Fernandopulle, *Uninsured in America...*, *op. cit.* (*supra*, n. 21), cover abstract.

24. OECD, 2000 figures, available online: http://www.oecd.org/dataoecd/7/42/35530071.xls

25. OECD, 2003 figures, available online: http://www.oecd.org/dataoecd/7/41/35530083.xls

26. *Ibid.*

27. D.L. Barlett & J.B. Steele, *Critical Condition, op. cit.* (*supra*, n. 21); S.S. Sered & R. Fernandopulle, *Uninsured in America...*, *op. cit.* (*supra*, n. 21); R. Kuttner, "Must Good HMOs Go Bad?", Part 1, *The New England Journal of Medicine*, 1998, 338, pp. 1558-1563; R. Kuttner, "Must Good HMOs Go Bad?", Part 2, *The New England Journal of Medicine*, 1998, 338, pp. 1635-1639; S. Woolhandler, T. Campbell & D.U. Himmelstein, "Costs of Health Care Administration in the United States and Canada," *The New England Journal of Medicine*, 349, pp. 768-775.

28. *A. Molnar,* Giving Kids the Business: The Commercialization of America's Schools, *Boulder: CO, Westview Press, 1996.*

pious myth, so often uttered, of the private sector "doing better with less[29] " seems to have its limits.

Like Margot and Nathan, Bernard-Henri Lévy loves America. He loves it so much that he has decided to "go on the ground, to judge on the spot", to "oppose to the chimera the body and the face of the concrete America of today[30] ". This is a noble approach, the result of which seems to me to be especially relevant to the issues we are dealing with here. Unfortunately, I fear that Bernard-Henri Lévy's crossed America is as deceptive as Margot or Nathan's fantasized America. By running too fast, one often misses the essence of things, a bit like those Parisian motorists, irascible contempors of the old Lugdunum, which they only cross on the road of their vacations through a clogged tunnel and a hideous industrial corridor. In his trip report, Bernard-Henri Lévy informs us, on the basis of Guy Sorman's writings and a conversation with Tracy, a waitress at the Grand Junction motel restaurant, that "the American social security system exists", that it "covers most of the active population" and that "social spending per capita is about equal to what it is in most European countries, including France[31] ". BHL, as he is often called, then tells us "that one is poor in the United States below the threshold of an annual income - $19,300 [about 14,850 euros] - which in a country like France would correspond rather to that of a modest wage earner[32] ". Tracy's ex-husband is presented to us as an apparently typical case[33]. A former miner who has been depressed for eight years, he no longer works but receives 60% of his former salary from the state and his company, i.e. $2,000 per month (about 1,550 euros). In addition to this subsidy, our man would be covered by the Medicare and Medicaid health programs, he would receive food aid in the form of monthly vouchers (food stamps) and he would live in social housing

---

29. Myth still developed today in a news program on a major French national radio station, "Les grandes gueules", RMC, November 22, 2006, 11 am - 2 pm.

30. Bernard-Henri Lévy, *American Vertigo*, Paris, Grasset, 2006, p. 19.

31. *Ibid*, p. 204.

32. *Ibid*, pp. 394-395.

33. *Ibid*, p. 202.

Introduction

with largely subsidized rent. A rather generous and efficient coverage. In any case, Mr. Levy tells us, "half - if not two-thirds - of the 37 million American 'poor' are destined not to remain poor and own their homes[34]. The others, the only real poor, are "exsanguinated beings", "wrecks" for whom "the very idea of having a roof over their heads or of one day finding a job has only the consistency of mirages[35]". In short, in the United States, the poor are not so poor as all that, the social safety net is as generous as in Western Europe (or even more so) and the only truly miserable people are vagrants excluded from the world and from work.

I have great respect for Bernard-Henri Lévy and his often remarkable work. However, a few clarifications are necessary with respect to the preceding sentences. First of all, poor Americans would surely be delighted to have the standard of living of "modest Europeans". The proposed poverty line of $19,300 is for families of four in 2004. The figure was then less than half for an individual considered alone ($9,645 or 7,400 euros)[36]. It is probably important to point out that 43% of the 37 million poor Americans actually live on an income that does not exceed half the poverty line[37]. In other words, about 5.5 percent of the U.S. population, or 16 million people, live in what is officially called "extreme poverty.[38] Near poverty" (125% of the official poverty line) affects 50 million people, or nearly 17% of the population[39]. For those who find it difficult to imagine what these figures mean, it may be interesting to point out that 50 million souls is more than

---

34. *Ibid*, p. 395.

35. *Ibid*.

36. US Census Bureau, Internet Release, 2006, http://www.census.gov/hhes/www/poverty/threshld/thresh04.html

37. US Census Bureau, Internet Release, 2006, http://www.census.gov/hhes/www/poverty/histpov/hstpov22.html and http://www.census.gov/hhes/www/poverty/poverty05/pov-05fig04.pdf

38. US Census Bureau, Internet Release, 2006, http://www.census.gov/hhes/www/poverty/histpov/hstpov22.html

39. US Census Bureau, Internet Release, 2006, http://www.census.gov/hhes/www/poverty/histpov/hstpov6.html

the population of Spain. It is five times the population of Belgium[40]. A family of four living at the poverty line has a little less than $1.50 for each of its members and for each meal[41]. For 16 million people, the figure is around 70 cents (less than 55 euro cents). Faced with such an extravagant figure, it is of course reassuring to think that poverty only affects those who are "adrift". However widespread this myth may be[42], it is unfortunately wrong: 37% of the poor over 16 years of age are working; 12% even have a full-time job[43]. In total, 25 percent of American wage earners are trapped in low-wage occupations. This is twice as many as in France or Germany and five times as many as in Sweden[44]. These "working poor" are indeed destined to leave their condition. Unfortunately, they never get very far and their journey does not go beyond, in most cases, the periphery of a poverty into which they cyclically fall back[45]. Their children, for the most part, suffer the same fate[46]. America has long since ceased to be the land of all possibilities. We

---

40. European Union, website, 2006, http://europa.eu/abc/keyfigures/index_fr.htm

41. *M.R. Rank,* One Nation Underprivileged..., op. cit. *(supra, n. 10) at 23.*

42. J. Iceland, *Poverty in America..., op. cit. (supra,* n. 9), at 3-4; William O'Hare, "A new look at poverty in America," *Population Bulletin* 1996, 51, at 1-48.

43. US Census Bureau, Internet Release, 2006, http://www.census.gov/hhes/www/poverty/histpov/hstpov18.html

44. Timothy M. Smeeding, Lee Rainwater & Gary Burtless, "United States Poverty in a Cross-National Context," *Luxembourg Income Study, Working Paper Series,* 2000, No. 244, Maxwell School of citizenship and public affairs, Syracuse University, Syracuse, NY.

45. Ann Huff Stevens, "Climbing out of Poverty, Falling Back In: Measuring the Persistence of Poverty over Multiple Spells," *Journal of Human Resources,* 1999, 34, pp. 557-588; Fredrik Andersson, Harry J. Holzer & Julia I. Lane, *Moving Up or Moving On: Who Advances in the Low-Wage Labor Market?* (New York: Russell Sage Foundation, 2005); M.R. Rank, *One Nation Underprivileged? (supra,* n. 10), pp. 94-95; J. Iceland, *Poverty in America..., op. cit. (supra,* n. 9), pp. 48-49.

46. B. Shulman, *The Betrayal of Work..., op. cit. (supra,* n. 10), pp. 82-89; Alison Aughinbaugh, "Reapplication and extension: intergenerational mobility in the United States," *Labour Economics,* 2000, 7, pp. 785-796; Peter Gottschalk & Sheldon Danziger, "Income Mobility and Exits from Poverty of American Children," *in* B. Bradbury, S. Jenkins & J. Micklewright (eds.), *The Dynamics of Child Poverty in Industrialized Countries* (Cambridge, UK: Cambridge University Press, 2001), pp. 135-153; Gary Solon, "Intergenerational mobility in the United States," *American Economic Review,* 1992, 82, pp. 393-408; Lawrence Mishel, Jared Bernstein & Sylvia Allegretto, *The State of Working America 2006-2007,* supra, n.13. *(supra,* n. 13), see chap. 2.

still believe this because, as psychologists and other advertisers know, a few tangible and concrete individual examples impress our reason much more than a mass reality with an abstract taste[47]. We also believe it because this tale is repeated to us, day after day, in a recurrent way. As President George W. Bush pointed out, for example, not long ago: "You bet, that people who work hard and make the right decisions in life can achieve anything they want in America[48]." An idea shared, moreover, by Nicolas Sarkozy, recently elected president of the French Republic and solemnly declaring, "Yes, I love Americans, I love their energy... I love the fact that anything is possible[49]." This omnipotence would illuminate even the most unexpected areas of our daily lives. Thus, for example, "in the United States, bars and restaurants are full of apprentice actors, whose high expectations do not prevent them from doing their job with a smile, while waiting for glory. Back home [in France], it's more tense and vengeful, because social mobility is less[50]. Unfortunately, the numbers are stubborn and "although it is surely possible for someone to rise from rags to riches, this tends to be the exception rather than the rule[51]. In America, the poor have a very unfortunate habit of remaining poor from year to year and from father to son. Of all developed countries, the United States has the lowest inter-generational social mobility[52].

One could argue, on the basis of Bernard-Henri Lévy's assertions, that poverty does exist, but that the American social system is generous enough to offer the indigent an acceptable standard of living. This is not the case. As I have already said, 47 million people do not have health cove-

---

47. Barry Schwartz, "The Paradox of Choice: Why More is Less," *First Ecco Paperback Edition*, 2005, New York, Harper Collins, pp. 56-61.
48. Quoted in Richard A. Oppel Jr. in *New York Times*, December 18, 2000, p. A19.
49. Quoted in *Marianne*, September 16-22, 2006, p. 8.
50. Service less and less understood, *ISA* (women's magazine), January 2008, p. 147.
51. M.R. Rank, *One Nation Underprivileged...*, *op. cit.* (*supra*, n. 10) at 70. Rank uses the phrase "rags to riches" here. This expression, translated as "from rags to riches", has no equivalent in French. It translates into English as a rapid passage from poverty to wealth. This idea is so dear to the Americans that they have even integrated it into their semantic space.
52. The State of Working America 2006-2007, op. cit. (supra, *n. 13), see chap. 2.*

rage[53]. The vast majority of these individuals come from disadvantaged households with incomes below twice the poverty line[54]. When it comes to assessing the capacity of social systems to address poverty, Uncle Sam's country comes last in the West[55]. In fact, of all the industrialized countries, America has the greatest wealth, the largest percentage of poor people[56] and the least generous welfare system[57]. As John Iceland summarizes in the preamble to his seminal work on poverty in America, "while the United States has virtually the world's highest per capita gross national product, it has higher levels of absolute and relative poverty than other wealthy countries in Northern and Western Europe[58]. This difference is expressed even when US measurement standards are applied[59]. It persists "because many occupations, including full-time ones, pay low wages and because government support is lower[60]. Poor Americans do not live like modest Europeans. As Paul Krugman, the distinguished Princeton economics professor and *New York Times* columnist, has masterfully demonstrated, they do not even live like poor Europeans[61]. The social assistance granted to the poor does not allow them, in the majority of cases, to escape from

---

53. *C. DeNavas-Walt, B.D. Proctor & C.H. Lee,* Income, Poverty, and Health Insurance Coverage, op. cit. (supra, *n. 22).*

54. "Who Are the Uninsured? A Consistent Profile across National Surveys," Kaiser Commission on Medicaid and the Uninsured, Washington, DC, August 2006, available online: http://www.kff.org/uninsured/upload/7553.pdf

55. Veli-Matti Ritakallio, "Trends of Poverty and Income Inequality in Cross-National Comparisons," *Luxembourg Income Study, Working Paper Series,* 2001, No. 272, Maxwell School of Citizenship and Public Affairs, Syracuse University, Syracuse, NY.

56. T.M. Smeeding, L. Rainwater & G. Burtless, "United States Poverty in a Cross-National Context," *op. cit. (supra,* n. 44); *United Nations Development Programme,* UNDP Poverty Report 2000 (New York: United Nations Publications, 2000); *The State of Working America 2006-2007, op. cit. (supra,* n. 13), especially table 8-17.

57. *M.R. Rank,* One Nation Underprivileged..., op. cit. (supra, *n. 10), at 60-62; J. Iceland,* Poverty in America..., op. cit. (supra, *n. 9), at 65.*

58. *Ibid,* p. 7.

59. *Ibid,* p. 146.

60. *Ibid,* p. 65.

61. Paul Krugman, "For Richer," *New York Times,* October 20, 2002, available online: http://www.pkarchive.org/economy/ForRicher.html

abject poverty[62]. This inadequacy does not prevent some noble souls from calling for the abolition of these aids on the grounds that they push the poor into laziness[63] and alter the proper functioning of the market[64]. The poor, that awful leech-like profiteer, is indeed much more "flexible" and "motivated" when he is starving and his children are cold. In a remark that he is famous for, the inimitable Ted Stanger stated that in France, social assistance "undermines the energy and imagination, the creativity of the country. For example, if Baudelaire were alive today, he would probably be on welfare. Would he have written *Les Fleurs du mal*? I don't think so. He would have been more concerned with getting more help, which is quite possible. And like that, he would not have had the time nor the imagination nor the artistic suffering to do his poems[65]. No comment!

Tracy's ex-husband, of whom Bernard-Henri Lévy speaks, seems to me, at best, to represent a very singular epiphenomenon. In fact, the relevance of this case is difficult to determine in the absence of additional information: does this man have children, has he remarried, does his wife work, has he contributed during his active life to a pension system subsidized by his employer or the federal government, etc.? 2,000 can be 2.5 or 0.6 times the official poverty line depending on whether you live alone or are the sole source of income for a family of 9[66]. I believe that we must be all the more circumspect here since many studies and testimonies underline, not the solidarity, but the extreme harshness of the American economic model. For those who doubt this point, I cannot recommend enough the

---

62. J. Iceland, *Poverty in America...*, *op. cit.* (*supra*, n. 9), at 130-132; M.R. Rank, *One Nation Underprivileged...*, *op. cit.* (*supra*, n. 10), pp. 60-62.
63. See, for example, Charles Murray, *Losing Ground: American Social Policy, 1950-1980*, New York, Basic Books, 1984. In France, Nicolas Baverez, *Que faire : Agenda 2007*, 2006, Paris, Perrin, chapter 4.
64. See, for example, A. Lindbeck, P. Molander, T. Persson, O. Petersson, A. Sandmo, B. Swedenborg & N. Thygesen, *Turning Sweden Around*, Cambridge (MA), MIT Press, 1994.
65. Ted Stanger, invited by Sophie Larmoyer, *in* " Carnets du Monde ", Europe 1, October 1st 2006.
66. US Census Bureau, Internet Release, 2006, http://www.census.gov/hhes/www/poverty/threshld/thresh05.html

excellent book in which Barbara Ehrenreich describes, with a rare talent, her immersion in the America of the working poor[67]. Far from the hackneyed stereotypes, the author makes us discover a brutal world, populated not by drunks and slackers, but by productive and moving humans, eviscerated on the altar of profit. These paupers are paid such miserable wages that they can't even feed or house themselves[68]. Of course, one might say that this only happens to others, the ignorant, the incompetent, the backward. Michelle Kennedy may have thought so from her middle-class position, until a divorce pushed her into poverty, forcing her to live with her three children in a car parked in the parking lot of the restaurant where she had finally found a job as a waitress. Despite earning, at best, two-thirds of Tracy's husband's income including tips, Michelle was denied all her welfare claims[69]. Caroline was more fortunate. However, she had to *voluntarily* remove her last few good teeth in order to meet Medicaid requirements and obtain funding for braces. The resulting prosthesis proved to be poorly designed and unusable. Caroline was offered a repair, but at a price she could not afford[70].

The case of Donna and Jack is a little different. They worked as waitresses and cooks. However, they had no social security coverage, as is often the case for low-wage professions. When Donna became ill, she underwent surgery in Fort Myers and received a bill for $57,000. When the couple was unable to pay the debt, the hospital sued. Donna and Jack lost their home and everything they owned[71]. The same thing happened to Suzanne Gibbons. The 58-year-old nurse had health insurance, but it covered only a portion of her costs. After a stroke and heart condition, Suzanne was left

---

67. Barbara Ehrenreich, *Nickel and Dimed: On (Not) Getting By in America*, New York, First Owl Books Edition, 2002.
68. See also David K. Shipler, *The Working Poor: Invisible in America* (New York: Vintage Books, 2005).
69. *Michelle Kennedy,* Without a Net: Middle Class and Homeless (with Kids) in America *(New York: Penguin Books, 2005) at 94.*
70. D.K. Shipler, *The Working Poor...*, *op. cit.* (*supra*, n. 68) at 52.
71. D.L. Barlett & J.B. Steele, *Critical Condition, op. cit.* (*supra*, n. 21) at 22.

Introduction

with tens of thousands of dollars in uncovered debt. She lost her home and was declared personally bankrupt in 2001[72]. As Steffie Woolhandler, a member of a group of Harvard researchers who recently published a study on the shortcomings of health coverage in the United States[73], humorously puts it, "We found that, too often, private insurance is an umbrella that melts in the rain.[74]

In practice, while hospitals generally refuse to treat the truly indigent, they eagerly track down the assets of their indebted middle and lower class patients (houses, salaries, savings, etc.)[75]. This effort is all the more lucrative when applied to uninsured individuals. Indeed, the latter are often charged prohibitive rates that are out of all proportion to those offered to insurance companies[76]. For a heart bypass operation, for example, the latter will pay between $55,000 and $60,000. The uninsured patient will see this range explode to between $123,000 and $177,000. The law of supply and demand, no doubt.

In an edifying book on the state of the American health care system, Barlett and Steele report the extravagant case of a patient who underwent surgery for a cyst on the back of his neck at a Catholic hospital with the gentle name of "Lady of the Resurrection Medical Center[77]". The patient received a bill for $74,396. The same operation would apparently have cost an insurance company $6,900, 10 times less! When our man was unable to pay the bill, the hospital obtained a very Catholic wage garnishment of

---

72. Bonnie Miller Rubin, "Medical Bills Pave Way to Poorhouse, Study Says: Many Bankruptcies Linked to Illness," *Chicago Tribune*, February 2, 2005.

73. David U. Himmelstein, Elizabeth Warren, Deborah Thorne & Steffie Woolhandler, *MarketWatch: Illness And Injury As Contributors To Bankruptcy*, Health Affairs, Project HOPE - The People-to-People Health Foundation, *February 2005*, available online: http://content. healthaffairs.org/cgi/content/full/hlthaff.w5,63/DC1

74. Steffie Woolhandler, quoted in Bonnie Miller Rubin, "Medical Bills Pave Way to Poorhouse...," *op. cit. (supra*, n. 72).

75. D.L. Barlett & J.B. Steele, *Critical Condition, op. cit. (supra*, n. 21) at 15-24.

76. "Outsourcing Your Heart," *Time*, May 29, 2006, pp. 44-47; D.L. Barlett & J.B. Steele, *Critical Condition, op. cit. (supra*, n. 21), pp. 15-24.

77. D.L. Barlett & J.B. Steele, *Critical Condition, op. cit. (supra*, n. 21) at 18-19.

$300 per month. If we forget the interest, this patient will need 20 years to pay his debt. Including interest at a rate of 15%, which for the American market is relatively low, a lifetime of repayment will not be enough to get our man back on track. At that rate, a $300 monthly payment doesn't even cover the interest. Three hundred dollars in perpetuity sounds like a sentence of eternal misery for an already poor worker. The hospital will gain a few bandages. There are no small profits in liberal lands.

Cured but ruined; not everyone is so lucky. When letters containing anthrax arrived in Congress in 2001, members of that institution were promptly evacuated, tested and placed on antibiotics. The black employees of the sorting center through which the letters passed were treated somewhat differently. They were not tested and treated until after they had experienced two deaths. One of these deaths was denied a prescription for antibiotics by his insurance company[78]. In the United States, it is not the doctors but the insurers who make the final decision on care[79]. I don't know if there is a relationship, but it is striking that the poorest people in this country live 9 years less than the richest[80]. Similarly, it is startling to observe that the infant mortality rate is 5.8/1,000 for children of white mothers, but 14.6/1,000 for children of black mothers[81]. On a more general level, nearly 20,000 human beings would die each year in America from being too indigent to be cared for[82]. This is 6 times the number of victims of the September 11, 2001 attacks (3,034)[83]. It is also

---

78. D.K. Shipler, *The Working Poor...*, *op. cit.* (*supra*, n. 68) at 209.
79. D.L. Barlett & J.B. Steele, *Critical Condition*, *op. cit.* (*supra*, n. 21), pp. 161-189.
80. Christopher Jencks, "Does Inequality Matter," *Daedalus* 2002, 131, pp. 49-65, p. 61.
81. Center for Disease Control and Prevention, "Infant Mortality Rates, Fetal Mortality Rates, and Perinatal Mortality Rates, According to Race," *United States, selected years, 1950-1999*, National Center for Health Statistics, Health Data, 2001, table 23, http://www.cdc.gov/nchs/data/hus/tables/2001/01hus023.pdf
82. Shannon Brownlee, "The Overtreated American," in *The Real State of the Union*, op. cit. (*supra*, n. 8), pp. 129-138, see p. 129; D.L. Barlett & J.B. Steele, *Critical Condition*, *op. cit.* (*supra*, n. 21), p. 3.
83. P. Grangereau, " Bush faithful to his divine mission ", *Libération*, 23 August 2006, p. 11.

the equivalent of a city like Lons-Le-Saunier, razed annually from the face of the earth for the crime of poverty.

In light of the above, I think we can question our propensity to see the American socio-economic system as a universal panacea. Is this really the model we want to import to Europe? Are we ready to accept that thousands of people die every year because they are too poor to access the health care system? Are we ready to park our least privileged children in educational ghettos of such mediocrity that one wonders if the institutions concerned still deserve the title of school? Are we really, as we often hear, "behind the times", "in decline", prostrate in "refusing to adapt to the new situation resulting from globalization and the fall of the Soviet empire", "stuck in the sanctuary of [our] pseudo social model[84] "? Perhaps, but let me not only doubt it, but also hope that everyone will take the time to reflect on these questions. They seem to merit even more sustained attention, given that the researchers, sociologists and journalists who have studied the failings of the American model mostly recommend surprisingly European solutions (universal social coverage, a minimum wage indexed to inflation, federalized education, etc.)[85]. Perhaps we are not so far behind after all.

Before I close these few introductory words, I would like to make it clear that I am in no way a member of the sad column of visceral and primary anti-Americans. I have lived in the United States for nearly eight years. My daughter, born in this country, is American. I was educated at MIT in Boston, Emory University in Atlanta and the University of California in San Francisco. My father fought for four years alongside GIs he saw "fall on the beaches of Sicily and the slopes of Cassino. He never stopped teaching me to respect these men and their values. In 1945, my mother, a German, desperate about the Nazi madness, welcomed the arrival of

---

84. N. Baverez, " Japon, Allemagne, France, le fossé de la réforme ", *Le Point*, n° 1722, 15 September 2005, p. 35.

85. *M.R. Rank*, One Nation Underprivileged..., op. cit. (supra, *n. 10*); *D.K. Shipler*, The Working Poor..., op. cit. (supra, *n. 68*); *B. Shulman*, The Betrayal of Work..., op. cit. (supra, *n. 10*); *S.S. Sered & R. Fernandopulle*, Uninsured in America..., op. cit. (supra, *n. 21*).

the "Boys" as a blessing. Six decades later, that "liberation" still evoked sincere tears of gratitude in her. I know what I owe to the United States as a European and as a unique individual. This country has taken me in and adopted me, and I love it like a second family. This love, however, is not without its clouds. Contemporary America has, I believe, lost part of its soul. By affirming the primacy of the "market" over the state, it has, it seems to me, sacrificed its humanistic foundations for the sake of more obscure individualistic values, whose poisonous fruits are called pauperization, indifference, profit, brutality and (in many cases) barbarity. To my dismay, I fear that it is these fruits, beyond our self-righteous views, that some are trying to impose in Europe under the guise of liberalism, economic competition or globalization. Perhaps the critics of "old Europe" are right. Perhaps our social models must be abolished in favor of a mindless economic Darwinism. Perhaps we should, as the editorialist of a major American newspaper recently proposed, stop all food aid to the poorest people on the nauseating pretext that this leads them to laziness and obesity[86]. Perhaps we should accept that millions of people working hard, full time, have no social security coverage, no paid leave, no maternity leave, no health insurance and an annual salary below the poverty line[87]. Everyone should decide for themselves. For my part, I have discovered throughout an 8-year journey the truth of the Prodigal Son: the grass is not always greener elsewhere. Paradoxically, America taught me how beautiful Western Europe was with its humanist tradition, its generous taxes and its luxuriant public services. Of course, not everything is perfect on the "old continent". Reforms are undoubtedly needed to save our social systems, overcome exclusion, rediscover a new collective solidarity and dissolve unemployment. However, it would be madness to let a media chimera

---

86. Mona Charen, "American Poor Are Getting Fat and Lazy on Governments Handouts," *St. Louis Post-Dispatch*, January 27, 2003, Section B, p. 7.

87. *J. Iceland,* Poverty in America..., op. cit. *(supra, n. 9); The State of Working America 2006-2007, op. cit. (supra, n. 13); B. Shulman,* The Betrayal of Work..., op. cit. *(supra, n. 10); D.K. Shipler,* The Working Poor..., op. cit. supra, *n. 68).*

dictate these reforms. I know of no place in the world where people live better than in Western Europe. I hope that this message will gain some audibility with those who have not had the chance to cross the Atlantic to judge for themselves the reality of an America that we fantasize about but know so little about. My greatest fear would be, I admit, that our ignorance would allow the socio-economic brutality of the "new world" to sweep over our children, more than it has already done. May Europe protect them from this disaster by preserving its soul and its values.

CHAPTER 1
WORK: THE REAL LAW OF THE MARKET

Marc works in real estate. He would like to recruit "one or two people", but the costs seem too high and the administrative burden too dissuasive. In particular, Marc fears that he will not be able to lay off employees "when the economy turns around". For him, the hundreds of pages of the Labor Code are a Kafkaesque nightmare, a veritable Maginot line erected on the road to employment. To make matters worse, "our" unemployed are, for the most part, "professional welfare recipients who have no interest in looking for a job and make ends meet by working under the table". In the last presidential elections, Marc chose to vote, "out of disgust for these iniquitous practices", for a far-right party that he says he has hated all his life. He plans to do as a friend who was driven to the United States by disgust. There, "they don't help the lazy", the government "takes care of its business" and the unemployment rate remains confined "under 5%".

Marc is right about at least one thing. Jobs are easy to find in the United States. You can't walk down a shopping street without encountering a merchant looking for labor. "Help wanted" is a constant and imperative message. That it is in Florida, in Maine or Minnesota, it took only some days to Barbara Ehrenreich to find, not one, but several jobs[88]. In the same way, when Thierry left Paris to do his post-doctoral training in Georgia, he thought he was condemning his wife to unemployment. Futile apprehen-

---

88. *B. Ehrenreich,* Nickel and Dimed: On (Not) Getting By in America, op. cit. *(Introd., n. 67).*

sion. Despite her stubbornly poor English, it took her only one afternoon to find a job as a cleaning lady in a luxury hotel. After three months, she was fired without notice or compensation. Within a week she was working again, in a nursing home.

Faced with such examples, it is difficult to deny Marc's sourness. In contrast to our "administered economy", the American model seems to be a prodigious machine for producing employment. Nicolas Baverez, described by *L'Express as* "the best essayist in France[89]", has not been wrong. In his latest book, this author forcefully asserts the virtues of the American liberal model[90]. France must adapt or perish under the yoke of an inexorable decline. In the course of his words, we learn that "the urban riots that devastated three hundred French cities during the three weeks of November 2005 (...) testify to the failure of the American model of social justice.) testify to the failure of the French pseudo social model[91]", that French cicadas work 384 hours less each year than American ants (i.e. 11 weeks of 35 hours)[92], that "the increase of one point in the minimum wage causes the loss of 15,000 jobs[93]", that "the best weapon against poverty is work[94]", that "the limitation of access to higher education to 38% of an age group and the selection by failure of 44% of students contribute to unemployment and the shortage of qualified labour[95]", that "the welfare system today strongly discourages activity[96]", and that in the United States a welfare reform based on a system of negative taxes for the working poor and a time limit on federal assistance (5 years in a lifetime) have since 1996 "produced excellent results since the number of families in great distress has fallen from 5 to 1.9 million, bringing the poverty rate down from

---

89. *L'Express*, n° 2880, 14-20 September 2006, p. 62.
90. N. Baverez, *What to do: Agenda 2007, op. cit.* (Introd., n. 63).
91. *Ibid.* at 117-118.
92. *Ibid*, p. 123.
93. *Ibid.*
94. *Ibid*, p. 132.
95. *Ibid*, p. 127.
96. *Ibid*, p. 130.

15.1% to 11.3%[97]". To best accompany this reform, "specific financial and educational support programs for poor children" were launched[98].

What can we say in the face of these "obvious" facts?

What can we say about this strange selectivity that forgets that "our" riots looked like an amiable procession of choirboys compared to the scenes of war that struck, for example, Miami, Los Angeles, or Cincinnati?

What can we say about this apology for a socio-economic model that in the United States burdens millions of poor people and ineluctably impoverishes a middle class that has been painfully established by the will of a vigorous state[99]?

What can we say about these American ants who work more than the French, Germans, Dutch or Danes, but only to neutralize the devastating effects of a liberalism which, for 30 years, has caused the costs of education, health and housing to skyrocket[100]?

What can we say about this incomprehensible blindness that condemns a priori any increase in the minimum wage and affirms that work remains in the liberal world a bulwark against misery, while millions of individuals working full time live in indigence and remain confined under the poverty line[101]?

What can we say about this terrible cynicism that discerns inactivity as the mark of indolence when unemployment is mainly the result of the structural bankruptcy of a job market structured like a game of musical chairs[102]?

---

97. *Ibid*, p. 132.
98. *Ibid*.
99. For a detailed discussion, see within this section: "Anna: At the Heart of Reality"; "Poverty: And Yet They Work".
100. *Ibid.* and, within the second section: "Health: Pay or Die"; "School: Better Rich and Dumb than Poor and Bright.
101. For a detailed discussion, see within this section: "Anna: At the Heart of Reality"; "Poverty: And Yet They Work".
102. For a detailed discussion, see within this section: "Causality: A Structural Failure".

What about the incredible legend that sees higher education as a cure for unemployment when the economy overwhelmingly creates underpaid, unskilled jobs[103]?

What can we say about these mysterious financial and educational support programs when we know that the American State contributes only marginally to the financing of schools (8%[104]) and that there are proportionally more children in poverty in the United States, after taking into account various social aids, than in any other developed nation[105]?

What about these oversimplifications that praise a reform without seeing, for example, its devastating effects on millions of single mothers who are pushed into poverty-stricken jobs far from home, to the direct detriment of children they have no way to care for (let alone educate)? After a documented and extensive study of this famous 1996 reform, Alan Weil and Kenneth Finegold conclude that "many of those who find work lose other supports intended to help them, such as food stamps and health insurance, leaving them no better off - and often worse off - than they were when they were not working[106]". In the United States, 15% of single mother families with children live below the poverty line, while the mother works full time - or more[107]!

Finally, what can we say about these impressive figures, which are not sourced anywhere and which seem quite unusual in relation to the official measures of the Bureau of Census[108]? The number of families in extreme poverty, i.e., with incomes below 50 percent of the poverty line, was

---

103. *Ibid.*

104. For a detailed discussion, see in the second section: "School: Better to be rich and stupid than poor and brilliant".

105. For a detailed discussion, see within this section: "Hugo: cursed from father to son".

106. Alan Weil & Kenneth Finegold, *Welfare Reform: the Next Act* (Washington, DC: Urban Institute Press, 2002), Introduction; see also Robert Moffitt, "From Welfare to Work: What the Evidence Shows," *Brookings Institution Policy*, January 2002, Brief No. 13.

107. US Census Bureau, Internet Release, 2006, http://pubdb3.census.gov/macro/032006/pov/new07_100_01.htm

108. US Census Bureau, Internet Release, 2006, http://www.census.gov/hhes/www/poverty/poverty.html

7.532, 7.708, 7.324, and 7.835 million in 1995, 1996, 1997, and 2004, respectively. This brings us, in percentage terms, from 10.8 percent to 10.2 percent[109]. The overall poverty rate, meanwhile, fell from 13.8 percent to 12.7 percent[110]. This is a far cry from the extravagant values previously stated (*i.e.,* a decrease from 5 million to 1.9 million families in severe distress and a drop in the poverty rate from 15.1% to 11.3%).

May Nicolas Baverez forgive me for questioning his work in this way. May he also forgive me for bitterly stigmatizing the flaws of a thought that, in my opinion, is more conventional than substantiated. May he forgive me for not lending credence to his fantasy of a France "stuck in the sanctuary of [its] pseudo social model" when recent and rigorously documented studies show that France over the last 30 years has been profoundly transformed under the effect of ever more resolute liberal policies[111] (we are still far from the "ideal" model of the United States, I admit). May he forgive me for being so fussy when I see figures thrown in front of the reader without source or guarantee (especially when they are false). I probably owe this unpleasant rigidity to the acerbic remarks of my scientific peers for whom an undocumented figure has neither interest, nor value, nor truth. As a preamble to his book, Mr. Baverez offers us a magnificent quotation from Bossuet: "The greatest insult that can be done to the truth is to know it, and at the same time to abandon it or to forget it." Let me contrast this principle with a more recent reflection by another great man, John Fitzgerald Kennedy: "The great enemy of truth is often not the lie - deliberate, manufactured and dishonest - but the myth - persistent, persuasive and unrealistic[112]."

---

109. US Census Bureau, Internet Release, 2006, http://www.census.gov/hhes/www/poverty/histpov/hstpov13.html

110. US Census Bureau, Internet Release, 2006, http://www.census.gov/hhes/www/poverty/histpov/hstpov2.html

111. Pepper D. Culpepper, Peter A. Hall & Bruno Palier, "La France en mutation 1980-2005", Paris, Presses de Sciences Po, 2006.

112. John F. Kennedy, Yale, 1962, quoted *in* M.R. Rank, *One Nation Underprivileged...*, *op. cit.* (Introd., n. 10), p. 13.

Henry de Castries: at the heart of the myth

In a recent interview, Henry de Castries, son of noble lineage and member of the very closed club of the best paid bosses of the CAC 40, explained that he believed in "equality of opportunity, but not in equality of destiny, because they depend largely on the efforts that each person is ready to make[113]". Put in less "select" terms, this idea states that abundance is a direct precipitate of work and poverty a mechanical consequence of laziness. Recently, Christine Lagarde, newly appointed Minister of the Economy, explained, in accordance with this postulate, that "work makes the individual solely responsible for his or her own life path[114]". This principle is at the heart not only of the liberal vulgate, but also of American mythology. In the United States, everyone is rewarded according to their merits and hard work. This fable has its roots in the legend of the Rockefellers, Gates and Fords. It is also based on a few pitiful facts, such as that of the 19 young children deprived of everything and locked up in the middle of cockroaches in a disgusting garret, by six undeserving mothers living on the $4,500 in social assistance they received each month for their children[115]. In matters of opinion, a few striking examples carry infinitely more weight than a plethora of insipid statistics[116]. Our leaders know this better than anyone else when they use and abuse references that are, to say the least, nebulous. Take Nicolas Sarkozy, for example. Our man likes to point out, from the height of his presidential office, that there are 500,000 unfilled jobs in France. In 2004, François Fillon, then Minister of Labor (and now Nicolas Sarkozy's Prime Minister), presented a less ambitious evaluation, since it was limited to 300,000 units. In 2005, the National

---

113. Interview given to the newspaper *Les Echos*, quoted in *Marianne*, 16-22 September 2006, p. 7.
114. Quoted in *Marianne*, August 11-17, 2007, p. 31.
115. Tracy Shryer, "19 Children Found Living in Roach-Infested Apartment," *Los Angeles Times*, February 3, 1994, Section A, p. 10.
116. B. Schwartz, "The Paradox of Choice: Why More is Less," *op. cit.* (Introd., n. 47), pp. 56-61.

Employment Agency (ANPE) proposed a figure of around 200,000 cases. So, 200, 300, 500 thousand? It doesn't matter, in fact, if we consider, as Sonya Faure points out in *Libération*, that the figure of 500,000 "doesn't mean much, but it allows governments to pass on the idea that if the unemployed really wanted to work, they could."[117]

If we admit that wealth depends solely on work done, then poverty denounces a guilty idleness. In this framework, money becomes the marker of our moral virtues and indigence the stigma of our unworthiness. It is no longer God who "saves the poor by his poverty[118]", but the market which "delivers the sinner by his suffering". There is, let us admit it, a certain logic to this adage. Indeed, by turning away from misery, society forces the poor to make amends. Indifference is no longer an institutional shame but a saving grace. The absence of any empathy would, in the final analysis, be the only way to guide these rascals of misery on the path to redemption. This reasoning probably explains why millions of indigent people in the United States are allowed to be deprived of the most basic care every year[119]. It also arguably legitimizes the compensation rule used after the September 11, 2001 attacks, according to which the life of a poor person is worth three times less than that of a rich person[120]. Finally, it perhaps justifies the economic aberration which, in certain years, leads the American tax authorities (IRS) to audit more modest families (less than $25,000/year) than wealthy families (more than $100,000/year), even though the latter generate a higher volume of adjustments[121]. It is true that the poor are to be distrusted. The poor are as treacherous as the rich are honest.

In short, the American myth teaches us that everyone is responsible for their own fate. In the polite language of economists, this is tantamount

---

117. Sonya Faure, "L'obscur calcul des emplois non pourvus," *Libération*, January 5, 2008.
118. La Bible de Jérusalem, Paris, Éditions du Cerf, 1973, Job, 36, 15.
119. D.L. Barlett & J.B. Steele, *Critical Condition*, *op. cit.* (Introd., n. 21); S.S. Sered & R. Fernandopulle, *Uninsured in America...*, *op. cit.* (Introd., n. 21); B. Shulman, *The Betrayal of Work...*, *op. cit.* (Introd., n. 10); D.K. Shipler, *The Working Poor...*, *op. cit.* (Introd., n. 68).
120. D.K. Shipler, *The Working Poor...*, *op. cit.* (Introd., n. 68), p. 90.
121. *Ibid.* at 15-16.

to saying that poverty escapes the sphere of structural deficiencies (lack of jobs, low wages, low growth) and becomes rooted in the space of individual deficiencies (inadequate training, lack of flexibility, questionable morality). As all the opinion polls conducted over the past 30 years have shown, this idea is unambiguously supported by the American public (and particularly by the wealthy)[122]. Unfortunately, consensus is not right. "The plurality of voices is not a proof worth anything, for truths that are a little difficult to discover, because it is much more likely that a single man has encountered them than a whole people," wrote Descartes in his famous *Discourse on Method*[123]. Galileo, Darwin, Wegener and Mendel know something about this, as they were right, alone, against the rest of the world in their time.

Let's think for a second about Mr. de Castries' fable. If it were true, we would have to blame an epidemic of laziness for the disaster that, in 1929, pushed millions of men and women into extreme poverty. We would have to sacrifice all of Bourdieu's work. We would have to desert Zola and shoot Ken Loach. But most of all, we would have to abandon our senses by refusing to see the millions of impoverished workers in the United States who babysit in day care centers, clean offices, serve in restaurants, work in call centers, toil in the fields, and wear themselves out lining the shelves of supermarkets. These people are the lifeblood of the modern economy. The ones I met were not lazy, uneducated, or morons. They were just the unavoidable victims of a brutal and wicked economic model. As Beth Shulman points out in a lucid book entitled "The Betrayal of Work," these

---

122. Joe Feagin, *Subordinating the Poor: Welfare and American Beliefs* (Englewoods Cliffs, NJ: Prentice Hall, 1975); Martin Gilens, *Why American Hate Welfare: Race, Media, and the Politics of Antipoverty Policy* (Chicago: University of Chicago Press, 1999); Kevin B. Smith & Lorene H. Stone, "Rags, Riches, and Bootstraps: Beliefs About the Causes of Wealth and Poverty," *Sociological Quarterly*, 1989, 30, 93-107; Daniel T. Lichter & Martha L. Crowley, "Poverty in America: Beyond Welfare Reform," *Population Bulletin*, 2002, 57, 1-36.
123. Text available online on the website of the academy of Nice: http://www.ac-nice.fr/philo/textes/Descartes-Discours.htm

people represent "super-exploited America…our prosperity rests, in part, on their misery[124]."

Before supporting the preceding remarks somewhat, it seems important to briefly question the persistence of the American myth. Clearly, this is not accidental. I believe that it obeys the mechanisms that drive rumor. In fact, if the myth of rewarded work has such a tough hide, it is because it is useful to us. It reassures us collectively on different levels. First, it pacifies the egos of the sons of fine bloodlines by stipulating that success derives its brilliance not from family ancestry, but from individual worth. Second, it reassures the hard-working by pushing the spectre of poverty away from their immediate world. Third, it offers hope for a better future to all those who remain destitute despite grueling labor. Fourth, and finally, it absolves the community of any responsibility for the fate of the poor. When everyone is treated according to his or her merits, the individual cannot absolve himself or herself of responsibility. The condition of indigence falls exclusively and fully on the one who bears it. This saves the conscience of the honest man. Compassion, empathy, mercy, the poor do not deserve any of these impulses. Only contempt suits him.

Anna: in the heart of reality

When it comes to illustrating the intimate nature of a socio-economic model, no theory can substitute for the reality of lived experiences. It is of course easy to consider the darkest of these existences as atypical aberrations. I would very much like, in accordance with this inclination, to be able to say that Anna, about whom I will have the opportunity to speak below, is only an accidental epiphenomenon. I would like to, but that would be a joke, as the dozens of similar examples recently published

---

124. B. Shulman, *The Betrayal of Work…*, *op. cit.* (Introd., n. 10), p. 4.

in several books with a strong ethnographic dimension show[125]. Anna is not a singular incongruity, she is not an artifact. She is a major, generally ignored precipitate of the American economy. On a U.S. scale, "Anna" can be broken down into millions of examples, each more distressing than the last[126]. If there were only one piece of evidence for this statement, it would be the genesis of this book. Indeed, unlike the authors who preceded me in the land of the working poor[127], I did not go to meet the poor. It is, in a way, the poor who came to me, through chance encounters. I did not carry out any methodical interview, nor any systematic investigation. I just accepted to see and hear these people who prepared my hamburgers, cleaned my office or looked after my daughter at the nursery. What strikes me most is how easy it was for me to remain blind to the outrage of their misery for years. What amazes me, too, is how easily I was able to swallow the myth of saving work without batting an eye. As Heather Boushey and her colleagues point out in a lengthy report entitled "Hardship in America: The Real Story of Working Families," "Lawmakers in the United States have embraced the idea that work is the solution to poverty, and the role of government is to promote employment rather than to provide income support to poor families. For many families, however, work may not be

---

125. B. Shulman, *The Betrayal of Work...*, *op. cit.* (Introd., n. 10); D.K. Shipler, *The Working Poor...*, *op. cit.* (Introd., n. 68); S.S. Sered & R. Fernandopulle, *Uninsured in America...*, *op. cit.* (Introd., n. 21); B. Ehrenreich, *Nickel and Dimed, op. cit.* (Introd., n. 67); M. Kennedy, *Without a Net...*, *op. cit.* (Introd., n. 69); M.R. Rank, *The Realities of Welfare in America*, New York, Columbia University Press, 1994.

126. Michelle Conlin & Aaron Bernstein, "Working... and Poor," *Business Week*, May 31, 2004, available online: http://www.businessweek.com/magazine/content/04_22/b3885001_mz001.htm; B. Shulman, *The Betrayal of Work...*, *op. cit.* (Introd., n. 10); *The State of Working America 2006-2007, op. cit.* (Introd., n. 13), chap. 3, table 3.7; M.R. Rank, *One Nation Underprivileged...*, *op. cit.* (Introd., n. 10), pp. 53-59; Bureau of Labor Statistics, "The Profile of the Working Poor 2003," Report 983, 2005, available online: http://www.bls.gov/cps/cp-swp2003.pdf

127. B. Shulman, *The Betrayal of Work...*, *op. cit.* (Introd., n. 10); D.K. Shipler, *The Working Poor...*, *op. cit.* (Introd., n. 68); S.S. Sered & R. Fernandopulle, *Uninsured in America...*, *op. cit.* (Introd., n. 21); B. Ehrenreich, *Nickel and Dimed, op. cit.* (Introd., n. 67); M. Kennedy, *Without a Net...*, *op. cit.* (Introd., n. 69); M.R. Rank, *The Realities of Welfare in America, op. cit.* (*supra*, n. 38).

sufficient to provide a decent standard of living[128]." Perhaps it is high time that we accept to open our eyes to this socio-economic reality that so disturbs our quiet certainties.

When I met Anna, I was staying in a hotel in Atlanta. One morning, when I had left a document in my room, I came by again, "unannounced. Anna was standing by the bed, holding a book by Beth Shulman that I had left on the bedside table. The cover depicted a housekeeper and the title read, "The Betrayal of Work[129]". I don't know who was more embarrassed by this brief confrontation, Anna or myself. A few days later, I saw Anna again, "in civilian clothes", in front of the hotel. It was 2:15 p.m. and she had just finished her shift. I asked her if she would like to have a coffee. I told her that I would like to talk to her about the book she had seen in my room. She kindly agreed but told me that she was not allowed to sit at the hotel bar. Anna was decent enough to clean guests' rooms, not to share their space. So we took up residence in a nearby fast food restaurant. Anna told me that she "didn't have much time" because she had to get home to take care of her son. I told her that I understood and explained that America was the ideal economic model for many Europeans, the one to strive for. I added that I had actually been a little surprised by the content of Shulman's book. I asked Anna if the author had not exaggerated a bit, if life was really that hard for the "working poor". As a response, Anna whispered, "I won't get paid for 5 days and I have exactly $18 left. I need $6 for Hugo's - my son's - lunch and $5 to put gas in the car. That leaves me with $7 for Hugo's 5 dinners and 5 breakfasts. When you're at that point, when you don't even have 50 cents to buy a coffee, when you're counting all the time and for everything, then yes, I guess you could say life is hard." I invited Anna to eat that day and the next. Two years later, I don't know what happened to her. All I have left of her life are a few

---

128. Heather Boushey, Chauna Brocht, Bethney Gundersen & Jared Bernstein, *Hardships in America: the Real Story of Working Families* (Washington, DC: Economic Policy Institute, 2001), p. 1.

129. B. Shulman, *The Betrayal of Work..., op. cit.* (Introd., n. 10).

scattered notes, mechanically transferred from our five "interviews" to the pages of Shulman's book. Anna is like the Little Prince. Sometimes, at night, I look at the sky and wonder if she still works in that hotel. I also wonder if her son will go to university as she wishes. I am often reminded of a saying by Alexander Chase: "The rich man may never go to heaven, but the poor man is already doing his time in hell"[130].

Anna is American, born of Mexican parents. When I met her, she was 39 years old. Her childhood was not a happy one. It followed the fickle rhythm of seasonal agricultural production. In the cotton fields of the South or the orange groves of Florida, life was apparently harsh and work often extended far beyond the cycle of the sun. School was not a priority. It never is when hunger grips the stomach. Anna remembers the promiscuity, the filthy barracks, the constant transhumance and the suffering that accompanied the workers' lives. Her mother, for example, had horribly deformed hands and her father was always bent over because his back hurt so much. Anna's parents bravely went through their physical decline. When they could no longer go forward, glorious America spat them out on the side of the road, without pension or gratitude. It is no longer "walk or die" as in Stephen King's novel, but "walk and die" as in a nightmare that does not say its name. For those who doubt the generality of Anna's story, and for those who think that times have changed in liberal lands, I suggest reading David Shipler's recent chapter on these "harvests of shame[131]". Anna's parents still have emulators. The fields of America are full of regular and undocumented workers who toil away with misery as their only horizon of existence. To call these people lazy is an insult to their suffering. As one farmer interviewed by Shipler explained, "You say, 'Well, this guy is taking advantage of these people. And he does. But on the other side of the arrangement there's, 'Where else is this guy going to go?' (...) I mean, he has no marketable skills. He has a roof over his head. It may not

---

130. Quoted *in* M.R. Rank, *One Nation Underprivileged...*, *op. cit.* (Introd., n. 10), p. 48.
131. D.K. Shipler, *The Working Poor...*, *op. cit.* (Introd., n. 68), chap. 4, "Harvest of Shame".

be a nice roof, but it's a roof. He's warm at night, he's fed every day. For me, that would be a crappy life, but for some of these people, I guess it's okay. I guess. It's kind of sad to say that[132]." Nice euphemism!

Today, Anna's parents have passed away. For almost two decades, Anna dutifully sent them a little money every month. Nine years ago, Anna had a son, Hugo. This child, she would like to send to university, so that "he can have a real life, with a good job". A "real life", a strange expression when you think about it. As if Anna's life didn't matter. As if being poor meant being nothing. As terrible as it seems, this nihilism seems to me to be consubstantial with the condition of the working poor. Only the assumption of insignificance can justify a wage of $5.15 an hour (the minimum wage in the United States; less than 4 euros against more than 8 in France[133]). If I were not nothing, then what I suffer would be intolerable. Society behaves like those abject husbands who manage to persuade their wives that no one could "want" them, that they are nothing but dead weight and that they deserve each and every one of the blows with which their bodies are covered every day. This atrophy of the self, David Shipler and Barbara Ehrenreich describe it with a terrifying thoroughness. At the turn of the words, we meet these women brutalized by life, sometimes sick, working hard with hunger in the belly and ready to tolerate all the humiliations to obtain an embryo of approval of an odious small chief[134]. We find Ann Brash explaining that the reason people don't always call to say they can't come to work is probably "because they don't think they're important enough to matter (...). It's more than low self-esteem, it's invisibility[135]." Moreover, when I caught Anna with Shulman's book in her hand, it was concern that I discerned on her face. As she would later admit to me, this concern reflected the fear of having been "seen," the fear of having broken

---

132. *Ibid.* at 113-114.

133. National Institute of Statistics and Economic Studies (INSEE), http://www.insee.fr/fr/indicateur/smic.htm

134. B. Ehrenreich, *Nickel and Dimed, op. cit.* (Introd., n. 67), e.g., chap. 2, "Scrubbing in Maine."

135. D.K. Shipler, *The Working Poor..., op. cit.* (Introd., n. 68), p. 129.

the implicit rule of invisibility, and the fear that I would report her and imagine that she wanted to steal the book, because "for a man like me, a woman like her doesn't read. Anna was never praised for her work, her punctuality or her diligence. Never has a hotel executive spoken to her. Never did she feel like anything more than "a meaningless, disposable, worthless housekeeper. In her book, Barbara Ehrenreich recounts this view of "housekeepers". "I ventured to ask why so many [business] owners seem hostile or dismissive of us," she says. "They think we're stupid" was Holly's response. "They think we have nothing better to do with our time." Even Marge suddenly seemed serious. "We're nothing to these people," she said. "We're just housekeepers. (...) At one place we stopped for refreshments, actually a small restaurant with a counter, I tried to order iced tea to go, but the waitress just stood there talking with a colleague, ignoring my 'excuse me. There is also the supermarket. I used to stop there on my way home from work [still in my clothes], but I couldn't stand the looks that could easily translate into: What are you doing here? Hey, no wonder she's poor, she's got a beer in her cart"[136].

For her misfortune, Anna is not only a "cleaning lady", she is also a single mother and therefore suspected of being a "slut", a girl of little, without principle or morals. Fortunately, people like Charles Murray are there to open our eyes and to condemn the ignominious life of this kind of woman. This author is best known to the general public for having co-authored a book a few years ago on the genetic superiority of white intelligence over black intelligence[137]. At a recent symposium, Murray went a step further to point out that there is "a dirty little secret about out-of-wedlock births to poor women. That dirty little secret is that many of these women are rotten mothers. (...). There are a great many children who are left to fend

---

136. B. Ehrenreich, *Nickel and Dimed, op. cit.* (Introd., n. 67), pp. 99-100.
137. R.J. Herrnstein & C. Murray, *The Bell Curve: Intelligence and Class Structure in American Life*, New York, Free Press, 1994. For a strong refutation of this work: Claude S. Fischer, Michael Hout, Martin Sanchez Jankowski, Samuel R. Lucas, Ann Swidler & Kim Vos, *Inequality by Design: Cracking the Bell Curve Myth* (Princeton, NJ: Princeton University Press, 1996); S.J. Gould, *The Ill-measurement of Man* (Paris: Odile Jacob, 1997, new ed.).

for themselves, all day and through the night, not because the mother is out looking for a job, but because she is out partying[138]." Clearly, this assertion is too excessive not to seem grotesque. In substance, however, the message is consistent with another more widely accepted representation that the poor are the bearers of corrupt values and distorted morals[139]. To illustrate this point, consider the example of Anna's son. Let us imagine that he becomes a delinquent and/or fails in his schooling. Common sense tells us that this will be because of the educational indignity of a resigning, neglectful and "rotten" mother. The idea is not new. For example, in the late eighteenth century, wealthy tutors visited impoverished families to instill courage and probity in them through spatial contiguity[140]. At that time, the poor were perceived as a sub-human physiological curiosity, a sort of rudimentary biped whose primitive impulses had to be curbed. This idea was seriously challenged for the first time after the 1929 crisis. It became clear that poverty was also the result of structural factors that the poor could not control[141]. If one accepts this evidence, then, one might suggest that Anna's son has less to fear from his mother's supposed deficiencies than from the extreme brutality of a ruthlessly prescribed economic system. The problem of school success illustrates this point. Anna would like Hugo to go to university. A beautiful dream, to which unfortunately the objective realities of life offer little hope. First of all, the exorbitant price of higher education means that in the United States "the smartest poor kids go to college with the same frequency as the dumbest rich kids[142]". Second, academic success owes much to cultural and domestic environments[143]. Anna has no formal education. She reads with difficulty and her verbal

---

138. Quoted *in* M.R. Rank, *One Nation Underprivileged...*, *op. cit.* (Introd., n. 10), p. 18.

139. D.T. Lichter & M.L. Crowley, "Poverty in America...," *op. cit.* (*supra*, n. 35).

140. *Walter Trattner,* From Poor Law to Welfare State: a History of Social Welfare in America, *New York, Free Press, 1994.*

141. *Ibid.*

142. T. Draut, *Strapped...*, *op. cit.* (Introd., n. 9), p. 35; for more details, see in the second part of this work: "School: better to be rich and stupid than poor and brilliant".

143. See the next part of this section: "Hugo: cursed from father to son".

"fluency" remains limited. She could, of course, hire an outside tutor as a stopgap measure, but this is not within her meager means. To make matters worse, Hugo is attending a difficult high school in suburban Atlanta. The education he receives does not seem, for lack of means and perhaps of political will, to be compatible with Anna's projects[144]. It is not easy to access the University when one is poor in America. Clearly, Hugo has every conceivable handicap on his head and the statistics do not speak for him! I will have the opportunity to come back to this point later.

I hope that a closer look at Anna's daily life will be enough to convince the most reluctant that there is nothing unworthy or "rotten" about this woman, on the contrary. During the week, Anna gets up at 5 am. She prepares her son's clothes, puts $1.25 in an envelope for the canteen, and then around 6:00 a.m., she leaves the house. She arrives at the hotel around 6:45 a.m. where she works as a housekeeper. Her day officially begins at 7:00 a.m. Just before going on duty, Anna calls Hugo to wake him up and make sure he won't miss school. She calls him a second time at 7:30 a.m. and again at 8:00 a.m. if necessary. Anna normally finishes work at 1pm. However, the pace of her work makes it impossible to keep to this schedule. In fact, Anna never leaves her post before 1:45-2:00 pm. This overtime is obviously not paid to her. She does not dare to "ask for it" for fear of being fired, as often happens to employees who dare to ask for a salary bonus[145]. She would easily find another job, she says, but she cannot afford to lose a week or two of pay. In addition, her current schedule allows her to care for her son in the afternoons, even though he often has to come home from school alone. Anna cannot hire a nanny or apply for the after-school program[146]. This program would cost her $2 per day, which seems low but is excessive for the family's finances.

---

144. For the problem of "poor" schools, see the second part of this book: "School: better to be rich and stupid than poor and brilliant".
145. B. Shulman, *The Betrayal of Work...*, *op. cit.* (Introd., n. 10), p. 20.
146. School ends in the United States at about 2:00 p.m. There is an after-school care system, the cost of which is usually means-tested.

Anna receives a cheque for $358 twice a month for her work. Her contract, which can be revoked at any time without notice, offers no health insurance, no paid leave, and no benefits of any kind (retirement pension, parental leave, etc.). To get by, Anna takes on a second job as a housekeeper in a retirement home on weekends. Hugo remains alone, under the distant care of a neighbor. For 16 hours of work, Anna receives $90. Again, she has no benefits or coverage of any kind. So if we add it all up, Anna works seven days a week for an official total of 46 hours and a salary of $270. This leads to a total monthly salary of $1,070 (or 825 euros). Not long ago, Anna left a third job as a cashier that she had been working for just over 2 years, on weekdays from 4:00 pm to 8:00 pm. She had been forced to take this job because of unforeseen financial expenses, which I will discuss below. Anna had to give up this income because Hugo's school results had plunged dangerously and because she "couldn't take it anymore". Her physical condition, which I will also come back to, did not allow her to stand in front of her cash register after having spent 6 hours cleaning rooms. No doubt this is the kind of softness that Mr. de Castries and Mrs. Lagarde have in mind when they dogmatically link effort and destiny[147]. By giving up her third job, Anna hopes to be able to get some help. According to her calculations, she should receive about $50 in food stamps each month and $2,500 in Earned Income Tax Credit (EITC) for the year. Although substantial, these supports will not lift her above the poverty line ($13,461 for a mother with one minor child[148]). Her application for Medicaid (health insurance for the poorest) has already been rejected. No doubt this is the kind of decision that should satisfy Mr. Baverez, who is quick to contemplate social assistance for the poorest[149]. Anna will indeed have to work a lot if she develops appendicitis or needs a

---

147. H. de Castries, quoted in *Marianne*, 16-22 September 2006, p. 7; C. Lagarde, quoted in *Marianne*, August 11-17, 2007, p. 31.

148. US Census Bureau, Internet Release, 2006, http://pubdb3.census.gov/macro/032006/pov/new35_000.htm

149. N. Baverez, *What to do: Agenda 2007, op. cit.* (Introd., n. 63), p. 130.

hip replacement one day. In the latter case, she will have to pay 4 to 5 years of salary to be treated[150], which means that she will probably have to keep her hip and plan to buy a little chair with wheels. I will come back to this problem in the second part of this book[151].

You have to dig deep into Anna's expenses to find any financial eccentricity. Her biggest expense is rent ($450), followed by her car loan ($180) and various incompressible costs (gas, phone, water, electricity, $150). The only "questionable" expense in the family budget is cable TV ($40), "the only leisure activity available when you are deprived of everything. Of course, one might think that Anna does not need a car, but that would be to ignore the reality of her situation. The life of the poor in the United States is like a large mosaic. Each piece illuminates its neighbor. At the center of the work is housing. The problem is basically quite simple. More and more people are crowding into cities whose spatial boundaries cannot be extended indefinitely. The poor are therefore being pushed further and further out of the cities. Anna would love to live near her work. Unfortunately, a studio apartment would cost her, at the very least, $1,000 a month, or about 94% of her salary! The standard definition of "affordable" housing puts this threshold at 30%[152]. This criterion is wishful thinking for over 80% of disadvantaged families[153]. The majority of these families spend more than 50% of their resources on rent[154]. Anna is doing quite well from this perspective with a burden of "only" 42%. For her rent to be considered affordable, she would have to earn $1,500 per month. A recent study found that the federal minimum wage ($5.15/hr) would have to be increased, on average, by more than three times to allow the poorest workers working 40 hours a week to

---

150. "Outsourcing your Heart," *op. cit.* (Introd., n. 76), pp. 44-47.
151. See the second part of this book: "Health: pay or die".
152. National Low Income Housing Coalition, Out of Reach 2005, Washington, DC, National Low Income Housing Coalition; for introduction and key tables, see: http://www.nlihc.org/oor/oor2005/
153. *Ibid.*
154. *Ibid.*

rent a median-priced two-bedroom apartment at an "affordable" price. In Georgia, the low-cost state where Anna lives, a factor of 2.6 would be required. The catch-up would have to reach 4.6 in California[155]. Put the other way around, these numbers indicate that it takes 2.6 full-time jobs to house a family at a price that is considered "affordable" in Georgia, when one is at minimum wage. This implies that a family with two parents working full time at the minimum wage borders, can only afford decent housing in this state at great sacrifice. As Barbara Ehrenreich says, "When rich and poor compete for housing in an open market, the poor don't stand a chance[156]."

When I worked in Atlanta, I sometimes drove through Anna's neighborhood. Like most poor neighborhoods, it had a "menacing appearance. There was "dilapidated housing, vacant houses with broken or boarded-up windows, abandoned or burned-out cars, and men hanging out on street corners[157]." I would, I confess, have been terrified if I had to live there. Officially, such places are called extreme poverty when 40% of the people living there are poor. As Paul Jargowsky has shown, "the popular and politically exploitative image [of these] ghettos as places where everyone drops out of school, and everyone is on welfare is a gross distortion of reality.... The data do not suggest that ghetto residents constitute an 'underclass' hopelessly antagonistic to the mainstream culture[158]." Anna is living proof of this! Despite working two jobs, she cannot afford to get out of her "crappy" suburb. Many others are in her situation. When you look at the numbers closely, you see that between 1970 and 1990, the number of people living in pockets of extreme poverty in the U.S. more

---

155. *Ibid.*
156. B. Ehrenreich, *Nickel and Dimed, op. cit.* (Introd., n. 67), p. 199.
157. Paul Jargowsky, *Poverty and Places: Ghettos, Barrios and the American City* (New York: Russell Sage Foundation, 1997), p. 11.
158. Paul Jargowsky, "Beyond the Street Corner: the Hidden Diversity of High Poverty Neighborhoods," *Urban Geography* 1996; 17: 579-603, p. 598.

CHAPTER 1 WORK: THE REAL LAW OF THE MARKET

than doubled, to a staggering 10.4 million people[159]. Curiously, the trend was then reversed and the years 1990-2000 saw an impressive decline. The number of people living in extreme poverty dropped by 25 percent to 7.9 million[160]. This seems like a significant success. Unfortunately, it is not. In fact, the reduction in pockets of extreme poverty has occurred in urban centers, but not in the surrounding suburbs[161]. In large cities such as Detroit, Chicago, Cleveland or Dallas, the number of pockets of poverty has even increased outside the city[162]. The decline in the inner city is explained by the rising cost of housing, which has gradually pushed the least advantaged members of the middle classes into the originally most impoverished urban neighbourhoods. The result was a mechanical dilution of the poverty rate, with no real reduction in poverty. Consistent with this idea, figures show that the number of poor people in the United States rose from 31.7 million to 33.9 million between 1990 and 2000[163].

Finding a job in the heart of a ghetto of extreme poverty is an almost insurmountable challenge. Like many of her fellow villagers, Anna is forced to work outside of her city. This is only possible with a car. Indeed, public transportation in Atlanta is very basic, especially in the slums. To buy the car, Anna used $2,000 in federal EITC money, plus $5,000 in credit, which she repaid over four years at, as I said, $180 a month. Informed readers may find these figures a bit extravagant. Indeed, $180 over 4 years is a credit rate of 30%, which is about 10% higher than the usury rate applicable in France. Based on these values, we can predict that Anna will have repaid $8,641 at the end of her contract. Her car, whose total cost will finally approach $10,650, will then be more like a wreck than a Formula 1 car.

---

159. Paul Jargowsky, "Stunning Progress, Hidden Problems: the Dramatic Decline of Concentrated Poverty in the 1990s," Center on Urban and Metropolitan Policy, The Living Cities Census Series (Washington, DC: Brookings Institution, 2003), p. 4.
160. *Ibid.*
161. *Ibid.* at 11-13.
162. *Ibid.*
163. *Ibid*, p. 4.

The previous figures are sadly valid. Anna is really subject to a 30% annual credit rate. She owes this privilege to liberal dogma. The latter suggests that competition lowers prices to the benefit of consumers. Thanks to the market economy, consumers are offered a wide freedom of choice, which they can use to punish contractors who are too "greedy" in favour of the most competitive companies. During the 1980s, this approach was applied to the banking system. Over time, this change proved to be "especially bad for individual investors and borrowers - and fantastically good for CEOs[164] and shareholders[165]". It all started with a Supreme Court decision allowing financial institutions to charge credit rates in the state of domicile[166]. In other words, a bank in Georgia, with a registered office in Delaware, can charge interest rates in Delaware. Fortunately, Delaware, like twenty-nine other states, has no usury laws[167]. Our bank is therefore entitled to charge its customers any interest rate it wants. In theory, however, this rate is supposed to depend on objective criteria such as salary, level of indebtedness, a possible history of "bad debts", etc. These criteria are supposed to allow the bank to charge the customer any interest rate it wishes. These criteria are supposed to allow an objective definition of a risk level for each borrower, the "*credit rating*". The worse the score, the higher the risk for the lender and the higher the rate[168]. For poorer people like Anna, the punishment is often in the range of 29% to 34%[169]. Even when the initial rate is more reasonable, companies will stop at nothing to maximize their profits. For example, a person who has taken out a loan at the "prime" rate of 12% will see this commitment revalued to 30% or 35% if his or her

---

164. "Chief Executive Officer.

165. T. Draut, *Strapped...*, *op. cit.* (Introd., n. 9), p. 100.

166. Vincent D. Rougeau, "Rediscovering Usury: an Argument for Legal Controls on Credit Card Interest Rates," *University of Colorado Law Review*, Winter 1996.

167. Lucy Lazarony, "States with Credit Card Caps" (data obtained from the American Banker Association), 2002, http://www.bankrate.com/brm/news/cc/20020320b.asp

168. Patrick McGeehan, "Soaring Interest Compounds Credit Card Pain for Millions," *New York Times*, November 21, 2004

169. T. Draut, *Strapped...*, *op. cit.* (Introd., n. 9), p. 101; D.K. Shipler, *The Working Poor...*, *op. cit.* (Introd., n. 68), pp. 23-27.

repayment is late, even if only by a few minutes. What's more, financial institutions keep a constant eye on their borrowers who sometimes see their interest rates soar following a dispute with a competing company. Forget about the electric bill on your desk and your credit rate could go up (a clause called "universal default"). The kind of endorsement Tamara Draut discovered at the bottom of a credit application from a major U.S. bank sums up the problem quite well. This rider states, "We reserve the right to change the terms (including APR [Annual Percentage Rate]) at any time for any reason, in addition to increased APRs that may occur for failure to comply with the terms of your account[170]." Like thousands of other Americans, Ed Schwebel thus saw his credit rate skyrocket from 9.2% to 18% without notice or explanation. For Steve Stachan, the increase was even more drastic, as his rate suddenly jumped from 5.25% to 20.21%[171]. Of course, these changes are retroactive in the sense that they affect the entire amount of money that remains to be repaid. It is hardly surprising that the profits of credit institutions are at record levels[172]. If the consumer has the impression that he is the turkey in a neoliberal farce, let him be reassured, this is not necessarily false. For those who still have illusions about the supposed regulatory virtues of the market, let me borrow a final example from Tamara Draut. In 2001, the Federal Reserve lowered its policy rate eleven times, from 6.24% to 3.88%. One would have expected that the unbridled competition would have pushed the banking companies to pass on these 2.36 points of decrease to the consumer. But no! During the same period, interest rates offered to individuals decreased by only 0.82%, from an average of 15.71% to 14.89%[173].

To sum up, Anna works a lot, earns little, lives in a tough suburb, pays a lot of rent for her income and owns a car bought through financial insti-

---

170. BankOne, quoted *in* T. Draut, *Strapped...*, *op. cit.* (Introd., n. 9), p. 102.
171. P. McGeehan, "Soaring Interest Compounds Credit Card Pain for Millions," *op. cit.* (*supra*, n. 81).
172. *Ibid.*
173. T. Draut, *Strapped...*, *op. cit.* (Introd., n. 9), p. 105.

tutions that, with their omnipotence, allow themselves to charge usurious rates that the sharks of the old mafias would not have disowned. Once she has paid all her fixed costs, Anna ends up with $250 each month. Add $50 in food stamps, and that's $300. In other words, Anna and Hugo have $10 a day to eat, dress, take care of themselves and buy what they need (school supplies, detergents, etc.). Having tried for myself to live for a month on only $300, I can testify that it is more of a feat than a blessing. Every day is a difficult balancing act. Like millions of poor people, Anna is constantly asking herself whether she would rather eat, order oil for her small space heater, buy a gift for her son's birthday, or relieve her toothache. In the latter case, the question is not whether she will be able to go to the dentist, but whether she will be able to afford some over-the-counter oral painkillers. The literature has amply validated the existence of this type of trade-off in poor families[174]. It has even given it a name: "*the eat-or-heat dilemma*" (a play on the words "*eat*" and "*heat*").

When nothing goes wrong, Anna manages to balance her budget. The problem is those little grains of sand in everyday life, those insignificant details that most of us don't pay attention to. The smallest bump in the road, the smallest jolt in the road, quickly turns into an insurmountable disaster for Anna. Two years before we met, Anna started to suffer from back pain. One morning, the pain was so severe that she had to give up going to work. After 36 hours in bed, she finally went to the emergency room at the behest of her neighbor. The doctor diagnosed sciatica. He did not examine Anna. He didn't even ask her to take off her sweater. He didn't ask for any additional X-rays or prescribe any anti-inflammatory medication. The doctor simply sent the patient home with a recommendation for oral painkillers and a two-week leave of absence. The cleaning

---

174. Martha Shirk, Neil G. Bennett & Lawrence Aber, "Lives on the Line: American Families and the Struggle to Make Ends Meet," Boulder, CO, *Westview Press*, 1999; Karen Seccombe, *So You Think I Drive a Cadillac? Welfare Recipients' Perspectives on the System and its Reform*, Needham Heights, MA, Allyn and Bacon, 1999; Kathryn Edin & Laura Lein, *Making Ends Meet: How Single Mothers Survive Welfare and Low-Wage Work*, New York, Russell Sage Foundation, 1997.

company that employed Anna on weekends fired her immediately. Shocking as it may seem, the practice does not seem unusual. Denise, for example, was pregnant when she slammed into the handle of a tank she was cleaning[175]. As Susan Sered and Rushika Fernandopulle report, the impact caused a miscarriage. The miscarriage came on top of severe back pain, which was also a result of Denise's work. The doctor asked her to rest until she had fully recovered. The company (Caterpillar, to name one) requested an immediate return. Denise proved unable to meet this ultimatum. She was fired without further ado. The law of the market, no doubt, the sacrosanct principle of supply and demand, an ideal world freed from the constraints of the Labor Code, the innovative world of the disposable worker. Who would dare, after that, to contest the obvious advance of the American economic model over that of Europe? But let's close this little parenthesis and come back to Anna. She was lucky enough to keep her main job at the hotel. However, no sick pay was paid to her during her absence, which is apparently the rule for a majority of the working poor in the US[176].

All told, her illness cost Anna a whopping $1,700: $850 for her emergency room visit, $100 for medication, $350 in unpaid wages at the hotel, and $400 in unpaid wages after she was laid off (including the time she was off sick, it took Anna four weeks to find a job at the nursing home where she was still working when I met her). To meet these expenses, Anna applied for and received a $2,000 loan, which she paid back over two years at a rate of $115 per month (which must be about 33% interest). The burden of these repayments forced her to take a third job, which she held until her debt was paid off. This job allowed her to save some money "for her son later on". Anna had tears in her eyes as she explained to me that she recently had to spend this money when her car broke down. Her goal now is to save "at least half" of the

---

175. Reported in S.S. Sered & R. Fernandopulle, *Uninsured in America...*, *op. cit.* (Introd., n. 21), pp. 159-162.
176. B. Shulman, *The Betrayal of Work...*, *op. cit.* (Introd., n. 10), p. 31.

$2,500 she should get in tax credits. With the rest, she would like to "spoil" Hugo a bit by buying him a Playstation and some clothes. I wish I could capture the infinite sadness that suddenly flooded Anna's voice when she told me this. I wish I could describe that dam that suddenly broke and offered me a flood of irrepressible tears. I would like to be able to transcribe this terrifying guilt, this irrevocable conviction of being only a waste, an incompetent, a weight, a bad mother. I would really like to be able to tell Anna's suffering. In that restaurant, I would have liked to be able to hold her in my arms in the midst of all those people who looked on without seeing, lowering their heads or laughing under their breath. I would have liked to tell them that this suffering was neither feigned nor crazy. I should probably have filmed these interviews. I could then, perhaps, have captured the strength of those tears that seized me away from my guards. More than any words in a book, Anna's collapse is a testament to the inexcusable cruelty of a system without morals or ethics. This woman should not suffer like this. Her life shouldn't be this hard, not in a country that's awash in affluence. There is no justification for such brutality.

Hugo : cursed from father to son

In the United States, more than in any other country, the poor keep replaying the dream of a better life. Generation after generation of paupers bend their backs in the hope that their children will climb the social ladder. Anna's parents, for example, accepted a life of drudgery to offer their daughter the opportunity of a presentable future. A useless sacrifice, finally burned in the gehenna of slaughtered futures. Anna has failed. All that remains is for her to lose herself in turn, for Hugo. The last one has to get out of it. It is necessary so that all was not vain. It is necessary to give a sense to all these botched lives.

I hear everywhere that the American model is the one that offers Hugo the best chance of success. I see several weaknesses in this claim. First, there are more children in poverty in the United States than in any other developed country[177]. The most frequently cited study states that Uncle Sam's country has 1.7 times more poor children than its closest competitor, Canada; the difference is 2.1 with Spain, 3.2 with Holland, 5.7 with France, 9.2 with Belgium, and 11.3 with Sweden, to take just a few examples[178]. In America, 17 million children under the age of 18 (23%) live in near poverty, that is, with a level of resources below 1.25 times the official poverty line[179]. If we take 100% of this threshold, the figure "drops" to 13 million (18%)[180]. If we focus on extreme poverty, we get the implausible number of 6 million children (8%) living on incomes below half the official poverty line[181]. America has more children in ultimate distress than Denmark, Ireland, or Finland have inhabitants[182]. For every 100 children under age 5, 20 live below the poverty line, or 1 in 5, or 4 million[183]. Unfortunately, this is not a typing error, but a sad reality after all, 1 in 5 children under the age of 5 is raised in poverty in the United States. An admirable picture for the world's leading economic power. If only the American system guaranteed its poor, as is often believed in Europe, the promise of broad social mobility. The

---

177. J. Iceland, *Poverty in America...*, *op. cit.* (Introd., n. 9), pp. 65-68; B. Bradbury & M. Jantti, "Child Poverty Across Twenty-Five Countries," 2001, *in* B. Bradbury, S. Jenkins, J. Micklewright (eds.), *The Dynamics of Child Poverty in Industrialized Countries, op. cit.* (Introd., n. 46), pp. 62-91; T.M. Smeeding, L. Rainwater & G. Burtless, "United States Poverty in a Cross-National Context," *op. cit.* (Introd., n. 44); *The State of Working America 2006-2007, op. cit.* (Introd., n. 13), figure 8G.
178. T.M. Smeeding, L. Rainwater & G. Burtless, "United States Poverty in a Cross-National Context," *op. cit.* (Introd., n. 44), table 2.
179. US Census Bureau, Internet Release, 2006, http://pubdb3.census.gov/macro/032006/pov/new01_125_01.htm
180. US Census Bureau, Internet Release, 2006, http://pubdb3.census.gov/macro/032006/pov/new01_100_01.htm
181. US Census Bureau, Internet Release, 2006, http://pubdb3.census.gov/macro/032006/pov/new01_50_01.htm
182. European Union, website, 2006, http://europa.eu/abc/keyfigures/index_fr.htm
183. US Census Bureau, Internet Release, 2006, http://pubdb3.census.gov/macro/032006/pov/new01_100_01.htm

idea would be that liberalism would guarantee equal opportunity for all. Being born poor would no longer be a definitive curse, but a transitory state that we could erase with our own will. Unfortunately, this myth is as beautiful as the facts are dismal. Comparative studies involving several European nations and the United States have shown that intergenerational social mobility is significantly lower in the latter country[184]. In other words, it is in America that children are most likely to remain trapped in their original condition. Nowhere are the consequences of the chance of birth more important.

Various markers of the lack of intergenerational social mobility in the United States can be found. Three seem especially telling.

1) The process of intergenerational wealth transfer means that children from the wealthiest families are approximately 40 times more likely to be among the wealthiest citizens as adults than children from disadvantaged backgrounds[185].

2) Children tend to stay within or near their parents' wealth quintile[186]. For example, 58 percent of children located in the bottom 20 percent of the U.S. population come from parents who were in the bottom 10 percent of the population. Only 5 percent of children from such parents end up among the richest 20 percent of the population. This substantial relationship between the incomes of a father and son can be expressed as a

---

184. Olli Kangas, "Distributive Justice and Social Policy," *Luxembourg Income Study, Working Paper Series*, 2000, No. 221, Maxwell School of Citizenship and Public Affairs, Syracuse University, Syracuse, NY; Gary R. Solon, "Cross Country Differences in Earnings Mobility," *Journal of Economic Perspectives*, 2002, 16, pp. 59-66; Bhashkar Mazumder, "Revised Estimates of Intergenerational Income Mobility in the United States," Federal Reserve Bank of Chicago, 2003, Working Paper, WP2003-16, available online: http://www.chicagofed.org/publications/workingpapers/papers/wp2003-16.pdf; *The State of Working America 2006-2007, op. cit.* (Introd., n. 13), chap. 2.
185. Jagdeesh Gokhale & Lawrence J Kotlikoff, "Simulating the Transmission of Wealth Inequality," *American Economic Review*, 2002, 92, pp. 265-269.
186. The State of Working America 2006-2007, op. cit. *(Introd., n. 13), chap. 2, figure 2B.*

correlation coefficient with a value of about 0.60[187]. According to Bhashkar Mazumder, an economist at the Federal Reserve Bank of Chicago, this correlation indicates that the United States is "exceptional in its relative lack of mobility."[188] For those who are reluctant to take the validity of this assertion at face value, the problem can be restated as follows. If the intergenerational correlation is 0.60 and the father is among the poorest 5 percent of individuals, then the probability that the son will one day belong to the wealthiest half of the population is only 11 percent. The probability that the son will be among the poorest 20 percent is more than 50 percent. The probability that he will reach the richest 20 percent stagnates at under 2 percent[189]. These figures are higher than those obtained, on comparable methodological grounds, in other countries such as Germany (correlation = 0.30), Finland or Canada[190]. For the latter two countries, the correlations are of the order of 0.20. This means that if the father is among the poorest 5% of individuals, then the probability that his son will one day belong to the wealthiest half of the population is 37%. The probability that this son will be among the poorest 20% is contained at 30%. The

---

187. B. Mazumder, "Revised Estimates of Intergenerational Income Mobility in the United States," *op. cit.* (*supra*, n. 97); B. Mazumder, "Earnings Mobility in the US: A New Look at Intergenerational Inequality," Federal Reserve Bank of Chicago, 2001, Working Paper, WP2001-18, available online: http://www.chicagofed.org/publications/workingpapers/papers/Wp2001-18.pdf; B. Mazumder, "Fortunate Sons: New Estimates of Intergenerational Mobility In the U.S. Using Social Security Earnings Data," *Review of Economics and Statistics*, 2005, 87, pp. 235-255.

188. B. Mazumder, "Revised Estimates of Intergenerational Income Mobility in the United States," *op. cit.* (*supra*, n. 97), at 4.

189. Gary R. Solon, "Intergenerational Income Mobility in the United States," *American Economic Review*, 1992, 82, pp. 393-408; Gary R. Solon, "Intergenerational Income Mobility in the United States," *University of Wisconsin-Madison IRP Discussion Paper* Nos. 894-89, 1989.

190. B. Mazumder, "Revised Estimates of Intergenerational Income Mobility in the United States," *op. cit.* (*supra*, n. 97), at 4; G.R. Solon, "Cross Country Differences in Earnings Mobility," *op. cit.* (*supra*, n. 97); *The State of Working America 2006-2007*, *op. cit.* (Introd., n. 13), chap. 2, figure 2G.

probability that he will reach the richest 20% is over 12%[191]. Another way of representing all these figures is to say that if the correlation between parents' and children's income is 0.60, then it will take a standard family of 4 individuals (2 parents, 2 children) between 9 and 10 generations - more than 2 centuries - to reach the middle class. If the correlation is less than half, then 4 to 5 generations will suffice[192].

3) There is a substantial relationship between the economic status of siblings. This relationship is expressed in the form of a correlation coefficient whose value is around 0.50[193]. This means, to remain faithful to the previous illustrations, that if a lambda individual is among the poorest 5% of the population, then the probability that his brother belongs to the better-off half of the population is only 17%. The probability that this brother is among the poorest 20 percent is 49 percent. The probability that he belongs to the richest 20 percent is only 3 percent[194].

In view of the elements reported above, it appears that the land of all possibilities is above all the land of all conservatism. Know the father and you will know the son. No country bears this assertion better than liberal America. In relation to this point, it is interesting to note that the strength of the correlations observed within a sibling[195] and between generations[196]

---

191. G.R. Solon, "Intergenerational Income Mobility in the United States," 1992, *op. cit.* (*supra*, n. 102); G.R. Solon, "Intergenerational Income Mobility in the United States," 1989, *op. cit. (supra,* n. 102).
192. The State of Working America 2006-2007, op. cit. *(Introd., n. 13), chap. 2.*
193. Bhashkar Mazumder, "Sibling Similarities, Differences and Economic Inequality," Federal Reserve Bank of Chicago, 2004, Working Paper, WP2004-13, available online: http://www.chicagofed.org/publications/workingpapers/wp2004_13.pdf
194. G.R. Solon, "Intergenerational Income Mobility in the United States," 1992, *op. cit.* (*supra*, n. 102); G.R. Solon, "Intergenerational Income Mobility in the United States," 1989, *op. cit. (supra,* n. 102).
195. Bhashkar Mazumder & David I. Levine, "The Growing Importance of Family and Community: An Analysis of Changes in the Sibling Correlation in Men's Earnings," Federal Reserve Bank of Chicago, 2003, Working Paper, WP2003-24, available online: http://www.chicagofed.org/publications/workingpapers/papers/wp2003-24.pdf
196. Daniel Aaronson & Bhashkar Mazumder, "Intergenerational Economic Mobility in the U.S., 1940 to 2000," Federal Reserve Bank of Chicago, 2006, Working Paper, WP2005-12, available online: http://www.chicagofed.org/publications/workingpapers/wp2005_12.pdf

has vigorously increased over the last two decades. For intergenerational mobility, for example, the increase was from 0.32 to 0.58[197]. Interestingly, the last 25 years have also seen the US government drastically reduce the magnitude of its social spending[198]. This contingency is not accidental, as shown by the existence of robust intergenerational mobility in European countries with high social interventionism[199]. In fact, when inequalities are no longer regulated by the community, the poorest find themselves in a situation of almost insurmountable handicap. Their bankruptcy is then not inevitable, but highly probable. As James Heckman, a prominent conservative economist at the University of Chicago, points out: "If I am born to educated and supportive parents, my chances of success are totally different from if I were born to a single parent or to abusive parents. (...) this is an example of market failure. Children do not 'buy' their parents, and as a result, there must be some form of intervention to compensate for these environmental differences[200]." An example originally proposed by Mark Rank illustrates perfectly, I believe, the relevance of this proposition[201]. Imagine a game of Monopoly involving three players. Normally, each of these players starts with zero assets and the same amount of money. However, if we integrate the vagaries of birth into this scheme, the problem changes drastically. One player ends up with 25,000 Euros, some real estate and the continuous advice of a coach who specializes in the game and its intricacies. The second player leaves with a standard sum of 2,000 Euros and a written guide to the best strategies to use. The third player is the least well off. He or she has a meager 250 Euros and an

---

197. *Ibid*, table 1.

198. J. Iceland, *Poverty in America...*, *op. cit*, (Introd., n. 9), chap. 7; M.R. Rank, *One Nation Underprivileged...*, *op. cit.* (Introd., n. 10), pp. 235-236.

199. B. Mazumder, "Revised Estimates of Intergenerational Income Mobility in the United States," *op. cit.* (*supra*, n. 97), at 4; G.R. Solon, "Cross Country Differences in Earnings Mobility," *op. cit.* (*supra*, n. 97); *The State of Working America 2006-2007*, *op. cit.* (Introd., n. 13), chap. 2, figure 2G.

200. Quoted *in* Alexander Stille, "Grounded by an Income Gap," *New York Times*, December 15, 2001.

201. M.R. Rank, *One Nation Underprivileged...*, *op. cit.* (Introd., n. 10), pp. 70-71.

empirical knowledge of the rules of the game. It is clear that the first player will win the game in the overwhelming majority of cases, even if his or her sidekicks are infinitely smarter and more diligent. No matter how good he is, player number three will be hard pressed to win. This player will have difficulty amassing properties. On the other hand, he will not be able to afford any misjudgments or bad luck. A bad choice or a capricious die will mean the end of the game for him. The second player will be better off. He will be able to buy some land and absorb a certain amount of misfortune without dying. If he is lucky, he may be able to eat away at the fortune of his more fortunate neighbor and eventually win the game. However, this neighbor will have to suffer from extreme bad luck or pathological stupidity to manage to lose. In order to preserve everyone's chances, a solution would perhaps be for a "banker" to intervene, upstream, to regulate the distribution of resources to the benefit of the least advantaged players. This interventionism would not erase the original inequalities, but would level out their importance. Everyone could then defend his chances with some hope of success. Our banker would occupy the role devolved since the war to the social systems of old Europe. These systems are, however, hated by American liberals on the grounds that social assistance is an incentive to laziness[202] and a distorting factor in the market mechanism[203]. Let the market work and everyone will be rewarded according to their merits.

The claim that the market rewards everyone according to their merit is not without its problems. In particular, who would dare to say that Anna is devoid of merit? Who would say that this woman lacks rigor and courage? Who would consider her lazy and deny the vigor of her efforts for herself and her child? Certainly not me! In fact, if we go beyond the semantic melody to look at the deep meaning of words, we realize that the notion of merit survives only by the grace of a despicable conceptual sham. In our Judeo-Christian imagination, the ideas of effort and merit

---

202. C. Murray, *Losing Ground...*, *op. cit.* (Introd., n. 63). In France, Nicolas Baverez, *Que faire: Agenda 2007*, *op. cit.* (Introd., n. 63), chap. 4.
203. *A. Lindbeck*, et al, Turning Sweden Around, op. cit.

are intimately superimposed. Work takes precedence over completion. We love the farmer who works his land hard. We honor the craftsman who takes pride in a fine work. To Anquetil the flamboyant we prefer Poulidor the hardworking. The first one breathes ease and facility while the second one sweats pain and torment. The effort is at the center of our values. We revere and glorify it, sometimes obscenely, often sincerely. "*Arbeit macht frei*" ("work makes you free"), proclaimed the gate of the Auschwitz camp. "I have lived because I have worked," thundered Zola[204]. We must put France back to work, Nicolas Baverez now tells us, on the grounds that France will know "neither sustainable growth, nor a return to full employment, nor catching up, without a significant increase in the volume of work[205]". At the sound of this very liberal wisdom, I cannot help but think of a sentence by Jeanson: "Work is a treasure. The work of others, that goes without saying[206]. This is a very wise assertion when one considers that the tremendous productivity gains recorded in recent years in the United States have only marginally benefited company employees. For example, between 2000 and 2004, productivity grew by 14 per cent while the median annual wage lost 1.2 per cent[207]. I will return to this point in detail later.

For a long time, I believed in rewarding effort. I believed in it until a gloomy notebook I received the year I turned 9. "Do what you can, but can't do much", the teacher had written. The young lady must not have been very Christian. Neither was my father, if I am to believe the memorable beating he gave me that day. Working wasn't enough, you had to succeed. Contrary to what I kept hearing, the "real" world didn't care about the effort made, it was only interested in the result obtained. Liberalism is the son of this bitter logic. For this economic model, effort has neither

---

204. Quoted *in* N. Baverez, *What to do: Agenda 2007, op. cit.* (Introd., n. 63), p. 117.
205. *Ibid*, p. 124.
206. H. Jeanson, *Soix-dix ans d'adolescence*, Paris, Stock, 1971, quoted *in* J.Y. Dournon, *Le Grand Dictionnaire des citations françaises*, Paris, Acropole, 1982.
207. *The State of Working America 2006-2007, op. cit. (Introd., n. 13), chap. 3, table 3.1.*

Mad in U.S.A.: The ravages of the American model

meaning nor value. The market does not pay for sweat. It rewards only the profit made. Woe betide those who, like Anna, have their sweat as their only wealth. The effort does not give them, even if it is massive, any recognition, any merit.

From an ethical point of view, the proven contempt for effort seems all the more unjust since our "merit" depends largely on factors that are beyond our control. If Mr. de Castries had been born into a poor family, would he have become what he is today? Would his intelligence, his perseverance, his judgment have overcome the prejudice of indigence? Let me doubt it, not because I doubt the qualities of the man, but because I know as a neurophysiologist the damage that poverty causes to the integrity of our psychological, physical and intellectual development. As a group of leading researchers point out in a recent collective report in the United States, "Today, this work [on the links between poverty and development] is undergoing a transition from the question of *whether* family resources affect child development to the question of *why* the research shows so consistently that this is the case[208]". For those who remain dubious, let me briefly discuss this issue.

When we are conceived, we receive a genetic heritage from our parents. This heritage defines a potential space for development. During our growth, this potential is progressively expressed on the basis of our encounters with the environment. If this environment is deficient, so is our development. It is clear that poverty leads to major environmental deficiencies. For example, being poor means, for many, suffering from inadequate nutrition. In the United States, food insecurity affects more than 13 million households (12%) according to the latest figures for 2004[209]. Most of these households (two-thirds) are faced with inadequate diets (staple foods, unbalanced

---

208. Jack P. Shonkoff & Deborah A. Phillips (eds.), *From Neurons to Neighborhoods: The Science of Early Childhood Development* (Washington, DC: National Academy Press, 2000), p. 267.
209. Mark Nord, Margaret Andrews, & Steven Carlson, "Household Food Security in the United States, 2004," United States Department of Agriculture, Economic Research Report, No. ERR11, October 2005, available online: http://www.ers.usda.gov/publications/err11/

diets, and various deficiencies) rather than inadequate diets. This relative "good news" indicates, however, that hunger is still felt by at least 4% of American families. While adults absorb most of this deprivation, a substantial number of children remain affected (275,000). For these children, food assistance is either insufficient[210] or too difficult to obtain[211]. All this is not without consequences. Indeed, insufficient and/or inadequate nutrition results in alterations in pre- and post-natal development. Factors such as height[212] or brain development[213] are heavily affected.

In addition to the problem of food, there is also the problem of habitat. Indeed, being poor often means living in biologically unhealthy environments, known to favor injuries, allergies, asthma[214] and various contaminations. Regarding the latter, epidemiological studies have shown, for example, that in 2005, 310,000 children under the age of 5 in the United States had dangerously high levels of lead in their blood[215]. Disadvantaged black children who frequently live in substandard housing were, on average, contaminated 2.3 times more frequently than white children (3% versus 1.3%)[216]. Overall, children from families with incomes below 130% of the poverty line were 3.5 times more likely to be contaminated with lead than their more affluent counterparts[217]. Medically, the effects of lead overexposure include loss of appetite,

---

210. D.K. Shipler, *The Working Poor...*, *op. cit.* (Introd., n. 68), p. 40.

211. Elisabeth Becker, "Millions Eligible for Food Stamps Aren't Applying," *New York Times*, February 26, 2001.

212. B. Bogin, P. Smith, A.B. Orden, M.I. Varela-Silva, J. Loucky, "Rapid Change in Height and Body Proportions of Maya American Children," *American Journal of Human Biology*, 2002, 14, pp. 753-761; Nicolas Herpin, *Le Pouvoir des grands*, Paris, La découverte, 2006.

213. J.P. Shonkoff & D.A. Phillips (eds.), *From Neurons to Neighborhoods...*, *op. cit.* (*supra*, n. 121), chap. 8 ("The Developing Brain").

214. D.K. Shipler, *The Working Poor...*, *op. cit.* (Introd., n. 68), pp. 226-227.

215. Center for Disease Control and Prevention (CDC), "Childhood Lead Poisoning," 2005, Fact Sheet, available online: http://www.cdc.gov/nceh/publications/factsheets/Childhood-LeadPoisoning.pdf

216. *Ibid.*

217. J.P. Shonkoff & D.A. Phillips (eds.), *From Neurons to Neighborhoods...*, *op. cit.* (*supra*, n. 121), chap. 10 ("Family Resources"), pp. 267-296, see table 10.1.

impaired nerve development, growth deficits, and organ damage, particularly to the liver. These disorders persist over the long term, particularly in their cognitive dimension[218]. It may be important to note that the number of 310,000 children is most likely underestimated. Indeed, recent studies have confirmed that lead ingestion-related disorders occur at levels well below the official tolerance threshold[219].

In addition to the above, there are a number of other factors that relate more or less directly to the nature of the cognitive stimulation provided to the child. These stimuli are absolutely necessary for the optimal development of brain functions. It has long been known, for example, that the brains of animals raised in enriched environments are larger, more complex, denser in synaptic connections, and ultimately more functionally capable than the brains of animals raised in less favorable environments[220]. It is also known that the brains of children who have suffered severe parental neglect or certain early institutional placements show substantial atrophy. One study showed that this atrophy was partially reversed when children were removed from their original environment before the age of 5 and placed in a more supportive environment[221]. This observation is compatible with the well-known notion of a "sensitive period". In fact, if the brain does

218. H.L. Needleman, A. Schell, D. Bellinger, A. Leviton & E.N. Allred, "The Long-Term Effects of Exposure to Low Doses of Lead in Childhood," An 11-year Follow-up Report, *The New England Journal of Medicine*, 1990, 322, pp. 83-88; D. Bellinger, K.M. Stiles & H.L. Needleman, "Low-Level Lead Exposure, Intelligence and Academic Achievement: a Long-Term Follow-Up Study," *Pediatrics*, 1992, 90, pp. 855-861; J.M. Coscia, M.D. Ris, P.A. Succop & K.N. Dietrich, "Cognitive Development of Lead Exposed Children from Ages 6 to 15 Years: an Application of Growth Curve Analysis," *Child Neuropsychol*, 2003, 9, pp. 10-21.
219. Richard L. Canfield, *et al*, "Intellectual Impairment in Children with Blood Lead Concentrations below 10 µg per deciliter," *The New England Journal of Medicine*, 2003, 348, pp. 1517-1526; L.M. Chiodo, S.W. Jacobson & J.L. Jacobson, "Neurodevelopmental Effects of Postnatal Lead Exposure at Very Low Levels," *Neurotoxicology and Teratology*, 2004, 26: 359-371.
220. For a review: J.P. Shonkoff & D.A. Phillips (eds.), *From Neurons to Neighborhoods...*, *op. cit.* (*supra*, n. 121), chap. 8; Bruce D. Perry, "Childhood Experience and the Expression of Genetic Potential: What Childhood Neglect Tells Us About Nature and Nurture," *Brain and Mind*, 2002, 3, pp. 79-100.
221. Quoted *in* Bruce D. Perry, "Childhood Experience and the Expression of Genetic Potential...," *op. cit.* (*supra*, n. 133), pp. 92-94.

not encounter the stimuli it needs to build itself at the required moment, it builds itself badly. In cases of extreme deprivation, it does not even build itself at all[222]. The perception and production of sounds is the best known example of this phenomenon. A child gradually loses the ability to distinguish and produce sounds that are not part of his or her mother tongue. Mathilde, originally from Germany, arrived in France at the age of 25. Half a century later, she was still making raclette with "pompétères" and "Reuplochon". As for the author of this book, after spending 8 years in the United States, he still insisted on confusing the beautiful beaches of California ("*beach*") with the dark girls of joy ("*bitch*"). When the train of ontogeny has passed, one unfortunately does not catch up with it anymore.

Of course, it is to be expected that the effects of poverty are not as drastic as those of extreme neglect. However, destitution is often accompanied by a form of cognitive understimulation. Disadvantaged parents generally lack the time, skills, energy, mental toughness and/or financial means to provide an optimal educational environment for their offspring, as Anna did. Consistent with this idea, several studies involving complex standardized scales have shown a strong relationship between family resources and the quality of the educational environment[223]. This relationship is estimated to explain 50% of the effects of poverty on the IQ of 5-year-olds[224] (these effects are detailed below). In support of this high figure,

---

222. See for example the seminal work of Hubel and Wiesel on the development of the visual system: D.H. Hubel & T.N. Wiesel, "The Period of Susceptibility to the Physiological Effects of Unilateral Eye Closure in Kittens," *Journal of Physiology* (London), 1970, 206, pp. 419-436; D.H. Hubel & T.N. Wiesel, "Single-Cell Responses in Striate Cortex of Kittens Deprived of Vision in One Eye," *Journal of Neurophysiology*, 1963, 26, pp. 1003-1017.
223. P. Garrett, N. Ng'andu & J. Ferron, "Poverty Experience of Young Children and the Quality of Their Home Environments," *Child Development*, 1994, 65, pp. 331-345; G.J. Duncan, W. Yeung, J. Brooks-Gunn & J.R. Smith, "How Much Does Childhood Poverty Affect the Life Chances of Children?", *American Sociological Review*, 1998, 63, pp. 406-423.
224. J. Brooks-Gunn, G.J. Duncan, P.K. Klebanov & N. Sealand, "Do Neighborhoods Influence Child and Adolescent Behavior?", *American Journal of Sociology*, 1993, 99, pp. 335-395; J. Brooks-Gunn & G.J. Duncan, "The Effects of Poverty on Children", 1997, *The Future of Children*, 7, pp. 55-71.

recent work by Guao and Harris found that the level of cognitive stimulation was by far the most important factor in explaining the influence of poverty on children's intellectual development. In the authors' words, "Poverty exerts a large negative effect on cognitive stimulation, and cognitive stimulation exerts a large positive effect on intellectual development; (...) most of the effect of poverty on intellectual development operates through this channel[225]."

The list of factors mentioned above to account for the adverse effects of poverty on child development is far from exhaustive. One could also have mentioned, at the expense of the less privileged, the attendance of schools and nurseries of sub-standard quality, the high proportion of single-parent families, untreated illnesses due to difficult access to the health system, increased risks of prematurity and exposure to dangerous substances during gestation (tobacco, drugs, alcohol), intra-family interactions vitiated by the existence of chronic stress inherent in the situation of indigence, etc.[226]. For years, conservative ideology has tried, especially in Anglo-Saxon countries, to deny the deleterious effects of all these factors on individual development. Some (pseudo)scientists have also been complacent in this endeavor. The master in this field was undoubtedly Cyril Burt, an influential English psychologist of the middle of the 20th century, who died in 1971 after being knighted by the Queen of England for his contribution to the influence of the crown. Sir Burt's specialty was the study of twins separated at birth and raised in different socio-economic environments. Not easy to find, but our great man, helped by two eminent collaborators, found 53 pairs of usable children. The study of these pairs showed that the IQ of two homozygous twins always remained very close, independently of the characteristics of the environment. Based on this observation, Burt

---

225. G. Guo & K.M. Harris, "The Mechanisms Mediating the Effects of Poverty on Children Intellectual Development," *Demography*, 2000, 37, pp. 431-447, citation p. 442.

226. For a more comprehensive review: J. Brooks-Gunn & G.J. Duncan, "The Effects of Poverty on Children," *op. cit.* (*supra*, n. 137); J.P. Shonkoff & D.A. Phillips (eds.), *From Neurons to Neighborhoods...*, *op. cit.* (*supra*, n. 121), chapters 10 and 13 ("Promoting Healthy Development Through Intervention").

proposed the concept of IQ heritability. In a later work, he drew the full implications of his observations by writing that "the wide inequality of income is largely, but not wholly, an effect of the wide inequality of innate intelligence. Clearly, these data "do not support the view (still held by many proponents of social and educational reform) that the apparent inequality in the intelligence of children and adults is, broadly speaking, an indirect consequence of unequal economic conditions[227]. This has the merit of clarity... except for one detail. Sir Cyril Burt, a great contemptor of the lack of moral sense of the poorest, had invented everything: travel, twins, statistics and female employees[228]! However, the message of the master was not completely lost and vigorous successors soon emerged. Among the best known are the incredible Richard Herrnstein and Charles Murray. Their joint work, *The Bell Curve*[229], is a worldwide best-seller. In this document (which I hardly dare to call a "work"), our two thieves propagate a triple message: 1) intelligence is inherited, just like height or eye color; 2) the degraded social situation of Blacks stems from the fact that, as a race, they have a lower IQ than Whites; 3) the apocalypse is waiting for us in the form of an army of mentally retarded people living off us and reproducing faster than the rabbits in our countryside. It is undeniable that the political microcosm was shaken. Unfortunately, the noise that this report made is matched only by the intellectual falsification that presided over its publication. Herrnstein and Murray did not, as Burt did, invent their data. They simply apprehended and presented them with incredible dishonesty[230]. As Stephen Jay Gould points out at the end of a

---

227. Cyril Burt, "Ability and Income," *British Journal of Educational Psychology*, 13, pp. 83-98, quoted *in* S.J. Gould, *The Ill-measurement of Man, op. cit.* (*supra*, n. 50), pp. 324-325.

228. Oliver Gillie, "Crucial Data Was Faked by Eminent Psychologist," London, *Sunday Times*, October 24, 1976; S.J. Gould, *The Mis-measurement of Man, op. cit.* (*supra*, n. 50), chap. V; Alexander Kohn, *False Prophets* (New York: Barnes & Noble Books, 1997); Anna Alter, "Le QI des jumeaux selon Cyril Burt", *Marianne*, 484, 29 July-4 August 2006.

229. R.J. Herrnstein & C. Murray, *The Bell Curve..., op. cit.* (*supra*, n. 50).

230. For a discussion, C.S. Fischer, M. Hout, M.S. Jankowski, S.R. Lucas, A. Swidler & K. Vos, *Inequality by Design..., op. cit.* (*supra*, n. 50); S.J. Gould, *The Ill-measurement of Man, op. cit.* (*supra*, n. 50), especially pp. 379-406.

meticulous critique of the "hereditarist" arguments presented in *The Bell Curve*: "This book is a manifesto for conservative ideology, and if it distorts the facts to such an extent, it is because of its overriding objective: to make propaganda above all. It echoes the dismal and fearsome hype orchestrated by the ideological laboratories of the right for a number of measures such as: eliminating or reducing unemployment benefits; ending aid to ethnic minorities in an effort to provide true equal opportunity in school and work; ending the federal aid program for disadvantaged schoolchildren and other forms of early education aid; and cutting aid to support the slowest learners, coupled with transferring the funds thus raised to gifted schoolchildren and students[231]." Ironically, this was published at a time when the United States, under Bill Clinton, was implementing welfare reform that drastically limited coverage for the poorest[232].

With a minimum of bad faith, it is possible to affirm, and I can testify to this, that Burt's deception and the intellectual dishonesty of the Herrnstein-Murray duo are by no means sufficient to condemn the "hereditary" theory. Even Mendel and Newton, in their time, would have taken some liberties with uncooperative numerical realities[233]. It is sometimes necessary, in order to establish a noble truth, to help the figures a little. The sin of Burt and his companions could in this context be all the more venial as the relationship between poverty and intellectual indigence is clearly established. Poor children are 1.5 times more likely to experience developmental delays and learning disabilities than their better-off counterparts[234]. Similarly, there is a strong correlation between a household's level of resources and

---

231. *Ibid.* at 390.

232. J. Iceland, *Poverty in America...*, *op. cit.* (Introd., n. 9), pp. 132-133; S.S. Sered & R. Fernandopulle, *Uninsured in America...*, *op. cit.* (Introd., n. 21), pp. 52-56; A. Weil & K. Finegold, *Welfare Reform...*, *op. cit.* (*supra*, n. 19).

233. A. Kohn, *False Prophets*, *op. cit.* (*supra*, n. 141), pp. 36-45; Anna Alter, "Les petits arrangements de Galilée, Newton et Mendel," *Marianne*, 485, August 5-August 11, 2006.

234. J. Brooks-Gunn & G.J. Duncan, "The Effects of Poverty on Children," *op. cit.* (*supra*, n. 137); J.P. Shonkoff & D.A. Phillips (eds.), *From Neurons to Neighborhoods...*, *op. cit.* (*supra*, n. 121), chap. 10.

the success of its children on tests of IQ, verbal fluency, and academic performance. Depending on the item, the differences observed between extremely (0.5 threshold) and relatively (1.5 to 2 thresholds) poor children range from 6 to 13 points[235]. For reference, 15 IQ points represents the gap between the states of normality (100) and mental retardation (below 85). Of course, the consequences of poverty are all the more severe the longer and earlier the child is exposed to it (which, in "Burtian" terms, indicates, not that poverty alters development, but rather that the more genetically imbecilic one is, the more intensely poor one is). To predict the number of years of schooling that an individual will complete, the best way is to know the extent of family resources available when that individual was very young. The accuracy of the estimate will be optimal between 0 and 5 years of age and then degraded between 5 and 10 years and 10 and 15 years. It has been shown that for poor children, an increase in average family income of $10,000 between the ages of 0 and 5, or only $166 per month, increases the number of years of schooling completed by one unit[236]. It is likely that this increase in years of schooling does not only reflect an optimization of intellectual structures. Indeed, poverty also has a large influence on emotional functions. Being poor exposes the child to depression, psychological disorders, anxiety, conflict, aggressiveness, etc.[237]. This may explain why disadvantaged schoolchildren are twice as likely to be suspended or expelled from school as their well-to-do counterparts[238].

On the basis of the preceding elements, the question arises as to whether the link associating material poverty, intellectual indigence and emotional

---

235. J. Brooks-Gunn & G.J. Duncan, "The Effects of Poverty on Children," *op. cit.* (*supra,* n. 137) at 61.

236. G.J. Duncan, W. Yeung, J. Brooks-Gunn & J.R. Smith, "How Much Does Childhood Poverty Affect the Life Chances of Children?" *op. cit.* (*supra,* n. 136).

237. J. Brooks-Gunn & G.J. Duncan, "The Effects of Poverty on Children," *op. cit.* (*supra,* n. 137); J.P. Shonkoff & D.A. Phillips (eds.), *From Neurons to Neighborhoods...,* *op. cit.* (*supra,* n. 121), chapters 10 and 13.

238. J. Brooks-Gunn & G.J. Duncan, "The Effects of Poverty on Children," *op. cit.* (*supra,* n. 137).

prejudice is inescapable because it is anchored in our genes and our laziness, or reformable because it is linked to the deficiencies of an insufficiently stimulating environment. A first element of answer is provided by old standardized studies, carried out on animals. In a first study, rats were trained to find their way through a maze[239]. The median competitors were then eliminated and only the best and worst performing rats were kept. The "geniuses" were then crossed on one side and the "dunces" on the other. After repeating this operation over several generations, two lines of rats were obtained, one "brilliant" and the other "dull". When these lines were subjected to the maze test, a large difference was observed to the detriment of the "dull" rats. This result clearly supports the thesis of a genetically determined cognitive competence which could be said to measure the "intelligence" of rats. A second study was conducted to identify precisely the robustness of this skill[240]. The initial crossing procedure was then reapplied to three situations: 1) impoverished: the rats were raised in an environment that was as basic and unstimulating as possible (solitude, monochrome cages, no toys, etc.); 2) enriched: the rats were raised in a complex and attractive environment (pairings, colored toys, various stimuli); 3) control: the rats were raised in an intermediate "standard" environment. The "control" situation allowed replicating the results of the original experiment. The "impoverished" situation caused a massive failure of the bright rats who suddenly became as incompetent as their dull counterparts. The "enriched" situation had the exact opposite effect. The dull rats promptly became as good as their brighter counterparts. In other words, take genetically stupid rats, raise them in a stimulating environment and they will eventually prove to be as "smart" as genetically brilliant rats.

239. R.C. Tryon, "Genetic Differences in Maze-Learning Ability in Rats," *Yearbook* of the National Society for the Study of Education, 1940, 39, pp. 111-119.
240. R.M. Cooper & J.P. Zubek, "Effects of Enriched and Restricted Early Environments on the Learning Ability of Bright and Dull Rats," *Canadian Journal of Psychology*, 1958, 12, pp. 159-164.

Of course, humans are not rats, even if biology owes many of its greatest advances to our rodent friends. In humans, we cannot carry out experimental genetic crosses (even if Burt, Murray and Mengele dreamed of it), nor can we manipulate the environment at will. However, we can study the effect of an environmental mutation on cognitive performance. This is what a team from INSERM did in 1999[241]. Five thousand adoption files were then examined to identify 65 children adopted between the ages of 4 and 6. At the time of adoption, these children had IQ values ranging from 60 (average mental retardation) to 86 (mild mental retardation). Nine years later, these values had increased by an average of 14 points. Interestingly, a strong interaction was observed between IQ variations and the socioeconomic status of the adopting families. The most affluent homes led to an increase in children's IQ of almost 20 points. The change was contained to "only" 8 points in the least privileged homes. It is difficult to find a more striking demonstration of the influence of the environment on the intellectual development of children.

The previous study is far from isolated in its message. Over the last thirty years, a number of studies have confirmed that procedures for helping poor households considerably reduce the deleterious influence of poverty on the cognitive, affective and social development of children[242]. Among these studies, some have focused on intra-family relational dynamics, others have worked on direct financial aid protocols, and others have concentrated on educational assistance for young children. There seems to be no magic formula and the individualization of approaches seems to be the key to success in this field[243]. However, there is now clear

---

241. Michel Duyme, Annick-Camille Dumaret & Stanislaw Tomkiewicz, "How Can We Boost IQs of 'dull children'? A Late Adoption Study," *Proceedings of the National Academy of Sciences* (USA), 1999, 96, pp. 8790-8794.
242. J. Brooks-Gunn & G.J. Duncan, "The Effects of Poverty on Children," *op. cit.* (*supra*, n. 137); J.P. Shonkoff & D.A. Phillips (eds.), *From Neurons to Neighborhoods...*, *op. cit.* (*supra*, n. 121), chap. 13.
243. J.P. Shonkoff & D.A. Phillips (eds.), *From Neurons to Neighborhoods...*, *op. cit.* (*supra*, n. 121), chap. 13, pp. 360-361.

evidence that poor children do better academically if they are placed in schools attended by an affluent population than if they are left together in schools with a high proportion of disadvantaged students[244]. Some early educational support programs based on this distributive approach have produced quite impressive results. One such program has now been running for over 40 years. It is known as the High/Scope Perry Preschool Study[245]. It began between 1962 and 1967 with the selection of 123 black children who were severely disadvantaged and designated candidates for academic failure. Fifty-eight of these children were randomly selected and enrolled at ages 3 to 4 in a high-quality preschool program. The rest received no special support. At the end of the program, educational intervention ceased for the experimental group and all participants were "released" on a strictly equal basis. Assessments were then conducted annually between the ages of 3 and 11, and at 14, 15, 19, 27 and 40. The message of these assessments is basically quite simple: children who have been subjected to a high-quality preschool program outperform their "control" counterparts in all domains, cognitive, affective, occupational, family and social. The differences continue to be substantial 35 years after the end of an early educational intervention that lasted only 24 months. Among the most important long-term influences were: academic achievement (65% bachelor's degree vs. 45%), unemployment rate (at age 40: 24% vs. 38%), annual wage ($20,800 vs. $15,300), drug use (heroin: 0% versus 9%; hashish: 48% versus 71%), delinquency rate (32% versus 48% arrested for violent crimes; 14% versus 34% arrested for drug offenses), and parents' level of involvement in their children's schooling. This last point is particularly impressive in the sense that it suggests the existence of a positive intergenerational contagion. From a

244. S. Caldas, & C. Bankston, "Effect of School Population Socioeconomic Status on Individual Academic Achievement," *Journal of Educational Research*, May/June 1997, pp. 269-276.
245. Lawrence J. Schweinhart, "The High/Scope Perry Preschool Study Through Age 40: summary, conclusions and frequently asked questions," 2006, High/Scope Educational Research Foundation, summary available online: http://www.highscope.org/file/Research/PerryProject/3_specialsummary%20col%2006%2007.pdf

strictly financial point of view, it seems that the community's money has been well invested. In fact, the cost of the High/Scope Perry Preschool Study was $15,000 per child (in constant 2000 dollars). This may seem out of line. Yet a careful numerical analysis shows that the taxpayer benefited greatly from this expenditure. Indeed, if one adds the extra taxes collected on higher salaries ($14,000) and the savings on special education programs ($7,000), social benefits ($3,000), or delinquency ($171,000), the return on investment is 1,700%. In other words, every dollar invested has returned 17[246].

In conclusion, it is clear from the foregoing that the poor are neither pathological slackers irredeemably unworthy of compassion, nor fundamentally amoral genetic morons. The condition of destitution does not (unfortunately) reflect the extent of individual effort. When a child is raised in a poor home, he or she is likely to end up poor himself or herself. This is true in the United States, more than in any other developed country. Financial deprivation carries with it all sorts of environmental deficiencies. Each of these deficiencies conspires against the emotional, intellectual, social, and psychological development of the individuals who suffer from them. The poorest children are like dumb rats, raised in poor environments, who suddenly turn out to be as smart as their most gifted peers when they are placed in a privileged environment early on. All the research shows that the deleterious effects of destitution can be, if not abrogated, at least successfully combated. It is of course possible to suggest that the community does not have to help its poor. One can legitimately make a political statement out of rugged individualism. This is America's choice. It is a choice that America makes well enough to have more poor children and adults than any other developed country without blushing. However, it is also possible, on the contrary, to think that it is fair to ensure that each individual who has just been born has a decent development universe. Europe, with its much-maligned social

---

246. *Ibid.*

system and its luxuriant taxes, is the daughter of this logic. Those who would like to take us away from this humanistic path should, I think, have the courage to go forward with a clear face, without hiding behind a sea of pontificating liberal bullshit. To economic barbarity, let us not add intellectual forfeiture.

Poverty: and yet they work

In the United States, the federal minimum wage has been $5.15 per hour since 1997[247]. At current exchange rates, this is about 48% of the French minimum wage (8.27 euros)[248]. When the median wage is compared to the minimum wage, it appears that unskilled labor costs substantially less in America than in all Western European countries[249]. This probably explains why having a job is far from being a guarantee of financial sufficiency in Uncle Sam. In liberal countries, a single adult working full-time[250] at minimum wage earns $10,300, or 1.03 times the poverty line[251]. The ratio drops to 0.81 for a single mother with one dependent child[252] and 0.77 for a "standard" household of four with a full-time father and half-time mother[253]. This means that for many Americans, even full-time work is not an escape from poverty. According to official figures, nearly 2.5 million people in the United States work for an hourly wage at or below the minimum wage[254]. This problem has

---

247. US Department of Labor, Internet Release, http://stats.bls.gov/cps/minwage2005.htm

248. National Institute of Statistics and Economic Studies (INSEE), http://www.insee.fr/fr/indicateur/smic.htm

249. "The Cost of Labour," *The Economist*, April 2, 2005.

250. By full-time I mean 40 hours a week, 50 weeks a year.

251. The poverty line is $9,973 for a single person; US Census Bureau, Internet Release, 2006, http://pubdb3.census.gov/macro/032006/pov/new35_000.htm

252. The poverty line is $12,755 for a family of two; US Census Bureau, Internet Release, 2006, http://pubdb3.census.gov/macro/032006/pov/new35_000.htm

253. The poverty line is equal to $20,144 for a family of 4; US Census Bureau, Internet Release, 2006, http://pubdb3.census.gov/macro/032006/pov/new35_000.htm

254. Us Bureau of Labor, Internet Release, http://stats.bls.gov/cps/minwage2005.htm

prompted nearly 20 states to set a minimum wage higher than the federal wage, as permitted by law (with a maximum of $7.63 in Washington state)[255]. The very libertarian (and very expensive) San Francisco even felt compelled to impose an $8.50 base. Unfortunately, all this "good will" has not solved the problem of compensation for work. For example, over 73% of poor families with at least one minor child are connected to the labour market by at least one parent. In nearly 30 percent of indigent households with children, the working parent is employed full time[256]. Focusing on the 3.5 million poor single mother families with at least one child, the mother is employed in more than 50 percent of cases. Nearly 15 percent of these women, like Anna, work full time or more, that is, at least 40 hours a week, 50 weeks of the year[257]. These figures take on their full meaning when compared to the ideological message disseminated by the American press and many of its European followers[258]. Thus, in a study that is certainly old (1996), but more relevant than ever, Gilens was able to show, by studying four of the largest American news magazines (*Time*, *Newsweek*, *US News* and *World Report*), that only 15 per cent of individuals of working age were represented, in the articles related to poverty, as actually working. To be accurate, this percentage should have been more than 50 percent[259].

Exactly how many working poor are there in the United States? The answer depends on the criteria used: 4.5 million if we consider only individuals who worked full-time for the whole year[260]; 7.4 million if

---

255. Us Bureau of Labor, Internet Release, http://www.dol.gov/esa/minwage/america.htm

256. US Census Bureau, Internet Release, 2006, http://pubdb3.census.gov/macro/032006/pov/new07_100_01.htm; see also J. Iceland & Josh Kim, "Poverty Among Working Families: Insights From an Improved Measure," *Social Science Quarterly*, 2001, 82, pp. 253-267.

257. US Census Bureau, Internet Release, 2006, http://pubdb3.census.gov/macro/032006/pov/new07_100_01.htm

258. For example, Bernard-Henri Lévy, *American Vertigo, op. cit.* (Introd., n. 30), p. 395.

259. Martin Gilens, "Race and Poverty in America: Public Misperceptions and the American News Media," *Public Opinion Quarterly*, 1996, 60, pp. 515-541.

260. Bureau of Labor Statistics, "The Profile of the Working Poor 2003," Report 983, 2005, available online: http://www.bls.gov/cps/cpswp2003.pdf

we include those whose activity exceeded 27 weeks of full-time equivalent[261]; 30 million if we measure the number of workers receiving a wage below 65% of the national median wage. A cross-national study published in 2000, using this criterion, showed that America was ahead of all other industrialized countries with 25 percent of working poor[262]. The percentages were, for example, 19.5 percent for the United Kingdom, 13.5 percent for France and Germany, 7.5 percent for Norway and 5.5 percent for Sweden. It seems from these values that the remuneration of labour is inversely proportional to the freedom offered to market forces. The more liberal the economy, the greater the number of workers earning low wages.

Based on the post-war social model, when the father worked and the mother stayed at home, some authors have proposed to define as working poor all employees whose hourly wage was less than that required to raise a standard family of 4 above the poverty line ($9.60 in 2005). On this basis, 25% of the U.S. workforce can be considered working poor[263]. Recently, Mark Rank has refined the concept somewhat by taking into account the actual size of the family unit and determining the number of households for which the wage of the "head of household" was not sufficient to exceed the states of poverty (official threshold), near poverty (1.25 * threshold) and relative poverty (1.50 * threshold)[264]. The results are striking. For full-time workers, they reach 10%, 15% and 22%. If we count workers who worked half-time or more, we get: 15%, 21% and 28%. If we now count all workers who are in the labor market, i.e., who have either worked or actively sought work, we find: 20%, 27%, and 33%. Of course, the

---

261. *Ibid.*

262. T.M. Smeeding, L. Rainwater & G. Burtless, "United States Poverty in a Cross-National Context," *op. cit.* (Introd., n. 44), Figure 2.

263. M. Conlin & A. Bernstein, "Working... and Poor," *op. cit.* (*supra*, n. 39), available online: http://www.businessweek.com/magazine/content/04_22/b3885001_mz001.htm; B. Shulman, *The Betrayal of Work...*, *op. cit.* (Introd., n. 10); *The State of Working America 2006-2007*, *op. cit.* (Introd., n. 13), chap. 3, table 3.7.

264. M.R. Rank, *One Nation Underprivileged...*, *op. cit.* (Introd., n. 10), pp. 53-59.

situation worsens with household size. For a standard family of four in which one parent works full-time, the chances of being poor are 15%. The chances of being in near-poverty or poverty are 25% and 36% respectively. These figures are hardly surprising considering that 41% of American workers earn less than $12 per hour, which is less than the minimum wage required to support a standard family of four above the near poverty line (1.25 * threshold)[265].

The situation for U.S. assets was not always this difficult. In fact, it has deteriorated significantly over the past 25 years. The New World economy has destroyed many stable, well-paying manufacturing jobs with solid benefits (health insurance, paid leave, retirement) for low-wage, non-social benefit service jobs, often on a part-time basis[266]. Eighteen percent of Americans in the top half of the population in 1983 were below the poverty line 10 years later[267]. Since 1970, the incomes of the least educated in the United States have plummeted. Between 1971 and 2002, the median wage of a young adult, aged 25 to 34, fell in constant 2002 dollars from $35,087 to $22,903 (-35%) for a non-graduate, from $41,113 to $29,647 (-28%) for a bachelor[268], from $44,743 to $35,552 (-20%) for a student with no university certification, and from $51,218

---

265. The State of Working America 2006-2007, op. cit. *(Introd., n. 13), chap. 3, table 3.7.*

266. Karen Seccombe, "Families in Poverty in the 1990s: Trends, Causes, Consequences and Lessons Learned," *Journal of Marriage and the Family*, 2000, 62, pp. 1094-1113; B. Shulman, *The Betrayal of Work...*, *op. cit.* (Introd., n. 10), pp. 47-50; M. Lind, "Are We Still a Middle Class Nation?" in *The Real State of the Union*, *op. cit.* (Introd., n. 8), pp. 20-23; M.R. Rank, *One Nation Underprivileged...*, *op. cit.* (Introd., n. 10), p. 80; J. Iceland, *Poverty in America...*, *op. cit.* (Introd., n. 9), p. 77; Barbara Hagenbaugh, "U.S. Manufacturing Jobs Fading Away Fast," *USA Today*, Dec. 12, 2002, available online at http://www.usatoday.com/money/economy/2002-12-12-manufacture_x.htm; *The State of Working America 2006-2007*, *op. cit.* (Introd., n. 13), chap. 3, tables 3.27 and 3.28; David Friedman, "One-Dimensional Growth," in *The Real State of the Union*, *op. cit.* (Introd., n. 8), pp. 27-33.

267. Jacob S. Hacker, "The Insecure Family," in *The Real State of the Union*, *op. cit.* (Introd., n. 8), pp. 85-91, reference p. 87.

268. The High-School diploma.

to \$48,955 (-0.05%) for university graduates (bachelor's degree + 4)[269]. The pattern is somewhat less dramatic when all workers are considered. In this case, between 1973 and 2005 (in constant dollars), there was a decrease for non-graduates (-17%), relative stagnation for baccalaureate holders (-0.02%) and an increase for university graduates (+17%)[270]. In parallel with these fluctuations, "basic" expenses related to housing, health, transportation, or education have literally exploded. This combination of rising costs and falling individual incomes for the least educated has been so massive that neither the increase in the number of hours worked over the past 30 years[271], nor the shift from a single-financed economy (where only the father works) to a dual-financed economy (where both the father and mother work) has been enough to stabilize the standard of living of the middle class[272]. In constant dollars, one wage in 1970 left families with more discretionary income than two wages today, even if those two wages are equivalent, on paper, to 75 per cent more income[273]. It seems a little difficult, therefore, to conclude, as I often hear, that the market has golden hands. When one shifts from myth to fact, it becomes clear that the liberal potions applied since Reagan's presidency have proved to be a formidable vehicle, not for enriching, but for impoverishing the middle classes. The market surely has a very beneficial effect on the price of sausages and computers. Unfortunately, its omnipotence seems to suffer from some weaknesses in certain fundamental areas such as the remuneration and stability of work[274], access to

---

269. US Department of Education, National Center for Education Statistics, "The Condition of Education," 2004, table 14.1, available online: http://nces.ed.gov/pubs2004/2004077.pdf

270. *The State of Working America 2006-2007*, op. cit. *(Introd., n. 13), chap. 3, table 3.17.*

271. *The State of Working America 2006-2007*, op. cit. *(Introd., n. 13), chap. 3, table 3.1; Juliet B. Schor,* The Overworked American *(New York: Basic Books, 1993).*

272. Elizabeth Warren & Amelia Warren Tyagi, *The Two Income Trap, op. cit.* (Introd., n. 10).

273. *Ibid.*

274. J.S. Hacker, "The Insecure Family", in *The Real State of the Union, op. cit.* (Introd., n. 8); T. Draut, *Strapped..., op. cit.* (Introd., n. 9); B. Shulman, *The Betrayal of Work..., op. cit.* (Introd., n. 10); B. Ehrenreich, *Nickel and Dimed, op. cit.* (Introd., n. 67); D.K. Shipler, *The Working Poor..., op. cit.* (Introd., n. 68).

housing[275], energy[276], justice[277], health[278], or education[279]. I will return to some of these points later.

For the sake of completeness, it should be pointed out that American workers have the decency not only to be economical in use, but also to be widely corvéeable. Nicolas Baverez is absolutely right: people work more in the United States than in France[280]. In fact, if we wanted to be really fair, we would have to say that we work more in the United States than in any other developed country[281]. The number of hours worked annually is 1,804 in America, 1,546 in France, 1,437 in Germany, 1,551 in Denmark, 1,534 in Belgium, 1,360 in Norway, 1,367 in the Netherlands and 1,775 in Japan (a country known for its industriousness)[282]. This seems consistent with the fact that U.S. employees take less vacation than all their European

---

275. B. Ehrenreich, *Nickel and Dimed*, *op. cit.* (Introd., n. 67); D.K. Shipler, *The Working Poor...*, *op. cit.* (Introd., n. 68); National Low Income Housing Coalition, *op. cit.* (*supra*, n. 65); Janny Scott & Randal C. Archibold, "Across Nation Housing Costs Rise as Burden," October 3, 2006, *New York Times*.

276. Isabelle Duriez, "Aux États-Unis, le réseau électrique a du plomb dans l'aile", *Libération*, 31 July 2006; Laurent Mauriac, "Les États-Unis risquent de broyer du noir", *Libération*, 17 October 2006.

277. D.R. Dow, *Executed On a Technicality...*, *op. cit.* (Introd., n. 20); J. Reiman, *The Rich Get Richer and the Poor Get Prison...*, *op. cit.* (Introd., n. 19); for a detailed discussion, see within the second section: "Justice: Whether You Are Powerful or Wretched".

278. D.L. Barlett & J.B. Steele, *Critical Condition*, *op. cit.* (Introd., n. 21); for a detailed discussion, see within the second section: "Health: Pay or Die."

279. A. Molnar, *Giving Kids the Business...*, *op. cit.* (Introd., n. 28); for a detailed discussion, see within the second section: "School: Better Rich and Dumb than Poor and Bright."

280. N. Baverez, *What to do: Agenda 2007*, *op. cit.* (Introd., n. 63), p. 123.

281. There is a widespread myth that France is the least hard-working country in the OECD. Not long ago, on a French national channel (RTL Matin 7am-9:30pm, April 27, 2007), Nicolas Bouzou still claimed, for example, that France was the least hard-working of all OECD countries. François Bayrou made the same speech on April 28, 2007 on BFM TV, during the debate that opposed him to Ségolène Royal between the two rounds of the French presidential election. With all due respect to Mr. Bouzou and Mr. Bayrou (and their supporters), this assertion is false. The Germans, the Dutch, the Belgians or the Norwegians, to take only a few examples, work less than the French. A simple detour to the OECD website is enough to convince you of this; see http://caliban.sourceoecd.org/pdf//fact2007pdf//06-01-05.pdf

282. OECD, Factbook 2007, 2005 figures, available online: http://caliban.sourceoecd.org/pdf//fact2007pdf//06-01-05.pdf

counterparts[283]. In fact, the legal duration of paid vacations in the United States is 0 weeks and 0 days per year, compared to 5 weeks in France, Austria, Denmark and Sweden. The Germans have 4 weeks, as do the Italians, Belgians and Finns. On average, Americans take about half as much vacation time (3.9 weeks/year) as Germans (7.8 weeks), Italians (7.9 weeks), Dutch (7.6 weeks) or French (7.0 weeks)[284]. Anna, for example, was not entitled to any time off and her salary did not allow her to take an "unpaid" vacation. If she had, she would probably have been fired anyway.

In addition to paid leave, Europeans also have paid maternity leave (e.g., 16 weeks in France and 14 in Germany, paid at 100%; 28 weeks in Denmark, paid at 60%[285]). America was without such coverage until 1993. Since then, the law provides for 12 weeks of unpaid leave, but this is no exaggeration! The history of this legislation, known officially as the Family and Medical Leave Act (FMLA), is quite extraordinary and, in a sense, extremely revealing. As Tamara Draut explains, the business community vigorously opposed the enactment of this maternity coverage, claiming that it represented an intolerable invasion of the economic sphere by state power[286]. Fred Krebs, a member of the U.S. Chamber of Commerce, said, for example, that it was "Congress as the personnel director. They want to tell you who to hire, what benefits to give, and even the racial composition of your workforce[287]." Consistent with these fears, Republican House member John Boehner stated that "we don't need the federal government strangling the free enterprise system in our country any further[288]." It could hardly be clearer. After more than 10 years of debate and two presidential vetoes by George H.W. Bush (the father), the bill was finally

---

283. *The State of Working America 2006-2007*, *op. cit.* (Introd., n. 13), chap. 8, see in particular table 8.9.
284. *Ibid.*
285. Sheila B Kamerman, "Parental Leave Policies: An Essential Ingredient in Early Childhood Education and Care Policies," *Social Policy Report*, 2000, 14, pp. 3-15.
286. T. Draut, *Strapped...*, *op. cit.* (Introd., n. 9).
287. Quoted *in* T. Draut, *Strapped...*, *op. cit.* (Introd., n. 9), p. 156.
288. Quoted *in* T. Draut, *ibid.*

signed into law by Bill Clinton. As Tamara Draut points out, "the FMLA debate demonstrates our nation's reluctance to engage in family policy or to regulate any aspect of the employee-employer relationship... In all but two of the 29 OECD countries [30 as of December 2000] [Finland and Sweden[289]], providing paid maternity leave costs less than 1% of GDP (gross domestic product). To put that percentage in perspective, the three rounds of tax cuts implemented under the Bush administration in 2001, 2002, and 2003 cost 2.6% of U.S. GDP in 2004[290]."

In addition to low wages and the lack of paid vacation and maternity leave, there is a significant lack of pension and health care coverage. Unlike in most European countries, these two areas are largely dependent on the goodwill of employers in the United States. Employers are increasingly quick to cut social spending in order to increase their profits. Over the past 30 years, corporate contributions to employee health and retirement coverage have been inexorably eroded[291]. Wal-Mart, the world's leading retailer, is a sad and recent example. Despite record profits, the company is increasingly looking to cut back on pension funding costs[292] after cutting back hard on health care spending[293]. The employees most affected are, of course, those at the bottom of the ladder[294]. To illustrate this point, let us start with the problem of pensions. In the United States, pensions are based on three pillars: 1) the federal social security system, which covers virtually all working people; 2) individual savings plans, which mainly concern the most privileged; 3) employer-sponsored pension plans. The latter benefit from tax and monetary advantages (the employer pays a

---

289. S.B. Kamerman, "Parental Leave Policies...", *op. cit.* (*supra*, n. 198) at 10.

290. T. Draut, *Strapped...*, *op. cit.* (Introd., n. 9), pp. 157-158.

291. The State of Working America 2006-2007, op. cit. *(Introd., n. 13), chap. 3.*

292. Steven Greenhouse & Michael Barbaro, "Wal-Mart Memo Suggests Ways to Cut Employee Benefit Costs," *New York Times*, October 26, 2005.

293. Bernard Wysocki & Ann Zimmerman, "Wal-Mart Cost Cutting Finds Big Target in Health Benefits," *The Wall Street Journal*, September 30, 2003.

294. B. Shulman, *The Betrayal of Work...*, *op. cit.* (Introd., n. 10), pp. 176-178; Michael Calabrese & Maya MacGuineas, "Spendthrift Nation," in *The Real State of the Union, op. cit.* (Introd., n. 8), pp. 34-42.

sum of money proportional to that saved by the employee). In 1979, 51% of private sector workers had pension plans. By 2004, only 46% had such plans[295]. In essence, the breakdown of the latter figure reveals a large aggregation bias. Indeed, nearly 70 percent of Americans in the top 20 percent of income earners had a pension plan in 2004. The percentage fell to around 10% for Americans at the other end of the distribution, in the lowest 20% income bracket. Median wage earners were covered in one out of two cases[296]. For a majority of those not covered, the problem is not refusal to contribute but lack of supply. More than half of companies with fewer than 100 employees do not offer pension plans to their employees, for reasons of cost and sustainability[297]. Yet Social Security replaces roughly only 53% of a poor worker's income and 39% of an "average" worker's income (a percentage that is expected to fall to 30% by 2030)[298] for retirements at age 65. These figures probably explain why Robert continued at the age of 71, with his rheumatism and obvious physical wear and tear, to fill customers' bags behind the cash register of an Atlanta supermarket for $6 an hour. For a lifetime of work, this man received just over $550 a month from Social Security. Five times a week, he came by subway and spent six hours on his feet putting French fries, sausages and Coca-Cola in "good conscience" bags, guaranteed to be "biodegradable" with a lot of advertising. Small detail, Robert was one of those men who had, one day in June 1944, landed on a beach in

---

295. *The State of Working America 2006-2007, op. cit.* (Introd., n. 13), chap. 3; Alicia H. Munnell & Pamela Perun, "An Update on Private Pensions," Center for Retirement Research at Boston College, 2006, Issue in Brief 50, available online: http://www.bc.edu/centers/crr/issues/ib_50.pdf
296. *Ibid.*
297. *Ibid.*
298. A.H. Munnell & P. Perun, "An Update on Private Pensions," *op. cit.* (*supra*, n. 208); Alicia H. Munnell & Annika Sunden, "Private Pensions: Coverage and Benefit Trends," *in* "Conversation on Coverage," symposium organized by "The Pension Rights Center," July 24-25, 2001, Washington, DC, see table 8; available online: http://www.pensioncoverage.net/studies_and_statistics/Private_Pension_Coverage_Benefits_and_Trends.pdf; Social Security online, Benefit calculators, http://www.ssa.gov/OACT/quickcalc/index.html

Normandy. I was a little ashamed, I think, when he told me this before launching into a long diatribe against this liberalism which "treats men like animals, as we Negroes were treated before". I would have been even more ashamed if I had known that the tax breaks associated annually with pension plans reach $120 billion, of which $80 billion goes directly into the pockets of the richest 20% of Americans[299]. The poorest get nothing, but is this really surprising when we know that the whole tax system in the United States is afflicted with the same tendency to favor high incomes[300]? I don't know what happened to Robert, but I do know that the end of his life deserved better than that unfortunate $550 and the humiliation of having to fill bags of groceries to survive at over 70 years old. If Robert were still an isolated example, it would probably be a lesser evil. Unfortunately, this is not the case, as a violent indictment published in 2005 by *Time Magazine* shows. This remarkably well-documented work presents a long inventory of poor retirees, often robbed of their life savings by staggeringly cynical corporations and unbelievably lenient legislators[301]. At 69, Joy Whitehouse receives a pension of $942. To make ends meet, she collects used cans and other empty food containers from garbage cans and roadside stands. She earns about $60 a month. At 78, Betty Dizik also continues to work. Her pension, less than $1,000, just covers her medical expenses, not living expenses. "I'll be working for the rest of my life[302]. *Time Magazine* reporters conclude, "Soon she'll have plenty of company[303]."

As Betty Dizik's example shows, in addition to the problem of pensions, there is the problem of health insurance. In the United States, health insurance has traditionally been covered to a large extent by the employer.

---

299. M. Calabrese & M. MacGuineas, "Spendthrift Nation," in *The Real State of the Union*, *op. cit.* (Introd., n. 8), p. 37.
300. M. MacGuineas, "Radical Tax Reform," in *The Real State of the Union*, *op. cit.* (Introd., n. 8), pp. 51-62.
301. D.L. Barlett & J.B. Steele, "The Broken Promise," *Time*, October 31, 2005, pp. 31-47.
302. *Ibid*, p. 47.
303. *Ibid.*

However, this commitment is tending to be increasingly limited, if not completely eliminated[304]. Between 1979 and 2004, the number of workers covered by an employer-sponsored insurance plan fell by 13 percentage points, from 69 percent to 56 percent[305]. At the same time, the co-payment charged to employees for their coverage has risen quite a bit (from 14% to 22% according to available figures for the period 1992-2003)[306]. Of course, one must be wary of averages here too. Seventy-two percent of the highest paid workers (top 20 percent) had coverage in 2003, compared to only 19 percent of the lowest paid workers (bottom 20 percent). Interestingly, the latter had lower quality coverage. In 2003, employers spent half as much to insure a poor worker as they did a rich worker[307]. Being less well insured means in America being covered only after a minimum expense (e.g., $1,000), for an annual maximum (e.g., $250,000), and for only a portion of the expenses incurred (e.g., 80%)[308]. Lynette can attest to this. Lynette has had one-third of her salary (just over $800) taken away each month to cover her late husband's cancer treatments. Of her tragedy, she says, "If Rob had had appendicitis or a broken leg, we would have been adequately insured. But for something catastrophic like cancer, we weren't. I don't think anyone would have been able to do that. I don't think anyone is[309]." Gil and her husband must share this belief, who, despite having personal insurance at the prohibitive rate of $640 per month, have accumulated $160,000 in debt as a result of

---

304. Lisa Clemans-Cope, Bowen Garrett & Catherine Hoffman, "Change in Employees' Health Insurance Coverage, 2001-2005," 2006, Issue Brief 7570, Kaiser Family Foundation, available online: http://www.kff.org/uninsured/upload/7570.pdf
305. The State of Working America 2006-2007, op. cit. *(Introd., n. 13), chap. 3.*
306. *Ibid.*
307. *Ibid.*
308. "Underinsured in America: Is Health Coverage Adequate," 2002, Fact Sheet, 4060, Kaiser Family Foundation, available online: http://www.kff.org/uninsured/upload/Underin-sured-in-America-Is-Health-Coverage-Adequate-Fact-Sheet.pdf
309. Kerry Howley, "I Can't Afford to Get Sick," *Reader Digest*, April 2006, available online: http://www.rd.com/content/the-cost-of-health-care-in-america/

their youngest son's cancer[310]... and the trend is unfortunately not improving! Over the past decade, the price of private coverage has skyrocketed in the United States. For example, between 1998 and 2004, the cost of basic single coverage in Philadelphia increased by 71% to $4,660 per year. During the same period, the companies offering these plans earned an additional $2 billion in profits[311]. Not surprisingly, the number of uninsured people in the United States increased from 31 million to 46.6 million (13% to 16%) between 1987 and 2005[312]. In 2005, 21.5 million individuals (17.7 percent) between the ages of 18 and 65, working full time, had no coverage. For part-time workers, the figure was 6 million (23.5%)[313]. The vast majority of uninsured workers are uninsured because their company does not provide access to an insurance plan and because they earn too much to obtain Medicaid coverage but not enough to purchase a private or employer-sponsored coverage plan[314].

It would obviously be dishonest to say that the implementation of liberal potions in America has had only negative effects for the country's inhabitants. Indeed, the last 30 years have been a golden age for the wealthy. Jack Welch, former CEO of General Electric, is a good example[315]. During his apparently messy divorce, normally "private" figures became

---

310. "Working... and poor," *Business Week*, May 31, 2004, available online: http://www.businessweek.com/magazine/content/04_22/b3885001_mz001.htm

311. D.L. Barlett & J.B. Steele, *Critical Condition, op. cit.* (Introd., n. 21), p. 33.

312. C. DeNavas-Walt, B.D. Proctor & C.H. Lee, *Income, Poverty, and Health Insurance Coverage, op. cit.* (Introd., n. 22), Report P60-231, table C-1, available online: http://www.census.gov/prod/2006pubs/p60-231.pdf

313. *Ibid*, table 8.

314. "Who Are the Uninsured? A Consistent Profile across National Surveys," Kaiser Commission on Medicaid and the Uninsured, *op. cit.* (Introd., n. 54), available online: http://www.kff.org/uninsured/upload/7553.pdf; Institute of Medicine, "Coverage Matters: Insurance and Health Care," Committee on the Consequences of Uninsurance. Board on Health Care Services, 2001, Washington, DC, National Academy Press, "Report in Brief," available online: http://books.nap.edu/html/coverage_matters/reportbrief.pdf, see p. 2 in particular; for a concrete example, see S.S. Sered & R. Fernandopulle, *Uninsured in America..., op. cit.* (Introd., n. 21), pp. 40-44.

315. P. Krugman, "For Richer," *op. cit.* (Introd., n. 61), available online: http://www.pkarchive.org/economy/ForRicher.html

public. In 2000, in his last year of business, Welch reportedly received $123 million, mostly in stock and stock options. Anna would have to work nearly 10,000 years to amass such a sum! For his retirement, our man was graced with a lifetime apartment in Manhattan (with food, wine and cleaning), access to a private jet and other perks worth a total of $2 million. As extreme as this case is, it is far from isolated. For example, in 1970, in constant 1998 dollars, the average salary was $32,522. In the same year, the compensation of the 100 highest paid CEOs was $1,255,000. Nearly 30 years later, in 1998, the average salary had increased by a modest 10% to $35,864. At the same time, the pay of our CEO friends had exploded by nearly 3,000% to $37,509,000. This means that the incomes of the 100 highest paid CEOs rose from 39 times to 1,000 times the income of the average wage earner between 1970 and 1998[316]. If we include a larger panel of 350 large companies, the change is "only" 236 points (from 24 to 260) between 1965 and 2005[317]. This means, assuming a worker works 5 days a week, 52 weeks a year, that the average CEO earns more in a day's work than the average worker earns in a year's work. No other developed country reaches this level of disparity[318].

One might think that our CEO friends are only a striking but misleading epiphenomenon. They are not. Since the late 1970s, inequality between rich and poor has increased massively in the United States. This

316. Thomas Piketty & Emmanuel Saez, "Income Inequality in the United States, 1913-1998," *Quarterly Journal of Economics*, 2003, 118, pp. 1-39, available online: http://www.jourdan.ens.fr/piketty/fichiers/public/PikettySaez2003.pdf; P. Krugman, "For Richer," *op. cit.* (Introd., n. 61).
317. The State of Working America 2006-2007, op. cit. *(Introd., n. 13), chap. 3, figure 3Z.*
318. The State of Working America 2006-2007, op. cit. *(Introd., n. 13), chap. 3, table 3.47.*

increase has affected wages, income and wealth indiscriminately[319]. Let us start with the evolution of wages. This is classically analyzed on the basis of a segmentation of the population into percentiles. The 10th percentile defines the boundary between the lowest paid 10% of individuals and the highest paid 90%. Similarly, the 95th percentile defines the boundary between the lowest paid 95% and the highest paid 5%. The 50th percentile characterizes the median. Based on the percentile values, we can calculate the wage ratios between the highest and lowest paid individuals (95/10 or 90/10), the highest paid individuals and the median individuals (95/50 or 90/50), and the median individuals and the lowest paid individuals (50/10). The results then show, for the last 30 years, that the earnings of the highest paid individuals have increased substantially faster than the earnings of median and poor individuals[320]. Thus, between 1979 and 2005, the 95/50 and 95/10 ratios increased from 2.4 to 2.9 and from 4.2 to 5.8, respectively. When we look at the income ratio between median and poor wage earners (50/10), we see a similar but less pronounced general trend. Indeed, the 50/10 fraction grew only from 1.7 to 1.9 between 1979 and 2005. Interestingly, this weak growth does not reflect a kind of harmoniously distributed asthenia, but a reversal of the trend at the end of the 1980s. Thus, in contrast to the continuous growth of the 95/50 and 95/10 ratios, the 50/10 ratio experienced a bi-phasic evolution. An increase from 1.7 to 2.1 was first recorded over the period 1979-1989,

---

319. Thomas Piketty & Emmanuel Saez, "The Evolution of Top Incomes: a Historical and International Perspective," National Bureau of Economic Research, 2006, Working Paper, 11955, available online: http://www.jourdan.ens.fr/piketty/fichiers/public/PikettySaez2006.pdf; T. Piketty & E. Saez, "Income Inequality in the United States, 1913-1998," *op. cit. (supra*, n. 229); "Effective Federal Tax Rates, 1979-1997," The Congress of the United States, Congressional Budget Office, 2001, available online: http://www.cbo.gov/ftpdocs/30xx/doc3089/EffectiveTaxRate.pdf; P. Krugman, "For Richer," *op. cit.* (Introd., n. 61); *The State of Working America 2006-2007*, *op. cit.* (Introd., n. 13), chaps. 1, 3, 5; M.R. Rank, *One Nation Underprivileged...*, *op. cit.* (Introd., n. 10), pp. 157-163; T. Draut, *Strapped...*, *op. cit.* (Introd., n. 9), pp. 21-22.
320. *The State of Working America 2006-2007*, *op. cit.* (Introd., n. 13), chap. 3, see especially table 3.4.

followed by a slight decrease from 2.1 to 1.9 over the period 1989-2005. In other words, for more than 15 years, the income gap between poor and median wage earners has been narrowing. This reduction reflects the aforementioned trend of impoverishment of the middle classes. The top earners are receiving (and often granting themselves by virtue of their decision-making position) ever higher salaries, to the detriment of the remuneration of middle-class earners, who are getting closer and closer to the mass of the working poor.

Wages represent only a portion of the total income of each tax household. In addition to wages, it is therefore interesting to look at the evolution of income. This is what Thomas Piketty and Emmanuel Saez have done in a series of widely cited works[321]. The results show that the richest 10% of households accounted for 32% of total income between 1950 and 1970. By 2002, the proportion had risen to 42%. Interestingly, this increase was not evenly distributed across the decile. It was mostly in the bottom percentile, the wealthiest one percent of Americans (2.7 million people). While they received 8% of total income in 1970, they received 16% in 2002. If we scratch the surface, we discover that it is mainly the wealthiest 0.01% who have benefited from the windfall. In 1970, these taxpayers received 0.7% of total income (i.e., they earned 70 times the average income). By 2002, the percentage had risen to over 3 percent (300 times average income). As Paul Krugman points out in an editorial in the *New York Times*, this means that the 13,000 richest families had an income in 2002 equal to that of the 20 million poorest families[322]. It is interesting to note that this enormous increase in wealth has been accompanied by a massive decrease in the tax burden. In 1960, the wealthiest 0.01 per cent of taxpayers paid 70 per cent of their income in federal taxes. By 2005, the figure had fallen

---

321. T. Piketty & E. Saez, "The Evolution of Top Incomes: a Historical and International Perspective," *op. cit.* (*supra*, n. 232); T. Piketty & E. Saez, "Income Inequality in the United States, 1913-1998," *op. cit.* (*supra*, n. 229).
322. P. Krugman, "For Richer," *op. cit.* (Introd., n. 61).

to 35 per cent[323]. Over the same period, the tax rate for the middle class has remained hopelessly flat at around 16 per cent.

Beyond wages and income is wealth, the difference between assets (savings, stocks, bonds, real estate, etc.) and debt. In 1962, the top 5% and 20% of households held 55% and 81% of the national wealth, respectively. In 2004, they owned 59% and 85%. Over the same period, the share of the bottom 80 percent of households fell from 19 percent to 15 percent. Also between 1962 and 2004, the average wealth of the top 1 percent of Americans increased, in constant 2005 dollars, from $5,623,000 to $14,792,000, a gain of more than $9 million. At the same time, the average wealth of the bottom 80 percent of individuals painfully gained a few tens of thousands from $40,000 to $83,000. The poorest 20% of individuals, on the other hand, slipped a little deeper into debt, seeing their "wealth" rise from -$6,000 to -$11,000. At a more synthetic level, the wealthiest 1% of Americans had 125 times the median wealth in 1962. Forty years later, in 2004, the factor reached 190[324].

Beyond their clarity, the preceding data are obviously not very soluble in the crucible of political correctness. This explains why they are often attacked with remarkable bad faith. One strategy, for example, is to group the data in 10% or 20% increments to make the results more acceptable. Indeed, large aggregations allow the increase in gains involving mostly the bottom percentiles of the population to be diluted in the mass. For those who might be tempted to consider this argument specious, I can only suggest (once again) that they read the excellent article published by Paul Krugman in the prestigious *New York Times*. According to this eminent economist from Princeton University: "For the past 15 years, it has been difficult to deny the evidence of rising inequality in the United States.

---

323. Thomas Piketty & Emmanuel Saez, "How Progressive Is the US Federal Tax System: a Historical and International Perspective," *Journal of Economic Perspectives*, 2007, 21, pp. 3-24, available online: http://www.jourdan.ens.fr/piketty/fichiers/public/PikettySaezJEP2006.pdf
324. *The State of Working America 2006-2007, op. cit.* (Introd., n. 13), chap. 5, see especially tables 5.3, 5.4, and figure 5B.

Census data clearly show that a growing share of income is going to the top 20 percent of families, and within that 20 percent to the top 5 percent, with a declining share going to middle-income families. Nevertheless, denying this evidence represents a substantial and well-funded industry. Conservative *think tanks* have produced a large number of studies attempting to discredit the data, the methodology and, not least, the motives of those who report the evidence. Studies that appear to refute the claim of increasing inequality receive prominent attention in the editorial pages and are avidly cited by right-leaning government officials[325]."

Before concluding this section, it is perhaps worth noting that the inequality explosion described above has preserved the shamefully "interventionist" European countries such as France, Germany, Holland and Denmark[326]. At the beginning of the third millennium, the United States is by far the most unbalanced developed country in terms of wealth distribution. Two markers show this clearly. The first, well known to economists, is the so-called "Gini coefficient". This coefficient varies between 0 for perfect equality (everyone has exactly the same income) and 1 for complete inequality (a single individual receives all the income). In 2000, this index was equal to 0.368 in the United States, 0.288 in France, 0.277 in Belgium, 0.252 in Germany, 0.251 in Norway and 0.247 in Finland[327]. These differences are considerable, even if they remain difficult to understand from an intuitive point of view. A second marker is clearly preferable in this respect: the income gap between the richest 10 per cent of individuals and the poorest 10 per cent of individuals. This gap is calculated by dividing the frontier income above which the richest tenth of the population is found by the frontier income below which the poorest tenth

---

325. *Ibid.*

326. T. Piketty & E. Saez, "The Evolution of Top Incomes: a Historical and International Perspective," *op. cit.* (*supra*, n. 232); T. Piketty & E. Saez, "Income Inequality in the United States, 1913-1998," *op. cit.* (*supra*, n. 229); *The State of Working America 2006-2007*, *op. cit.* (Introd., n. 13), chap. 8.

327. *The State of Working America 2006-2007*, *op. cit.* (Introd., n. 13), chap. 8, see, in particular, table 8.16.

is found. In other words, if you have 100 individuals ranked in ascending order of income, you divide the income of the 90th by the income of the 10th. In the United States, the ratio is 5.4, compared to 3.5 in France, 3.2 in Germany, 3.0 in Sweden, and 2.8 in Norway[328].

To summarize, the liberal policies pursued in the United States for the past 30 years have resulted in the massive enrichment of the most privileged, the progressive impoverishment of the middle class and the creation of a huge cohort of working poor. Thus 25% of American workers, or 30 million people, work for wages that do not allow them to lift their families out of poverty. These people are indentured, they have no paid vacations, no health coverage, no rights. This situation explains why unskilled labor costs less in the United States than in all Western European countries. I often hear in France and in Europe about the burdens and constraints that stifle employment and ruin the spirit of initiative. Unfortunately, I never hear about the burdens and constraints that offer everyone, and in particular the poorest, a decent pension, insurance to take care of themselves, paid vacations to rest and rights to defend themselves. I never hear about the role of taxes in the process of national solidarity and levelling out the unequal excesses of the market. It may be interesting to point out here that America is the country that devotes the smallest part of its gross domestic product (GDP) to social programs. In Uncle Sam's case, 2% of GDP is used to help the less fortunate, compared to 8% in Germany, 9% in France, 12% in Norway and 14% in Sweden[329]. It is therefore not surprising that social programs are less efficient in the United States than in all other European nations[330]. This can be measured by estimating the percentage of the population that is lifted out of poverty by social assistance. In America, according to a 2001 study, a 38% reduction is achieved (*i.e.,* from 29% to 18% of individuals below the poverty line). In

---

328. *Ibid.*
329. *Ibid*, see, in particular, figure 8H.
330. *Ibid*, M.R. Rank, *One Nation Underprivileged...*, *op. cit.* (Introd., n. 10), pp. 60-62.

Germany, the reduction was 76% (29% to 7%), in France 79% (39% to 8%) and in Finland 89% (33% to 4%)[331].

Personally, I tend to find the financial redistribution by the state, through taxation, relevant and morally appropriate. Before asking whether we pay too much tax, we should perhaps ask ourselves why we pay so much tax. I can see why some people would disagree with this view. One can legitimately argue that the American model is superior to all others. It is fair to say that Jack Welch makes more money in one year than Anna does in ten thousand. It can be considered normal that millions of people work 40 hours a week, 52 weeks a year, without being able to house and feed their families. It is acceptable that people die or suffer because they cannot access the care they need due to lack of insurance. We can consider it moral that Robert, after having landed on the beaches of Normandy at the age of 18, fills bags of groceries at the age of 71 because his pension does not allow him to live decently. We can be satisfied with the fact that this happens in the richest and most powerful country on the planet. We can. We can, but we have to say it clearly. When I read that the economic model of old Europe must be Americanized under the pretext that "the best weapon against poverty is work[332] ", I admit that I tend to smile a little. When I learn that "the welfare system [in France] today strongly discourages activity, because of the small gap between the minimum wage and the minimum social benefits, as well as the multiple benefits whose benefit is linked to inactivity, such as the Universal Medical Coverage, the single parent allowance (...)[333] ", I say to myself that there are indeed two ways. The first one is to drastically reduce the social assistance to the most disadvantaged and to take away their right to be treated. This solves the impossible equation of a docile workforce and a ridiculous unemployment rate (not less than 5% anyway, because when the poor become really

---

331. V.-M. Ritakallio, "Trends of Poverty and Income Inequality in Cross-National Comparisons," *op. cit.*
332. N. Baverez, *What to do: Agenda 2007, op. cit.* (Introd., n. 63), p. 132.
333. *Ibid*, p. 130.

scarce, their price increases to the great displeasure of the market). When you have no right to anything, you often have no choice but to accept the unacceptable. This is the American way. The alternative is to make sure that work provides a decent income for everyone. Europe has been the daughter of this philosophy until now. It is increasingly being reproached for this heresy against the law: daring to regulate the wisdom of the almighty market, what an absurd extravagance! Among the worst pupils is obviously my beautiful France, victim of a "multiform bankruptcy" at the same time financial, economic, social, civic[334]. I must say, however, that I much prefer all these bankruptcies combined to the humanistic and ethical bankruptcy that is striking the new world.

Causality: a structural failure

"If you don't work at school, you'll end up a bum." "When you give them money, they will drink it." "It's easier to beg than to work." "There are plenty of unfilled jobs in the crafts, but people don't want to work anymore[335]." We have all heard these sharp remarks directed at the indigent in our cities. I find them interesting, because they underline the intimacy of the link that unites, in our collective imagination, individual failure and social decay. The poor would be, by his turpitude, only responsible for his misfortune. I believed it too. The new world has cured me of this illusion. For millions of Americans, poverty is the reflection, not of individual inadequacies, but of chronic structural malformations. Across the Atlantic, poverty is not an epiphenomenon on its way to extinction. It is a prescription in the process of spreading. It is the inevitable residue of a heavily unbalanced socio-economic structure. On the one hand, a weak, pusillanimous state, lacking in audacity and altruism, operates. On the

---

334. *Ibid.* at 119-120.

335. Daniel Bernard & François Vignal, "Artisans, traders, very small businesses: they could create hundreds of thousands of jobs", *Marianne*, 9-15 September 2006, p. 59-65.

other, an all-powerful, marmoreal market is active, guided only by the lure of profit. In the middle of the anvil are the people, powerless puppets, labeled "human resources" and managed according to the restructurings like any other perishable commodity. I am told that the struggle is fair between people and the market and that the State has no business getting involved. I am also told that the introduction of a restrictive labor code, the statutory prescription of paid vacations, or the nationalization of the health care system alter the proper functioning of the economy and therefore operate, in the long run, against the interest of workers. Yet, as I have already pointed out, the number of poor people is greater in the United States than in any other developed country, especially in Northern Europe. In 1976, 28 percent of the poor lived in extreme poverty (below 50 percent of the threshold). By 2004, the proportion had risen to 43 percent, or almost 1 in 2 poor people[336]. At the same time, the U.S. middle class has suffered a very serious erosion. Where one wage was sufficient in 1970 to raise a family out of poverty, it now takes two[337]. All this indicates that economic liberalization does not, contrary to what I keep hearing, benefit the mass of people. It benefits essentially, as the previous section has amply demonstrated, a wealthy elite, owners of the capital, of the tools of production and of the media through which the good word is transmitted to us. I myself have only recently accepted these facts, while researching for this book. To those who would see me as a dangerous communist (the "me" of a few years ago would surely have done so), I would say that I have long voted center-right and I would suggest reading an article already mentioned and published in the *New York Times* by Paul Krugman under the title "For the Richest". According to this economist, "Few people are aware of the magnitude with which the gap between the very rich and the rest has widened over a relatively short period of time. In fact, the mere mention of the subject exposes you to accusations of 'class warfare',

---

336. The State of Working America 2006-2007, op. cit. *(Introd., n. 13), chap. 6, figure 6D.*
337. Elizabeth Warren & Amelia Warren Tyagi, *The Two Income Trap, op. cit.* (Introd., n. 10).

'politics of envy' and so on. And very few people are willing to talk about the profound effects - economic, social and political - of this widening gap.... The concentration of income at the top is a major reason why the United States, for all its economic achievements, has more poverty and less life expectancy than any other advanced nation.... Our optimism about America, our belief that in the end our nation always finds its way, comes from the past - a past in which we were a middle-class society. But it was a different country[338]." It's hard to find a more abrupt indictment of the American-style market economy.

Basically, to say that the poor are responsible for their condition is to suggest that they would not be poor if they were less lazy, more competent, more courageous and/or more qualified. This is surely true. If Anna had a degree in law, nursing or computer science, her life would be much simpler and more prosperous. However, the problem would only be transferred to others. The market offers only limited access to excellent degrees and the lucrative jobs associated with them. The question then is not whether there will be poor people, but who will be poor, because it is inevitable that some will be poor. It is like a game of musical chairs: when the song stops, some are sitting and others are standing. Of course, we can ask ourselves who the losers are. We can point out their blunders and try to eradicate them. In the end, however, it makes no difference. There are always losers. No matter what the individual characteristics of the players are, the percentage of the castaways is written into the structure of the game[339].

As Timothy Bartik, an economist at the prestigious Upjohn Institute, points out, it is generally accepted that the United States creates, at least in times of growth, enough jobs to provide employment for all sincere applicants. This assumption is even an implicit pillar of the 1996 welfare reform for the indigent. According to this reform, collective generosity

---

338. P. Krugman, "For Richer," *op. cit.* (Introd., n. 61).
339. For a detailed discussion, M.R. Rank, *One Nation Underprivileged...*, *op. cit.* (Introd., n. 10), chap. 3.

(welfare) is limited to 5 years for a lifetime, including 2 consecutive years[340]. If an individual exceeds these durations, he or she is necessarily an odious parasite and the so-called YOYO rule is applied: "*You're On Your Own*". But the assumption of job sufficiency is seriously flawed. Even in times of strong growth, the U.S. economy does not create enough jobs for everyone who wants to work to do so. In the late 1990s, for example, when the U.S. economy was booming, an additional 9 million jobs would have been needed to provide full-time work for everyone[341]. In substance, this figure is infinitely less surprising than the jobs sufficiency thesis. Indeed, liberal orthodoxy suggests that the unemployment rate should not fall below a floor, around 4 to 5 per cent of the total number of workers, which in the United States is 5 to 6 million people. When the threshold is reached, the shortage of labour leads to pressure on wages[342]. This tension in turn produces, in theory, an increase in inflation. Prior to the development of this spiral, the Federal Reserve takes monetary measures to "slow down the economy", that is, in ordinary language, to maintain an incompressible pool of structural unemployed[343].

In addition to the cohort of structurally unemployed and the victims of the lack of jobs, there are millions of indigent workers. In the United States, nearly 30 million people work for poverty wages and non-existent social benefits[344]. I hear that all of these poor people belong to the least educated fringe of the population (Burt's friends would say the mire). I am

---

340. A. Weil & K. Finegold, *Welfare Reform...*, *op. cit.* (*supra*, n. 19), Introduction; S.S. Sered & R. Fernandopulle, *Uninsured in America...*, *op. cit.* (Introd., n. 21), pp. 52-56.
341. "Tomothy Bartik, Poverty Jobs and Subsidized Employment," *Challenge*, 2002, 45, pp. 100-111; T. Bartik, *Jobs For the Poor: Can Labor Demand Policies Help* (New York: Russell Sage Foundation, 2001).
342. The State of Working America 2006-2007, op. cit. *(Introd., n. 13), chap. 6, figure 6H.*
343. M.R. Rank, *One Nation Underprivileged...*, *op. cit.* (Introd., n. 10), pp. 152-156; Louis Uchitelle, "Companies Try Dipping Deeper Into the Labor Pool," *New York Times*, March 26, 2000.
344. The State of Working America 2006-2007, op. cit. *(Introd., n. 13), chap. 6; C. De-Navas-Walt, B.D. Proctor & C.H. Lee,* Income, Poverty, and Health Insurance Coverage, *op. cit. (Introd., n. 22).*

told that the "new economy" is in fact hungry for highly skilled and highly paid labor. On this basis, I am told that the antidote to misery lies in the academic training of the masses and the development of technological eminence. When exposed to this kind of logic, I often wonder what would happen if all men suddenly became over-efficient, perfectly qualified, omnipotent like God himself. One has to believe that everyday necessities would disappear, that the garbage would pick itself up, that freight trucks would move without a driver, that the hamburgers at my favorite McDonald's would be served by docile robots, and that the housekeeper so precious to my old mother would be replaced by a computerized white tornado (a tornado, of course, that would be smiling, capable of empathy, of extreme kindness and of reassuring words).

Unfortunately, the Bureau of Labor Statistics (BLS) gives little hope to my ramblings. Indeed, projections from this government institution indicate that 47% of available jobs in 2014 will be open to those with a bachelor's degree or less. Only 26% of all jobs will require a university qualification at the bachelor's level (compared to 24 in 2004)[345]. Among the 30 activities that are expected to grow the most between 2004 and 2014, 11 (37%) do not require a degree and are associated only with brief "on-site" training. These activities offer, in BLS terminology, "very low" wages, that is, wages in the bottom quartile of the income distribution (less than $20,190/year). In fact, of the 8,833,000 jobs projected to be created in the 30 fastest growing sectors of the economy, 3,503,000, or 40 percent, will involve unskilled, low-wage jobs (less than $20,190/year). If we exclude the need for nurses and higher education teachers from the picture, the proportion rises to 46%. It is difficult, therefore, to see the new economy and university education as a salvation against poverty. This conclusion raises questions about the strength of the technological myth. It then becomes clear that the magic of percentages is sometimes

---

345. Daniel E. Hecker, "Employment Outlook 2004-2014," *Monthly Labor Review*, 2005, Bureau of Labor Statistics, available online: http://www.bls.gov/opub/mlr/2005/11/art5full. pdf, see table 6.

conveniently misleading: 50% of almost nothing is less, in absolute terms, than 15% of a large numerical aggregate. So, for example, between 2004 and 2014, BLS statisticians expect a 48.4 percent increase in the number of highly skilled computer engineers. At the same time, the sales force is expected to grow by only 17.3 percent[346]. Now, 48.4% of 460,000 engineers is only 222,000 units, or roughly 3.3 times less than the 760,000 souls representing 17.3% of 4,256,000 vendors.

For those who are not convinced of the incoherence of the technological myth, allow me to take a small dive into the past. Indeed, although it is often difficult to compare myths with facts, history sometimes offers us the opportunity to look directly at the world in the light of our fantasies. The technological myth is one of the most beautiful examples of these too rare confrontations. The adventure began in 1983, when Ronald Reagan's Secretary of Education commissioned a report that caused a stir under the evocative title "A Nation at Risk. The message was basically quite simple: the performance of the public education system was both deplorable and catastrophic. In the words of the report, "If a hostile foreign power had tried to impose on America the poor educational performance that exists today, we might well have seen it as an act of war[347]." The media, conservative politicians, the American public, and "business" rallied to this cry with great unanimity[348]. Gradually, the idea grew that America would soon run out of skilled workers. In 1988, *Fortune Magazine* wrote explicitly, "It's like Pearl Harbor. The Japanese [invaded us] and America was caught short. Not on weapons and tanks and warships - those are yesterday's weapons - but on mental strength. In a high-tech age when nations compete on intelligence, American schools are producing an army of illiterates. Corporations that can't hire enough skilled workers

---

346. *Ibid*, table 3.
347. "National Commission on Excellence in Education, A Nation at Risk: the Imperatives for Educational Reform," Washington, DC, US Department of Education, 1983, p. 1.
348. For a remarkable discussion, A. Molnar, *Giving Kids the Business...*, *op. cit.* (Introd., n. 28), chap. 1 in particular.

now realize they must do something to save public schools. Not to be charitable, not to promote good public relations, but to survive[349]." Two years after this observation, David Kearns, CEO of Xerox, drove the point home by stating, again in *Fortune*, that by the year 2000 America would be "devoid of skilled workers[350]." A report published in 1987 by the very conservative Hudson Institute also stated its fear of a disastrous shortage of skilled workers during the decade 1990-2000[351]. In 1988, the prestigious *New York Times added* its voice to the conservative Cassandra's song with an article entitled "Impending Disaster for U.S. Jobs: Incompetent Workers to Work[352]". Curiously, the inevitable catastrophe announced by all sides did not happen. The decade from 1990 to 2000, famous for its growth, saw no shortage of skilled workers. The only shortage that occurred was, in fact, the shortage of available jobs. The market had probably undertaken, in its wisdom, to limit its need for intelligence to the strict minimum. Unlike many conservative outlets, the *New York Times was* quick to make amends in a 1994 article entitled "Low Wages and Closed Doors Welcome Young Job Seekers[353]." In 1995, the same newspaper ran a front-page headline, "Skilled Workers Watch Their Jobs Cross the Ocean[354]." This migration had nothing to do with a lack of labor. The "brains" were simply cheaper elsewhere. With some irony, Alex Molnar points out, as an epitaph to this article and to the technology myth, that "if American schools produced

---

349. Nancy J. Perry, "Saving the Schools, How Business Can Help," *Fortune Magazine*, November 7, 1988.

350. David T. Kearns, "Why I Got Involved," *Fortune Magazine* (special issue), Spring 1990, p. 46.

351. William B. Johnson, "Workforce 2000," Hudson Institute, Indianapolis, Ind. 1987.

352. Edward B. Fiske, "Impending Job Disaster: Workforce Unqualified to Work," *New York Times*, September 25, 1989.

353. Tamar Lewin, "Low Pay and Closed Doors Confront Young Job Seekers," *New York Times*, March 10, 1994.

354. Kate Bradsher, "Skilled Workers Watch Their Jobs Migrate Overseas," *New York Times*, August 28, 1995.

more highly skilled workers, the main consequence would likely be to raise the rate of discussion in unemployment offices[355]."

Thus, in view of the above, it seems relatively indelicate to denounce the role of individual deficiencies in the emergence of mass poverty when the number of jobs is insufficient to satisfy everyone's demand and when 25% of the jobs available combine indigent wages and non-existent social benefits. Again, when there are more players than chairs and when a quarter of the chairs stand on only two legs, it is inevitable that people will fall and losers will exist. Attempts to drown the fish of systemic deficiencies under an uninterrupted stream of clever untruths do not change anything. The system produces poor people, mechanically. In other words, poverty is not an individual failure, it is a structural bankruptcy. If all the children in America had the intelligence and pugnacity of Einstein tomorrow, poverty would not disappear. There would still be a shortage of jobs (the market would see to that if necessary) and poverty wages would still be the lot of 25% of workers. For those who still doubt this, let me briefly mention some studies on the dynamic rather than static aspects of poverty. The question raised by these studies is basically quite simple: who is poor, who becomes poor, who stays poor and who escapes the curse? The findings can be summarized in three points: 1) a substantial proportion of Americans experience poverty at some point in their lives; 2) the state of destitution is generally brief but recurrent; 3) those who escape poverty most often remain close to its boundaries. These three points are discussed in detail below.

One of the most striking aspects of poverty in the United States is its frequency. By age 60, 48 percent of Americans have spent at least one year of their adult lives in poverty[356]. This means that nearly one out of every two Americans faces destitution at least once in their lifetime. Interestingly, it is relatively rare for the scourge to spread over time. Indeed, the number

---

355. A. Molnar, *Giving Kids the Business…*, *op. cit.* (Introd., n. 28), p. 6.
356. M.R. Rank, *One Nation Underprivileged…*, *op. cit.* (Introd., n. 10), chap. 4.

of individuals who have spent more than 2, 3, or 4 consecutive years below the poverty line is 26.1 percent, 17.5 percent, and 9.8 percent, respectively[357]. In other words, prolonged periods of misery (4 years or more) affect *only* 10% of Americans. This relatively good news must be tempered, however, by the recurrence data. The numbers show that poverty often knocks on the door of its victims several times. For example, half of all individuals who leave poverty fall back into poverty within four years[358]. More generally, 78% of those who have experienced one year of poverty will experience a second later in life[359]. By age 60, 21% of the U.S. population will have spent 5 or more years of their adult lives in poverty. The percentage rises to 30% for individuals aged 75[360]. These figures are all the more dramatic given that Bill Clinton's 1996 welfare reform capped relief at a total of 5 years over a lifetime[361].

When the population is segmented by racial background, it becomes clear that not all New Worlders are equal when it comes to poverty. For example, 82% of Blacks aged 60 have spent at least one year of their adult lives in poverty. The percentage is 42% for whites. By age 75, the proportions are 91% and 53% respectively. For those who suspect a typo, it is perhaps worth emphasizing that 9 out of 10 black adults aged 75 have spent at least one year below the poverty line[362]. Approximately 50 percent of blacks versus 30 percent of whites who fall into poverty at some point will be poor for at least five years in the next 10 years[363]. Of course, all of these data must be modulated by education level. At age 60, those with a bachelor's degree or higher have a 42 percent chance of having experienced destitution. The percentage is 64% for the others. When race

---

357. *Ibid.*

358. J. Iceland, *Poverty in America...*, *op. cit.* (Introd., n. 9), pp. 48-49.

359

360. *Ibid.*

361. A. Weil & K. Finegold, *Welfare Reform...*, *op. cit.* (*supra*, n. 19); S.S. Sered & R. Fernandopulle, *Uninsured in America...*, *op. cit.* (Introd., n. 21), pp. 52-56.

362. M.R. Rank, *One Nation Underprivileged...*, *op. cit.* (Introd., n. 10), chap. 4.

363. J. Iceland, *Poverty in America...*, *op. cit.* (Introd., n. 9), pp. 65-68.

and education are combined, it appears that in America it is better to be white than educated to avoid destitution. By age 60, 50 percent of white men without a degree have experienced poverty, compared to 76 percent of black men with a bachelor's degree or higher. For women, the figures are 60% and 82% respectively[364].

The ease with which adults cyclically leave and return to poverty highlights the weakness of American social systems. The primary role of these systems is to smooth out the ups and downs of life, i.e., to smooth out the peaks of affluence and fill in the valleys of adversity. As I have already pointed out, the United States has the least generous and least effective capping system of all developed countries[365]. In Uncle Sam's case, 2% of GDP is taken to help the less fortunate. This is four times less than in France or Germany and seven times less than in Sweden[366]. In America, social assistance reduces the number of poor people by 38%, compared to 76% in Germany, 79% in France and 89% in Finland[367]. Unemployment insurance is no exception to the disaster. Between 1950 and 1960, 50 per cent of the unemployed received assistance following the loss of their job. Forty years later, after several reforms aimed at tightening eligibility criteria, the percentage had fallen to 35 percent[368]. The nature of the current criteria (hours worked threshold, minimum income threshold, cause of job loss) means that the working poor are effectively excluded from the compensation system. The qualification rate for this population is less than 20%[369]. Marcos, for example, is a "typical" employee who worked for 18 months

---

364. M.R. Rank, *One Nation Underprivileged...*, *op. cit.* (Introd., n. 10), chap. 4.

365. The State of Working America 2006-2007, op. cit. *(Introd., n. 13), chap. 8, M.R. Rank,* One Nation Underprivileged..., op. cit. *(Introd., n. 10), pp. 60-62.*

366. *The State of Working America 2006-2007, op. cit.* (Introd., n. 13), chap. 8, see, in particular, figure 8H.

367. V.-M. Ritakallio, "Trends of Poverty and Income Inequality in Cross-National Comparisons," *op. cit.*

368. US General Accounting Office, "Unemployment Insurance: Role of Safety Net for Low-Wage Workers Is Limited," December 2000, GAO-01-181, available online: http://www.gao.gov/new.items/d01181.pdf

369. *Ibid.*

for a private institution. He worked 25 hours a week for a salary equal to the minimum wage ($5.15). When he was laid off in June 2002, he did not receive any unemployment insurance benefits because he did not meet the eligibility criteria[370]. However, even if Marcos had been lucky enough to qualify, he would not have received much. Typically, unemployment benefits continue for a maximum of 26 weeks (the federal government can increase this figure during periods of high unemployment)[371]. It averages 47 percent of the original wage, provided that the state's earnings ceiling is not reached[372]. In 2002, for example, the ceiling was $190 per week for a single person in Alabama[373], which was the poverty line at that time[374]. Massachusetts was more generous with a limit of $512.

Beyond the weakness of social systems, the cyclical nature of poverty in the U.S. also shows the speciousness of rigid categorical classifications. If I make $9,972, I am officially poor. If I make $2 more, I am out of the statistics. In fact, longitudinal studies show that the poor generally lose their "official certification" without moving significantly away from the boundaries of destitution. For example, only one-quarter of the working poor who earned less than $12,000 per year between 1993 and 1995 had moved out of the low-income trap by 2001. Three-quarters of the original poor were still earning less than $15,000 per year at that time[375]. These results are consistent with those of other older studies[376]. In the most cited

---

370. Andrew Stettner, Heather Boushey & Jeffrey Wenger, "Clearing the Path to Unemployment Insurance For Low-Wage Workers," National Employment Law Project, Center for Economic and Policy Research, 2005, available online: http://www.cepr.net/publications/ABPreport2005.pdf

371. Maurice Emsellem, *et al*, "Failing the Unemployed," Economic Policy Institute, Center on Budget and Policy Priorities, 2002, available online: http://www.cbpp.org/3-12-02ui.pdf

372. *Ibid.*

373. *Ibid.*

374. US Census Bureau, Internet Release, 2006, http://www.census.gov/hhes/www/poverty/threshld/thresh02.html

375. F. Andersson, H.J. Holzer & J.I. Lane, *Moving Up or Moving On...*, *op. cit.* (Introd., n. 45).

376. For a discussion, B. Shulman, *The Betrayal of Work...*, *op. cit.* (Introd., n. 10), p. 102, and note 3, pp. 214-215.

of these studies, for example, it was shown that 70 per cent of workers in the lowest 20 per cent of the population in 1974 had not changed their situation by 1991. Those who were fortunate enough to move up had mostly moved up only one quintile to the bottom 40 percent.

In theory, there are many factors that can lead an individual or family into poverty: divorce, health problems, birth of a child, layoffs, etc. When all these factors are considered, it is the fluctuations in the labor market that primarily explain the cyclical nature of poverty in the United States. When all these factors are considered, it appears that fluctuations in the labor market are the main reason for the cyclical nature of poverty in the United States[377]. These fluctuations are greater in America than in any other developed country. For example, according to the 2002 OECD report, an American employee kept his or her job for an average of seven years, compared to almost 12 years for a French, Belgian, Italian or Swedish employee[378]. If we consider not the average, but the median, it appears that half of American workers have been in their jobs for less than 4 years[379]. Unsurprisingly, this value decreases for non-graduates and for jobs that do not require any particular skills. Thus, for example, the median tenure is 5.5 years for a skilled manufacturing worker and 1.9 years for a service worker in the hotel sector[380]. This difference is directly consistent with the observation that income volatility is twice as high in poor families as in rich households[381]. Here, it may be noted that the shift from a single-funded to a dual-funded family economy has only exacerbated the problem. Indeed,

---

377. Constance Newman, "Income Volatility Complicates Food Assistance," USDA, Amber Waves, 2006, 4, pp. 16-21, available online: http://www.ers.usda.gov/AmberWaves/September06/PDF/IncomeVolatilityFeatureSeptember06.pdf

378. Organisation for Economic Co-operation and Development *(OECD)*, "*Employment Outlook 2002 - Surveying the Jobs Horizon*," chap. 5, figure 5.4, available online: http://www.oecd.org/dataoecd/36/49/17652691.pdf

379. Bureau of Labor Statistics, "Employee Tenure in 2006," available online: ftp://ftp.bls.gov/pub/news.release/tenure.txt

380. *Ibid.*

381. C. Newman, "Income Volatility Complicates Food Assistance," *op. cit.* (*supra*, n. 290).

when both men and women work, the likelihood of losing a source of income is doubled[382].

From a practical perspective, income volatility is a serious problem for the U.S. government: it complicates the mechanisms of food assistance and leads to over-allocation bias[383]. The poor are definitely willing to do anything to abuse the system. This is a far cry from the extreme probity of the leaders of large corporations such as Enron, Vivendi, Worldcom or more recently Apple[384]. Fortunately, the rich man is honest and upright. For some time now, he has even become an ethnologist, like Mrs. Laurence Parisot, president of the main French employers' union, the MEDEF. Not long ago, this vigorous muse of the liberal cause told us with magnificent aplomb that "life, health and love are precarious; why should work escape this law"[385]? A few days later, the lady repeated her statement by telling us that "precariousness [was] a law of the human condition" and that the word "precariousness" was "intended to prevent us from thinking[386]". Poor Franklin Delano Roosevelt, apparently the outdated father of the American "New Deal" and apparently a dangerous leftist for suggesting that it was the responsibility of the community to protect families from the "hazards and vicissitudes of life[387]". In fact, I think Ms. Parisot misses two details. First, man has always sought to escape precariousness through the development of agriculture, animal husbandry, the divinatory arts, religion, medicine, or science. In fact, the great projects that have animated man for thousands of years have all aimed at securing individual and collective destinies. Secondly, no

---

382. J.S. Hacker, "The Insecure Family", in *The Real State of the Union, op. cit.* (Introd., n. 8), p. 87.

383. C. Newman, "Income Volatility Complicates Food Assistance," *op. cit.* (*supra*, n. 290).

384. Yann Philippin, "Apple wants to save its savior", *Le Journal du Dimanche*, December 31, 2006, p. 19.

385. Quoted in *Le Figaro*, August 30, 2005.

386. France Inter, Rue des Entrepreneurs, September 3, 2005.

387. Quoted by Jacob S. Hacker, in "Call It the Family Risk Factor," *New York Times*, January 11, 2004.

one can escape the principle of communicating vessels. As Jacob Hacker rightly pointed out in a remarkable editorial in the *New York Times, placing* the burden of precariousness on the worker is a way of exempting the company from the fluctuations of the economic climate[388]. What Ms. Parisot is telling us is no longer that "precariousness is a law of the human condition" but that "precariousness must be borne by the mass of employees, in order to preserve the profit margins of shareholders, CEOs and other holders of corporate capital". This is perhaps an excellent and legitimate idea. But it must be presented in its true nakedness so that everyone has the opportunity to form a fair opinion.

To the list of anti-precarity strategies, one could add the gregarious instinct that pushes men to group together within villages, nations, brotherhoods, corporations or unions. This alliance approach operates on two levels. Firstly, it allows, by mutualizing the risk, to dilute in the community mass the deleterious effect of individual catastrophes. Secondly, it increases the potential for action tenfold, by associating singular vigor. It is this second lever that mainly plays in the union aggregation. The idea is to give employees greater bargaining power. In fact, the result is rather positive. Indeed, when workers are strictly matched (type of job, level of education, region, marital status, etc.), a significant difference appears between union members and non-union members in the area of wages and social benefits[389]. According to low estimates, union members receive, on average, 15 percent more pay. They are 28 percent more likely to be covered by employer-sponsored health insurance. They are also twice as likely to have a company-subsidized pension plan. Finally, they benefit from an additional 15% of paid vacations[390]. With figures like these, workers would have to be severely decerebrate

---

388. *Ibid.*
389. *The State of Working America 2006-2007, op. cit.* (Introd., n. 13), chap. 3, see especially, tables 3.34-3.36; Bureau of Labor Statistics, "Union Members in 2005," available online: ftp://ftp.bls.gov/pub/news.release/union2.txt.
390. *Ibid.*

not to join a union. Yet the number of union members in the U.S. has dropped by half over the past 25 years, to about 15 per cent in 2005[391]. In the private sector, the number is even lower: 7.8 per cent. This is an astonishing paradox that can only be explained by the real "silent war[392]" that political and business America has been waging against the union movement for 25 years.

It all started in 1981 with the strike of 12,000 American air traffic controllers. In theory, this strike was illegal, as federal employees do not have the right in the United States to stop working. In practice, this kind of action was tolerated, as several congregations of civil servants had already tried their luck with success. Unfortunately for the controllers, Reagan (freshly elected) was not Carter (freshly defeated). While the latter had been conciliatory, the former proved intransigent. He issued an ultimatum to the strikers: return to work within 48 hours or you will be fired, replaced, and stripped of the right to hold a federal job for life. Only about a thousand controllers took the threat seriously. Eleven thousand thought Reagan was bluffing. They got their money's worth, and to this day they still bear the brunt of the president's anathema. Ron Taylor is one of them. Despite his hopes for clemency, this Vietnam veteran is still banned from holding federal office, 23 years after the fact[393]. The firmness of the ruling made it easier for private employers to do business. They began to fight union organizing projects more and more openly, with incredible harshness and remarkable impunity. The

---

391. *The State of Working America 2006-2007, op. cit.* (Introd., n. 13), chap. 3, see especially, figure 3W; Bureau of Labor statistics, "Union Members in 2005," *op. cit.* (*supra*, n. 302).

392. American Federation of Labor and Congress of Industrial Organizations (AFL-CIO), "The Silent War," September 2005, available online: http://www.aflcio.org/joinaunion/how/upload/vatw_issuebrief.pdf

393. David Kiley, "Air-Traffic Controller Still Feels the Sting Decades Later," *USA Today*, October 6, 2004, available online: http://www.usatoday.com/news/washington/2004-06-10-taylor-vignette_x.htm

various reports published in recent years on the subject are quite simply astounding[394].

To understand the problem, it is necessary to appreciate the complexity of the steps required of U.S. employees who wish to join together. The first step is to collect enough "authorization cards" from employees (at least 30%). These cards are used to launch an internal campaign that can last from a few weeks to several months, depending on management's pugnacity. At the end of the campaign, an election is (theoretically) held and the creation of a union is ratified (or rejected) by a simple majority (50%). The management of the company can then recognize the union as constituted (and deal with it) or reject the vote of the employees (and start an endless judicial guerrilla war). To fight against the gregariousness of their employees, companies generally do not bother with vain subtleties. As summarized in a 2000 report commissioned by Human Rights Watch from Lance Compa, a professor of international law at the prestigious Cornell University[395], "many workers who try to form or join a union in order to bargain with their employer are spied on, harassed, pressured, threatened, suspended, fired, displaced or otherwise victimized for exercising their right to freedom of association. Guerrilla warfare can begin as early as the hiring process, as at Wal-mart, the world's largest retailer. When they are hired, employees at this company are subjected to a video explaining that Wal-mart is a big family and "showing" how unions are harmful to the interests of employees. After being subjected to this video

---

394. Lance Compa, "Unfair Advantage," report prepared for Human Right Watch, August 2000, available online at http://hrw.org/reports/pdfs/u/us/uslbr008.pdf; Kate Bronfenbrenner, "Uneasy Terrain," September 2006, report for The US Trade Deficit Review Comission, available online at http://digitalcommons.ilr.cornell.edu/cgi/viewcontent.cgi?article=1002&context=reports; Chirag Metha & Nick Theodore, "Undermining the Right to Organize," Center for Economic Development, University of Illinois, Chicago, December 2005, report for "Human Right at Work," available online: http://araw.org/docUploads/UROCUEDcompressedfullreport%2Epdf; Robert J Flanagan, "Has Management Strangled US Unions," *Journal of Labor Research*, 2005, 26, pp. 33-63; AFL-CIO, "The Silent War," *op. cit.* (*supra*, n. 305).
395. L. Compa, "Unfair Advantage," *op. cit.* (*supra*, n. 307), quoted at 13-14.

during her dive into the world of the working poor, Barbara Ehrenreich notes, not without humor, "You come to wonder - and I imagine some of my young orientation buddies may wonder - why monsters like these shop stewards, these patent crooks, are allowed to go free on the land[396]." When a video isn't enough, employers move on to more sophisticated strategies. More than 80 per cent of them hire consultants specializing in union busting, the so-called "union-busters". In 30% of cases, the leaders are fired; 5 times out of 10, threats of relocation or layoffs are put forward; 6 times out of 10, the carrot of possible benefits or wage increases is brandished if the union is not formed; 9 times out of 10, employees are required to attend compulsory meetings in which it is explained to them that unions will rob them of their rights, their money, their freedom (themes dear to the heart of America) All of these strategies pay off handsomely. Their combined implementation results in a "no" vote rate of nearly 85%, even though employees are in almost all cases in favour of forming a union at the beginning of the campaign (more than 50% of authorization cards collected)[397]. The legal sanctions against offending employers are so symbolic and the time taken to resolve disputes so long that the law has almost no dissuasive effect. When employers dismiss an employee and are finally convicted, they are only required to pay the employee the difference between what he or she should have received had he or she not been wrongfully dismissed and what he or she has received in the meantime. In general, the bill is more than reasonable. For example, Ernest and Jean were paid less than $1,800 in 1999, after five years of proceedings, for having been wrongfully dismissed for their union activities[398]. On average, wrongfully dismissing an employee for

---

396. B. Ehrenreich, *Nickel and Dimed, op. cit.* (Introd., n. 67), p. 145.
397. C. Metha & N. Theodore, "Undermining the Right to Organize," *op. cit.* (*supra*, n. 307); see, for similar values, K. Bronfenbrenner, "Uneasy Terrain," *op. cit.* (*supra*, n. 307).
398. L. Compa, "Unfair Advantage", *op. cit.* (*supra*, n. 307), pp. 110-115.

breaking a union training process cost \$2,750 in 2002[399], less than the cost of some anti-union consultants for one day.

Businesses would be wrong to deprive themselves and our European liberals would be crazy not to call for a rapid alignment of our Labor Code with that of the United States. This would even allow them to replace strikers with other more conciliatory employees. For those who think this practice is outdated or illegal, I suggest a trip to Uncle Sam's country. As is often pointed out by employers at union meetings, it is possible in the United States to replace strikers with new employees during wage demands. This replacement, when it occurs, is permanent and irrevocable. In other words, when the strike ends, the strikers are out. Lance Compa's 2000 report for Human Rights Watch documented thousands of cases of workers who were never reinstated after a strike. International Paper, for example, a Maine-based company, replaced 1,200 strikers in three months. When the strike ended, they were left unemployed and without recourse. Maurice, an employee of the company as had his grandfather, father, brother and children, found it, I believe, "unbelievable that a company could forget all those lifetime contributions and replace us all in one fell swoop... It's like we had our own Holocaust[400]. In local schools, physical and verbal confrontations developed between the children of replacements and substitutes. Several years after the strike ended, one former worker summed up the situation: "I still have an intense hatred for International Paper and the Yellows who came like rats to steal our jobs when we left the plant. I will take that hatred to my grave. There have been suicides, early deaths, divorces, alcoholism, broken families, lost homes, and who knows what else. Thank God there has been no murder[401]." This is not a passage from *Germinal.* It is happening today and it is happening in America. Do

---

399. AFL-CIO, "The Employee Free Choice Act: Meaningful Remedies Against Employer Coercion," 2006, available online: http://www.aflcio.org/joinaunion/voiceatwork/efca/up-load/Coercion_Remedies.pdf
400. L. Compa, "Unfair Advantage", *op. cit.* (*supra*, n. 307), p. 295.
401. *Ibid*, p. 296.

we have to go back to Zola's time to seem modern to the liberal gurus? It would seem so. Thus, for example, Nicolas Baverez explains to us in astonishing terms that "at the heart of the British decline were the trade unions, which had gradually taken control of the economy and society[402]". Fortunately, Margaret Thatcher came along and put an end to these evil-doers and gave back to honest entrepreneurs the basic freedom to operate in peace. Needless to say, England is the country in Western Europe that is closest to the United States in terms of the extent of its inequality and the depth of its poverty? For example, after including social assistance, child poverty, which weighs most heavily on our destiny, affects 15.5% of children in England. France, with its "pseudo social model"[403], comes in at half that number (7.5%). Norway, Finland and Denmark do even better with 3.4%, 2.8% and 2.4% respectively.

To summarize, mass poverty in the United States has an eminently structural origin. In America, there is not enough work for everyone, 25% of jobs offer miserable wages without social security coverage, and when unemployment falls too low, the Federal Reserve struggles to raise it. In Uncle Sam, millions of people hover on the edge of poverty as the major macroeconomic factors sway. One day, they are above the poverty line, and they are paragons of virtue. The next day, they are destitute, asking for a helping hand, and they are suddenly portrayed as models of laziness. This is hardly serious. For the past 30 years, the situation of working people in the United States has been steadily deteriorating as a result of liberal potions. As Jacob Hacker points out, "Increasingly, unemployment is structural, not cyclical: long, devastating, and abrogated only when workers accept huge cuts in pay or hours[404]." It is not, as I keep hearing, the players who are indecently lazy or dishonest. It is the game itself that is undoubtedly truncated. No matter who the people are, it is in the essence of the system

---

402. N. Baverez, *What to do: Agenda 2007, op. cit.* (Introd., n. 63), p. 57.
403. *Ibid,* p. 118.
404. J.S. Hacker, "The Insecure Family", in *The Real State of the Union, op. cit.* (Introd., n. 8), p. 86.

that there are losers. It is in the flesh of these "losers" (ever more numerous) that the prosperity of the "winners" (ever more rare) is anchored. The game is all the more unequal because it is arbitrated by an anorexic labor code. To say that the struggle is fair between men and companies is a scandalous intellectual swindle. When Anna applies for a job and is told, "Okay, but it's going to be $6 an hour with no paid time off, no health insurance, no pension," what choice does she have? None. It's despicable, but that's the way it is. She either accepts or she sinks. In this context, isn't it indecent to point a vengeful finger at the fantasized spinelessness of "our" poor? Is it not despicable to try so hard to dissolve our collective responsibility behind the sad chimera of the effort made? Is it not obscene to see so much wealth concentrated in so few hands? To those who think I am exaggerating, I would like to remind them of one simple figure: the poorest 50% of Americans hold 4% of the national wealth; that is about 9 times less than the richest 1% of Americans[405].

Between official and unofficial figures: from Charybdis to Scylla

So far, we have talked about poverty in reference to the official definition of the term. This definition is based on simple criteria developed in the mid-1960s by Mollie Orshansky, a statistician and economist at the US Social Security[406]. Orshansky based her definition on the "Economic Food Plan" defined and costed by the U.S. Department of Agriculture for families of different sizes and organizations. This program was originally established "for temporary and emergency use when funds are low. It did

---

405. *The State of Working America 2006-2007, op. cit.* (Introd., n. 13), chap. 5, see, in particular, table 5.3.

406. Social Security Administration, Social Security Pioneers, Mollie Orshansky, available online at http://www.ssa.gov/history/orshansky.html; For a review of this topic, Gordon M. Fisher, "The Development of Orshansky Poverty Thresholds and Their Subsequent History as the Official US Poverty Measure," US Census Bureau, 1997, Poverty Measurement Working Paper, available online at http://www.census.gov/hhes/poverty/povmeas/papers/orshansky.html

not allow for restaurant dining, required meticulous organization of food storage and preparation, and was built to provide a nutritious but monotonous diet[407]." Along with these estimates, Orshansky also used official statistical data from 1955 ("Household Consumption Survey") showing that American households spent one-third of their budget on food. The poverty line was then defined by multiplying the minimum food basket cost for a given family composition by three.

In the opinion of a majority of experts, this approach to poverty is both biased and outdated. Without going into detail, this obsolescence is primarily due to the fact that the spending patterns of American households have changed dramatically since the 1960s. Today, not one-third, but between one-fifth and one-sixth of income is spent on food[408]. This has two consequences. First, the definition of destitution has, over the past 40 years, become much harder and more distant from the core of the middle class. In 1960, the poverty line for a standard family of four was 48 percent of median family income. Today, it is only 29%[409]. Second, Orshansky's equation underestimates the current poverty line by a factor of 2 (if food is one-sixth rather than one-third of expenditures, then the minimum food budget would have to be multiplied by 6 rather than 3 to obtain a valid poverty line). If one accepts this precept, not 37 (12.6%) but 91 million (31.0%) people in the United States are close to poverty[410]. Interestingly, this figure was recently validated by Boushey and colleagues

---

407. National Research Council, *Measuring Poverty: A New Approach*, Constance F. Citro & Robert T. Michael (eds.) (Washington, DC: National Academy Press, 1995), p. 24, available online at http://www.census.gov/hhes/www/povmeas/toc.html
408. H. Boushey, C. Brocht, B. Gundersen & J. Bernstein, *Hardships in America...*, *op. cit.* (*supra*, n. 41), at 6; J. Iceland, *Poverty in America...*, *op. cit.* (Introd., n. 9), p. 24; Jared Bernstein, Chauna Brocht & Maggie Spade-Aguilar, *How Much Is Enough? Basic Family Budgets for Working Families* (Washington, DC: Economic Policy Institute, 2000).
409. *The State of Working America 2006-2007*, op. cit. *(Introd., n. 13), chap. 6, p. 280.*
410. US Census Bureau, Internet Release, 2006, http://pubdb3.census.gov/macro/032006/pov/new01_200_01.htm

in a report published by the prestigious Economic Policy Institute[411]. In this report, the authors calculated the minimum budget that would allow families of different sizes to live "decently" depending on where they lived. The latter was defined as the ability to afford food, shelter, health care and child care. In Nassau-Suffolk, New York, the minimum budget was $48,606 in 1999, or 3.62 times the poverty line. In Hattiesburg, Mississippi, it was "only" $21,989, or 1.64 times the poverty line. On average, completing a "decent" life required an income level of 2 times the poverty line. But 30% of families did not reach this benchmark. For these families, this failure meant insufficient or poor quality food, substandard and/or insecure housing, poor or non-existent childcare, and poor or non-existent health coverage.

Recognizing the weaknesses of the official poverty line, in 1995 the U.S. Congress commissioned a panel of the American Academy of Sciences (NAS) to redefine the principles for calculating the poverty line. The panel proposed a new approach, which was more complex but apparently less questionable than Orshansky's[412]. Without going into detail, the idea proposed was to define the indigence threshold as a percentage of the median basic expenditure (food, housing, clothing) for a standard family of four (two children, two parents). The resulting threshold was then multiplied by a variable factor to include other potential needs. Depending on the different theoretical options chosen and the percentages adopted, we obtain a family of poverty lines. On average, these offer percentages of indigence 1 to 2 points higher than the Orshansky threshold. This implies that the official number of poor people is underestimated by at least 2.5 to 3 million[413]. The number of poor people in the U.S. is therefore estimated to be around 40 million.

---

411. H. Boushey, C. Brocht, B. Gundersen & J. Bernstein, *Hardships in America...*, *op. cit.* (*supra*, n. 41).
412. For a discussion, see J. Iceland, *Poverty in America...*, *op. cit.* (Introd., n. 9), pp. 30-32; for the original text, National Research Council, *Measuring Poverty...*, *op. cit.* (*supra*, n. 320), http://www.census.gov/hhes/www/povmeas/toc.html
413. The State of Working America 2006-2007, op. cit. *(Introd., n. 13), chap. 8, pp. 291-293.*

To summarize, the above figures suggest that there are between 40 and 91 million poor people in the United States. I believe that this wide range should be seen not as an uncertainty of measurement, but as a range of gradations. The low estimate (40 million) would then define a crass poverty, a poverty of absolute lack. This would mean hunger, unhealthy and/or insecure housing, lack of access to health care and closed horizons. The second estimate (91 million) would include a poverty of insufficiency and exclusion. This poverty would barely meet the basic needs of food and shelter but would deny access to the surrounding affluence and health care system. It would affect 50 million people. As David Shipler writes of these people, "Having a bowl of rice in a society where everyone else has half a bowl can be a sign of success and intelligence.... Having five bowls of rice in a society where the majority enjoys a decent, balanced diet is a tragedy[414]." Again, one might think that this kind of tragedy is legitimate. One can also argue that between 40 and 90 million indigents is an acceptable number. One can. However, one can also look with anguish and suspicion at an economic system that makes America produce, at once, more wealth and more poverty than any other developed country.

____

414. D.K. Shipler, *The Working Poor...*, *op. cit.* (Introd., n. 68), pp. 8-9.

CHAPTER 2
JUSTICE-EDUCATION-HEALTH:
AMERICA BY EXAMPLE

Adulators of liberal America often highlight the problem of the welfare state and taxes. They would be wrong to deprive themselves of this opportunity, since the subject is so promising and easy. It cannot be denied that the level of compulsory taxation is substantially lower in the United States than in most European countries. In France, for example, the overall tax rate is, on average, over 57%[415]. This means, as Ted Stanger greedily (and somewhat exaggeratedly) points out in his latest book, that "a basic taxpayer... pays the equivalent of his entire income from January 1 to July 15 each year in taxes and contributions.[416]" For an American, the mowing stops in April, which is below the 40% levy[417]. I often hear that this tax parsimony is favourable to purchasing power and entrepreneurship. It would boost household consumption and reward the boldness of builders. From this point of view, France has not understood anything. Its fiscal voracity and backward-looking dogmas are undoubtedly at the heart of its sad decline[418]. I am willing to believe this. I also want to admit, a priori,

---

415. T. Piketty & E. Saez, "How Progressive Is the US Federal Tax System...," *op. cit.* (chap. I, n. 236), 21, pp. 3-24, table A5, available online: http://www.jourdan.ens.fr/piketty/fichiers/public/PikettySaezJEP2006.pdf
416. Ted Stanger, *Sacred Public Servants, op. cit.* (Introd., n. 16).
417. T. Piketty & E. Saez, "How Progressive Is the US Federal Tax System...," *op. cit.* (chap. I, n. 236), table A5.
418. T. Stanger, *Sacred Civil Servants, op. cit.* (Introd., n. 16); N. Baverez, *Que faire: Agenda 2007, op. cit.* (Introd., n. 63), in particular chap. 2.

that the State is a nuisance and taxes an offence. However, I cannot help thinking that, in the final analysis, we must pay for the doctors, nurses, teachers, researchers, judges, police officers, soldiers and all the equipment that all these people need.

Allow me to tell you a brief anecdote to illustrate the above. Shortly before the 2007 presidential election, while I was at my local newsagent's, a very nice lady in her seventies was bravely railing against "those socialists and their taxes". The same woman was angry three days earlier about having to wait 4 hours in the emergency room because of the lack of a doctor. The month before, she was ranting against insecurity, the laxity of judges and the lack of police officers. I admit that I was a bit impudent in pointing out to her that it was difficult to ask, at the same time, for more doctors, more policemen, more judges, less taxes and fewer civil servants. "And in America, how do you think they do it? Bush cuts taxes every year, and yet it works much better there than here, look at the research, the Nobel prizes, the hospitals, the schools, they crush us everywhere. We pay, we pay, but we get nothing. And then these civil servants, anyway, they're always on strike." I wisely refrained from specifying that I myself was a member of this cohort of infamous useless leeches, fattened at the expense of the nation's living forces. However, I took the liberty, under the reproachful eye of the tobacconist (who, since then, has taken me for a dangerous communist), to ask my interlocutor if she had lived in America. She answered that she hadn't, but if I didn't believe her, I could have just watched TV. Our muse of the "made in Bush" knew well what she was saying "and anyway her sister-in-law had worked in the United States"... Eternal refrain of the man who saw the man who saw the man who saw the bear. Unfortunately, one must sometimes be wary of television and second-hand accounts.

Taxes: everything is paid for

Molly lives in Atlanta. She is an executive secretary for a small company and the sole mother of two children. Her salary in 2005 was $3,000 gross per month. Caroline lives in Lyon. She has two daughters and works in a communications agency. Her monthly salary is 2,400 euros ($3,120 at the current rate). After the state's passage, Molly and Caroline lose 39% and 57% of their income respectively[419]. This leaves Molly with $1,830 and Caroline with 1,030 euros. To insure her daughters against illness, Caroline pays nothing. Molly has to pay $550 per month. This seems like a reasonable investment when you consider that for an uninsured person, a simple appendectomy can cost $14,000[420]. Caroline has enrolled her two daughters in the local public school. After classes (4:30 p.m.), they stay in school until 5:45 p.m. Caroline pays absolutely nothing for this service. Molly is not so lucky. Both of her children attend a public school near her home. For study hall from 1:30 to 6:00 p.m., Molly pays $650 a month. She would have liked to put her children in a "better school," but the $1,600 per month per student fee charged by the private school in her neighbourhood has made that wish unattainable. If Molly's children do get into college, her mother will have to pay a minimum of $5,000 (per head) in tuition. For a prestigious private university, it would be $30,000 or $40,000. Caroline would pay less than 200 euros. Polytechnique and the ancient Sorbonne are infinitely more accessible than any American university. Unlike Caroline, Molly gets nothing if she gets sick. When Molly gave birth to her second child, she had to limit her maternity leave to three short weeks: one before the birth thanks to unpaid leave and two afterwards on the basis of the 10 days of paid leave granted annually by the company. By law, Molly was entitled to 12 weeks of maternity leave, but this did not include any allowance or emolument. It was of course impossible for this

---

419. T. Piketty & E. Saez, "How Progressive Is the US Federal Tax System…," *op. cit.* (chap. I, n. 236), table A5.
420. S.S. Sered & R. Fernandopulle, *Uninsured in America…, op. cit.* (Introd., n. 21), p. 12.

single mother to survive for 3 months without any income. Let's remember that the French system grants Caroline 16 weeks without loss of salary. On another level, Molly's company does not offer a subsidized retirement plan. If we play a little simulation game and assume that our two women retire at age 65 after 160 quarters of loyal service at a constant salary equal to their current salary, it appears that Molly will receive 39% of her salary, or $1,160 (in 2007 dollars)[421]. 1,825 ($2,372 at current rates)[422].

Those who think that the previous elements are far-fetched should give me credit for a few more moments. I will have the opportunity to substantiate my claims below, particularly in quantitative terms. What is important here is to understand that in the United States, as in Europe, everything is paid for. The tax burden is lower for Molly. However, she has only rudimentary social security coverage (no statutory paid leave and maternity leave, no health coverage, restrictive and flimsy unemployment coverage, low pension, etc.). In the end, I am not sure that Molly is better off than Caroline. On the contrary! Far from mowing down the middle classes, taxes offer them purchasing power by allowing a pooling of resources in the key sectors of education, health, social coverage and/or justice. It is a bit like the principle of insurance. By giving "a little", one avoids having to pay a lot in the long run. The wealthy can probably afford to take their chances, without any cover, in the game of misfortune. They can afford to lose a large amount of money by trying to save it. For the middle and modest classes, this bet on luck is madness. It means, when the dice are unlucky, giving up the fruits of a lifetime. For example, if Molly gets sick and chooses not to insure herself, she will lose everything: her savings, her home and, ultimately, her life.

If there is one thing I learned from my time in the United States, it is that taxes can be fair, useful and healthy. The taxing parsimony of which

---

421. Social Security Online, Benefit Calculators, http://www.ssa.gov/OACT/quickcalc/index.html

422. "Retirement Simulator", *Les Echos*, http://www.lesechos.fr/patrimoine/calcul/retraite/e_retraite.html

American liberals claim to be famous masks a harshness of which the overwhelming majority of Europeans are unaware. The laws of the market know neither mercy nor compassion. They are as barbaric as they are ruthless. In America, people die because they do not have enough money for health institutions to treat them[423]. In America, the likelihood of being sentenced to death depends, for the same blood crime, on the wealth of the plaintiff and his ability to hire private lawyers[424]. In America, the infant mortality rate is twice as high for blacks as for whites[425]. In America, a poor, bright child is less likely to graduate from college than a rich, dumb child[426]. I don't think there is a better description of this system than the one provided by Devon when Susan Sered and Rushika Fernandopulle asked him about what it means to live without health insurance, "I feel like the way the system is set up is like a weird version of natural selection, in which the people who are the poorest can't afford to keep themselves healthy, and as a result they die[427]."

Justice: depending on whether you are powerful or miserable...

In continental Europe, the judicial system follows an inquisitorial logic. In this case, a professional judge, in theory impartial, investigates the case at the taxpayer's expense, for both the prosecution and the defence, with the main concern being the emergence of the truth. In the United States,

---

423. S.S. Sered & R. Fernandopulle, *Uninsured in America...*, *op. cit.* (Introd., n. 21); D.L. Barlett & J.B. Steele, *Critical Condition*, *op. cit.* (Introd., n. 21).
424. *D.R. Dow,* Executed On a Technicality..., op. cit. *(Introd., n. 20); J. Reiman,* The Rich Get Richer and the Poor Get Prison..., op. cit. *(Introd., n. 19).*
425. Center for Disease Control and Prevention, "Infant Mortality Rates...," *op. cit.* (Introd., n. 81), table 23, http://www.cdc.gov/nchs/data/hus/tables/2001/01hus023.pdf
426. M.A. Fox, B.A. Connolly & T.D. Snyder, "Youth Indicators 2005: Trends in the Well-Being of American Youth," US Department of Education, National Center for Education Statistics, 2005, table 21, available online: http://nces.ed.gov/pubs2005/2005050.pdf; T. Draut, *Strapped...*, *op. cit.* (Introd., n. 9), pp. 34-35.
427. S.S. Sered & R. Fernandopulle, *Uninsured in America...*, *op. cit.* (Introd., n. 21), p. 17.

the approach is completely different. Indeed, in this country, the procedure is of an adversarial nature. When a crime occurs, the police investigate and report their findings to the prosecutor. The prosecutor then assesses the nature of the evidence presented and, if he or she wishes, conducts further investigations. As the name suggests, the *prosecutor* "prosecutes". He is there to investigate against the accused. This imputation is obviously directly opposed to that of the defense. The latter is privately recruited by a defendant whose unwavering ally it wants to be. In order to accomplish its work, the defense investigates only on behalf of the accused, with the help, if necessary, of private investigators. At the end of the chain, if the prosecutor considers that his case is sufficiently consistent, he refers it to the judge. The judge then plays the role of arbitrator. During the trial, each party presents its arguments in a contradictory debate, "a battle between equal opponents, with the truth as the ultimate victory[428]". At the end of this process, the judge and jury decide "by conscience" on the guilt or innocence of the accused. Frequently, however, the confrontation ends in a settlement between the parties before a judgment is rendered.

Over the past ten years, numerous reports, books and articles have highlighted the appalling shortcomings of the American justice system[429].

---

428. Ken Armstrong, Florangela Daliva & Justin Mayo, "For Some, Free Counsel Comes at a High Cost," *Seattle Times*, April 4, 2004, available online: http://seattletimes.nwsource.com/news/local/unequaldefense/

429. Adam Liptak, "Study Suspects Thousands of Falses Convictions," *New York Times*, April 19, 2004; D.R. Dow, *Executed On a Technicality...*, *op. cit.* (Introd, n. 20); Richard Willing & Gary Fields, "Geography of the Death Penalty," *USA Today*, December 20, 1999; Amnesty International, USA, "Failing the Future: Death Penalty Developments, March 1998 - March 2000," Report AMR 51/003/2000, April 2000; Bill Moushey, "Win at All Costs," *Pittsburg Post-Gazette*, 10-part report, November 22-December 13, 1998; Ken Armstrong, Maurice Possley & Judith Marriott, "Trial and Error: A Shocking Expose of Prosecutorial Misconduct," *Chicago Tribune*, January 10-14, 1999; Steven Weinberg, "Harmful Error: Investigating America's Local Prosecutors," Washington, DC, Center for Public Integrity, 2003; K. Armstrong, F. Davila & J. Mayo, "An Unequal Defense...," *op. cit.* (Introd., n. 19), 3-part report, April 4-6, 2004; James S. Liebman, Jeffrey Fagan, & Valerie West, "A Broken System: Error Rates in Capital Cases, 1973-1995", Columbia Law School, *Public Law Research Paper*, No. 15, June 2000; John Grisham, *The Accused*, Paris, Robert Laffont, 2007.

Simply put, I know of no other developed (I almost said *civilized*) country in which a man can be sentenced to life, with a 25-year term of imprisonment, for being caught with 46 milligrams of cocaine, for trying to pay for groceries at the supermarket with a fictitious check for $94, or for stealing a box of vitamins, a pair of sneakers, a spare tire, or baby milk[430]. Nor do I know of any other democratic nation in which the conviction rate depends so heavily, for the same crime, on the financial wealth and racial status of the defendant[431]. In Texas, to take just one example, a prisoner is three times more likely to be acquitted in a criminal trial if he or she has a private attorney. He is also three times less likely to be sentenced to death following a guilty verdict[432]. In Texas, it was not until 1999 that a white man was sentenced to death for the murder of a black man[433]. In Georgia, it was shown that a murderer was 4 to 5 times more likely to be sentenced to death if the victim was white than if he was black[434]. In general, nationally, while whites account for less than 50% of homicide victims, they account for 80% of death sentences[435]. Since the advent of DNA testing, dozens of people wrongly convicted in criminal cases have been released from U.S. prisons. 25% of these lucky winners had confessed their "crime" to the police and 70% had been "formally" recognized by a prosecution witness[436]. With respect to the latter point, there is converging evidence that many prosecutors are willing to blithely break the letter of the law to secure convictions and re-election (judges and prosecutors are mostly elected in the United

---

430. Joe Domanick, *Cruel Justice: Three Strikes and the Politics of Crime in America's Golden State* (Los Angeles: University of California Press, 2004); for the examples discussed, see pp. 3-4.
431. *J. Reiman,* The Rich Get Richer and the Poor Get Prison..., op. cit. *(Introd., n. 19); D.R. Dow,* Executed On a Technicality..., op. cit. *(Introd., n. 20).*
432. *Ibid,* p. 8.
433. *Ibid,* p. 101.
434. *Ibid,* p. 195.
435. *Ibid.*
436. *Ibid.* at 97-98.

States)[437]. The most common strategies include falsifying and fabricating evidence, withholding exculpatory evidence and bribing witnesses. As Larry Pozner, president of the American Association of Criminal Defense Lawyers, pointed out in 1999, "the problem of lawbreaking prosecutors is more disturbing, and does more damage to society, than any common criminal.[438]

Beyond their criminal misdeeds, many prosecutors tend to seek very heavy sentences in order to secure a reputation as incorruptible vigilantes[439]. This tendency partly explains why the incarceration rate is substantially higher in the United States than in any other OECD country. For example, while the incarceration rate is below 100 per 100,000 in France (91), Germany (96), Finland (66), or Japan (58), it is 725 per 100,000 in the United States[440]. If we consider only the black population, the proportion reaches an extravagant 2,500 per 100,000[441]. An article in the prestigious *Washington Post* showed that spending on prisons in 1997 exceeded spending on universities[442]. At the same time, states such as California and Florida were spending more money to fund their prison

---

437. Bill Moushey, "Win at All Costs," *op. cit.* (*supra*, n. 15); K. Armstrong, M. Possley & J. Marriott, "Trial and Error...", *op. cit.* (*supra*, n. 15); S. Weinberg, "Harmful Error...", *op. cit.* (*supra*, n. 15); J. S. Liebman, J. Fagan, & V. West, "A Broken System...," *op. cit.* (*supra*, n. 15); NACDL, "Winning at Any Cost: Prosecutorial Excess Distorting America's Justice System," News Release by the National Association of Criminal Defense Lawyers (NACDL), available online at http://www.criminaljustice.org; Amnesty International, USA, "Failing the Future...," *op. cit.* (*supra*, n. 15).
438. NACDL, "Winning at Any Cost...," *op. cit.* (*supra*, n. 23), at 1.
439. R. Willing & G. Fields, "Geography of the Death Penalty," *op. cit.* (*supra*, n. 15).
440. OECD, Factbook 2007, "Economic, Environmental and Social Statistics: Prison Population"; available online: http://miranda.sourceoecd.org/vl=1979075/cl=12/nw=1/rpsv/factbook/data/11-03-03-T01.xls
441. Human Right Watch, "Race and Incarceration in the United States," February 22, 2002, available online: http://hrw.org/backgrounder/usa/race/pdf/table1.pdf; Bruce Western & Katherine Beckett, "How Unregulated Is the US Labor Market? The Penal System as a Labor Market Institution," *American Journal of Sociology*, 1999, 104, pp. 1030-1060.
442. Roberto Suro, "Institute Urges Change in Funding Priorities," *Washington Post*, February 24, 1997.

systems than to subsidize their university systems, which was far from the case in the 1980s[443].

Allow me to make a small aside to the above comments. The extreme rate of imprisonment, especially among the disadvantaged black population, removes from the market a large number of poor individuals who are declared candidates for unemployment. Including this parameter makes the unemployment rates of the major European countries look much more presentable compared to those of the United States. As Bruce Western and Katherine Beckett explain in a study published in the mid-1990s: "In contrast to claims of 'Eurosclerosis' and successful deregulation of the U.S. labor market, our estimates of unemployment among U.S. men consistently exceed European unemployment rates between 1975 and 1994. State intervention in the labor market through the penal system thus helps produce a falsely optimistic view of U.S. labor market performance compared to Europe[444]." It is strange that this "detail" has so easily escaped Laurence Parisot, Ted Stanger and Nicolas Baverez, to mention only a few of the names already mentioned in this book. I recognize, however, that it would not be politically correct to insinuate, in the midst of liberal fervor, that America produces as many (or more) unemployed people than our dear old Europe, despite its extreme flexibility and its famously weak labor code. Let's lie, disguise, conceal, pretend, arrange, omit, fudge, something will always remain. Unfortunately, media fame is also credibility for many voters.

Returning to the problem of justice, it seems clear that the propensity of accusatory structures to break the law and seek heavy sentences makes the role of defensive packages quite crucial. In fact, as a recent *Seattle Times* article points out, if lawyers don't do their jobs properly, "the

---

443. Fox Butterfield, "New Prisons Cast Shadow Over Higher Education," *New York Times*, April 2, 1995.
444. B. Western & K. Beckett, "How Unregulated Is the US Labor Market? (*supra*, n. 27), p. 1052.

[adversarial] system breaks down[445]." Unfortunately, this is what happens to less fortunate individuals. To understand this point, it is important to realize that the U.S. justice system imposes significant, if not exorbitant, procedural costs on defendants[446]. In particular, a proper exculpatory investigation requires the setting up of a counter-investigation that may involve, depending on the case: expert reports, psychiatric evaluations, complex technological analyses (e.g. DNA, graphology, ballistics), the hiring of private investigators, etc. Even if you exclude legal fees, the bill can quickly run into the thousands, even tens of thousands of dollars. Many defendants cannot afford such expenses. As a result, they are *de facto* "forced to forego legally founded rights or defenses[447]".

From a personal point of view, I find it unfortunate that defendants have to give up some means of defense because of lack of money. However, this inconvenience is nothing compared to the Kafkaesque situation experienced by many defendants under the administration of public defenders. Theoretically, these lawyers must be zealous and qualified. In practice, they often prove to be intellectually inept, morally cynical and technically incompetent[448]. The source of this state of affairs can be found in the liberal logic which, in the United States, regulates all socio-economic activities. In America, contrary to what the great democratic ideals state, justice is often treated like any other consumer good, according to a purely accounting

---

445. Ken Armstrong, Florangela Daliva & Justin Mayo, "Attorney Profited, But His Clients Lost," *Seattle Times*, April 5, 2004, available online: http://seattletimes.nwsource.com/news/local/unequaldefense/

446. Robert A. Kagan, "Should Europe Be Concerned About 'American-style Contradictory Legalism'?", *Law and Society*, 2001, 48, pp. 471-493, available online: http://www.reds.msh-paris.fr/publications/revue/pdf/ds48/ds048-08.pdf; Adam Liptak, "Debt to Society Is Least of Costs For Ex-Convicts", *New York Times*, February 23, 2006.

447. R.A. Kagan, "Should Europe be concerned about 'American-style contradictory legalism'?", *op. cit. (supra*, n. 32), at 475.

448. D.R. Dow, *Executed On a Technicality...*, *op. cit.* (Introd., n. 20); Amnesty International, USA, "Failing the Future...," *op. cit. (supra*, n. 15); K. Armstrong, F. Davila & J. Mayo, "An Unequal Defense...", *op. cit.* (Introd., n. 19); J.S. Liebman, J. Fagan, & V. West, "A Broken System...," *op. cit. (supra*, n. 15).

logic. The judicial universe is then reduced to a space of cost. Fairness or the duty of truth are of little importance, what counts in the final analysis is accounting efficiency. The astonishing logic of "representation contracts" perfectly illustrates this point[449]. The idea is to subcontract the defense of the poorest suspects to a lawyer, for a fixed sum. Typically, the contract is signed for a defined period of time (e.g. 5 years) and does not specify any quantitative threshold. This means that the lawyer must handle all cases that come to him or her, no matter how many there are. Most contracts allow for continued private practice and subcontracting.

A comprehensive study conducted in Washington state by reporters from the *Seattle Times*[450] found that the prevalence of agency contracts has exploded over the past 30 years. In 1973, six of the state's 39 counties had opted for this option. By 2004, 26 had done so. Yet, as early as 1973, the Washington Bar Association concluded that such retainers should be eliminated because they did not provide plaintiffs with an acceptable defense. The nature of the problem can be seen in a few figures. The D.C. Bar Association estimates (and there seems to be a consensus on this) that one lawyer cannot possibly cover more than 150 criminal cases per year. In many cases, lucky "retainers" reach two or three times that limit. Tom Earl, for example, was awarded the Grant County representation contract. In 2003, he handled 413 cases, not including his private practice. Our man didn't even take the time to meet with his clients, let alone talk to them. He did not conduct any investigations and obviously did not interview witnesses before the hearing. He often did not even bother to call back potentially "friendly" witnesses who had contacted his firm. This was a strange improvisation, considering that Tom Earl's clients often had their heads or a few decades in jail. In fact, in order to minimize his worries and spare himself the pain of a trial, our man pushed his clients to plead guilty. Faced with the poor work done by their lawyer, they often had no choice

---

449. K. Armstrong, F. Davila & J. Mayo, "An Unequal Defense...", *op. cit.* (Introd., n. 19).
450. *Ibid.*

but to accept this option and to comply with the arrangements imposed by the prosecutor. Eighty-eight percent of Earl's clients accepted a plea bargain, compared to a statewide average of 76 percent. Still, some defendants were foolish enough to want to assert their innocence. John Jackson was one of them. His case, as reported by the *Seattle Times,* is as edifying as it is painful. In 1995, our man was accused of selling drugs. In support of his case, the prosecutor presented two witnesses: a confidential informant and a police officer who said he had witnessed a sale. When the case arrived on Tom Earl's desk in November, he was on his 300th criminal case (not including his private practice). He had minimal time to devote to each case and no financial interest in investigating. In fact, anything he spent on investigative work was subtracted from the overall amount he received from the representation contract. Jackson was sentenced to six years in prison. He decided to appeal from the bottom of his cell. His case went to trial again 5 years later! The defense was entrusted to Nancy Tenney. She was a federal assistant in a public defense office. This meant that she was to the defense what the prosecutor was to the prosecution: a well-trained, salaried attorney with a competent staff. At the appeal hearing, Tenney questioned the notorious confidential informant and showed that he had a clear mental disorder. The man explained, for example, that he had warned the prosecutor about a list of high-profile crimes, including the Oklahoma City bombing, before they happened. Tenney also revealed that the informant had been treated for schizophrenia for 25 years. The lawyer also showed that the police officer's statement was untrue. From the location where he said he was placed, he would have had to see through walls to witness any transaction. Jackson was acquitted. To obtain this verdict, Tenney had taken three simple steps: 1) interview the prosecution witness; 2) research the witness's possible psychiatric history; and 3) visit the crime scene. Not rocket science, but enough to clear his client of suspicion. Earl had done nothing of the sort! In a sad irony, Jackson was acquitted after he had served his sentence and was already out of prison. He died the following year.

Through his cynicism and amorality, Tom Earl, a lawyer appointed by Grant County to defend the most vulnerable defendants, had robbed Jackson of 6 of the last 7 years of his life. Between 1999 and 2003, this lawyer tried 34 cases. He lost 32. This may seem like a lot, but it is still better than, among other examples, his colleague Guillermo Romero. The latter did not have a contract, but was regularly rehired by successive contractors as a subcontractor. Romero's only qualification was that he was "economic". As a lawyer he was inept, in the words of the Washington Bar Association. One day he asked for a "D and A" test, which stands for DNA. Romero explained to his clients that they could not appeal... when they could. He told them they could leave the state or the country... when they couldn't. Between 1997 and 2003, Romero tried 23 cases and won none. In 1997, to take just one example reported by the *Seattle Times*, he defended Lambert, a 15-year-old accused of killing an elderly couple. On the written transcript of the police interview, it appeared that Lambert said he went to his victims' house with the intention of killing them. This is a very damaging element of premeditation. Lambert had never said that, but since Romero had not bothered to listen to the tapes, he did not notice the mistake. Lambert apparently believed that he was facing the electric chair and that a life sentence meant a release after 15-20 years "like in the movies". He agreed to plead guilty, which earned him life without parole. Lambert was not, in his opinion, informed of the consequences of pleading guilty. He did not understand that he could not be sentenced to death because of his age at the time. He was not informed of the importance of being tried as a child, which would have guaranteed him a lighter sentence. He agreed to be tried as an adult, after a hearing that Romero had obviously prepared in spite of common sense. In the face of these facts, Judge Nielsen rejected Lambert's admission of guilt in 2003 and ordered that the teenager be released or retried. According to the judge, Romero's conduct at trial was "unprofessional", "clearly reprehensible" and characteristic of a "dereliction of duty". The Court of Appeal reversed this judgment in 2004, arguing that Lambert was, at the time of his first trial, old enough to know what he was doing[451]. As Adam Liptak points out in a *New York* Times article, "In Washington state, as in other states, minors who sign a contract to buy a stereo or a bicycle are allowed to change their minds. They are, in the words of the Supreme Court, 'incompetent to assign their rights.[452]. But juveniles are allowed to submit binding plea agreements that involve life without the possibility of early release[453]. According to the prosecutor who prosecuted Lambert, the teenager "had the right to plead guilty...children of these ages are trusted to decide on an abortion[454].

In short, because of the scandalously inconsistent lawyers, Jackson was sentenced to 6 years despite his innocence and Lambert was sentenced to life imprisonment with no possibility of early release despite his young age. Others have even less of a chance and their lives are lost. As David Dow, a University of Houston law professor and death penalty lawyer, points out, "America has two legal systems, one for the wealthy defendants and one for the poor.... Wealth is important because in many cases the outcome of a trial depends less on what actually happened than on the skill of the lawyer[455]. (...) Everyone who has been sent to death row in Texas or elsewhere has common characteristics - bad lawyers, impatient appellate judges, poverty[456]." In a recent work, Dow gives us a non-fiction version of Kafka's famous "Trial." Every word of this work hides a nightmare for anyone who still believes in justice and the equality of men before the law. Consider the case of Carl Johnson, executed in Texas on September 19, 1995[457]. The transcript of the trial minutes gives the impression that his lawyer was not present. In fact, he was there, but he was sleeping. Prior

---

451. Adam Liptak, "Years of Regret Follow a Hasty Guilty Plea Made at 16," *New York Times*, October 3, 2005.

452. A difficult to translate phrase stating that "minors are... incompetent to contract away their rights".

453. Adam Liptak, "Years of Regret Follow a Hasty Guilty Plea Made at 16," *op. cit.* (*supra*, n. 37).

454. *Ibid.*

455. D.R. Dow, *Executed On a Technicality...*, *op. cit.* (Introd., n. 20), p. 7.

456. *Ibid*, p. 23.

457. *Ibid.* chapter 1.

to the trial, he had not conducted any investigations and had refused to meet with defense witnesses. During the hearing, the spectacle of their improvised interrogations was apparently very "entertaining. To crown his performance, our lawyer pleaded his client's innocence, apparently unaware that the latter had produced a written confession. It must be said that this was not the first time Johnson's defense attorney had done this. All of his death penalty clients had ended up on death row. In the early 1990s, this lawyer (*sic)* even "weighed in" on one in five death row inmates in Harris County, Texas. That didn't stop the authorities from assigning him clients over and over again. He must have been economical in his use, like Romero.

Of course, one would expect the competent courts to reject the results of such trials, given the inept performance of the defense. This is rarely the case. In fact, as David Dow sadly explains, evidence of incompetence is, in itself, insufficient to win a case. To "deserve" a new trial, the defendant must prove that with another defender, the verdict would have been different. This condition is very difficult (if not impossible) to meet. This explains why trials have been validated when the public defender had sexual relations with the defendant's wife, showed up drunk at the hearing, fell asleep during the debates, refused to meet with his client before the trial, refused to receive potential witnesses, did not conduct any investigation, and/or fulfilled one of his client's appeal requests despite common sense[458].

Take Johnny Joe Martinez, for example[459]. This man was sentenced to death, even though broad mitigating circumstances, related to his life history, should have given him a "simple" prison sentence. His first lawyer had "failed" to seek out this evidence and present it to the jury. The second lawyer made the appeal so poorly that he irreparably damaged any hope of sentence conversion. This lawyer never met with his client, conducted no investigation, interviewed no witnesses, sought no experts, including

---

458. *Ibid*, p. 8.
459. *Ibid.* chapter 3.

psychiatric experts, and steadfastly refused to answer Martinez's phone calls and increasingly desperate (and poignant) letters. The request for appeal was formulated in 6 pages, 15 to 20 times less than the usual standard in such cases. Martinez received a copy of the manuscript months after his appeal was denied. Speaking of Martinez's lawyer, David Dow notes that "his mistake was irreparable. His mistake led directly to Martinez's execution[460]. To understand this point, it is important to know that Martinez fell under a statute that prevented anything from being made in a second appeal that could have been made in the first. This means that anything that was overlooked by the lawyer cannot be represented afterwards. Sabotage the appeal and you will convict your client as surely as if you put a bullet in his brain yourself.

The situation becomes quite unbearable and ubiquitous when the elements thus neglected are likely to lead to the innocence of the accused. This is what happened to Gary Graham after he was charged with the 1981 murder of Bobby Lambert[461]. The prosecutor organized his case along two lines: 1) Graham had a gun of the same caliber as the one used by the murderer; 2) three witnesses, present at the crime scene, had testified against Graham. However, only one of them testified that he formally recognized the accused. Like many others before and after him, Graham was assigned an incompetent lawyer. The lawyer did not investigate the case, paid no attention to the police reports, and handled the case in a manner that made no sense. A second lawyer appointed for the appeal process showed the same culpable indifference. It was not until the "third round" that Graham finally got competent counsel. They discovered two things. First, a ballistics analysis conducted by the police showed that Graham's gun was not the one used in the murder. Second, two witnesses at the crime scene testified that Graham was not the shooter. These witnesses were standing close to the shooter at the time of the shooting (10 feet away) and had seen

---

460. *Ibid*, p. 59.
461. *Ibid.* chapter 4.

him in full view. The witness who recognized Graham only saw the shooter from a distance (10 to 15 m) in an area of low light. All of this information was in the file that the police gave to the defense at the first trial. Graham's original lawyers did not see fit to address it. His last defenders tried to get a new trial. No state, federal or supreme court would consider the merits of the case on the grounds that it could have been presented in the first appeal. Graham was executed for the murder of Bobby Lambert. His last words were, "Tonight they are murdering me[462].

One might think that the previous cases are only epiphenomena, aberrations of little significance. Unfortunately, they are not. Johnson, Martinez, and Graham were defended by inept but representative lawyers. As David Dow points out, they had "what most death row inmates have[463]." In North Carolina, according to a 2002 study, 20 percent of death row inmates were represented by lawyers who had already been sanctioned by the state bar[464]. In Texas, one-third of death row inmates executed during George W. Bush's term as governor were defended by lawyers who had been disciplined (disbarred, suspended, reprimanded, etc.)[465]. In the same state, a study of 251 cases showed that one-quarter of the appeal petitions submitted between 1995-2002 were less than 15 pages in length. Three-quarters of the petitions submitted had not been investigated or further investigated after the first trial[466]. In a more comprehensive and highly publicized report, James Liebman, Jeffrey Fagan and Valerie West studied the error rate in capital trials from 1973 to 1995[467]. In 68% of the cases, serious errors, prejudicial to the convicted, were identified by the appellate courts. The primary source of these errors was inept counsel (37%). The second factor was associated with prosecutorial misconduct (e.g., suppression of evidence exonerating the accused, falsification of evidence, etc.: 19%). : 19

---

462. *Ibid*, p. 115.
463. *Ibid*, p. 83.
464. *Ibid.*
465. *Ibid.*
466. *Ibid.*
467. J.S. Liebman, J. Fagan, & V. West, "A Broken System...," *op. cit. (supra,* n. 15).

%). When the overturned trials were retried, 82% of the defendants were sentenced to prison rather than to death. In 7% of cases, an acquittal was obtained (after an average of 10 years of proceedings).

One might think that the ability of the U.S. justice system to identify and correct its errors is quite reassuring. Yet, as Liebman and colleagues point out, "capital trials produce so many errors that it takes three judicial reviews to identify them - leaving serious doubts about whether we identify them all[468]." This issue seems all the more threatening because a series of laws enacted in 1996 have made appeal procedures much more difficult and uncertain. These laws were passed by the Clinton administration under pressure from security lobbies, victims' associations and populist politicians, who argued that criminals were constantly getting new trials, that this was costing honest taxpayers a lot of money, that unscrupulous lawyers were getting undue releases and pardons, that (appointed) federal judges were more concerned with the rights of murderers than those of victims, etc.[469]. This kind of rhetoric is more palatable to the public than the failure of a system that violates the constitutional rights of 7 out of 10 death row inmates. As a result of the 1996 legislation known as the Antiterrorist and Effective Death Penalty Act (AEDPA), the rate of legitimate appeals has dropped to 14%[470]. What has not changed [since 1996 and the implementation of AEDPA] is the fairness of the system. What has changed is whether death row inmates whose rights have been violated would prevail in their appeals. They now rarely prevail[471]." In other words, the system is not working any better than it did before, it still makes just as many mistakes, many lawyers remain grossly incompetent, many prosecutors continue to falsify the evidence to further their careers, but since 1996 juries have been less and less willing to recognize these violations as acceptable causes for invalidation. Need I remind you that prior to the

---

468. *Ibid*, Executive Summary.
469. D.R. Dow, *Executed On a Technicality...*, *op. cit.* (Introd., n. 20), p. xxi.
470. *Ibid*, p. xxii.
471. *Ibid.* at xxii-xxiii.

1996 laws, 82% of convicts whose rights were violated escaped the electric chair? Now most do not.

In short, it is better in the United States to be called O.J. Simpson or Michael Jackson than John Jackson or Garry Graham when dealing with the law. The first two owed it to the mastery of their lawyers to be acquitted during resounding trials. The two others owed it to the total ineptitude of their defenders to be condemned in the general indifference, in spite of the convincing evidence of their innocence. John Jackson served 6 years in prison and died broken a year after his release. Garry Graham spent 19 years in prison before being executed by lethal injection. Before he died, he told anyone who would listen, "I'm going to be executed because I'm black, because I'm poor, because I had no real defense[472]." This cry could be that of thousands of men and women handed over to the accounting logic of a society in which money is the absolute God, a society that awards many lawyers representation contracts, without limiting the number of cases that can be handled, without ensuring that the lawyers assigned are competent and without providing the necessary funding for the emergence of real adversarial investigations. The only criterion of interest is that of cost and, ultimately, profitability. It doesn't matter how incompetent a lawyer is, it doesn't matter if he takes on 300, 400 or 500 cases a year, it doesn't matter if he doesn't even have time to interview his clients, it doesn't matter if he falls asleep during hearings or is a notorious alcoholic, it doesn't matter if poor people are sentenced to death 3 times more often than others for the same crime, it doesn't matter, as long as the lawyer proves to be economical in use. I wonder, at the end of this dive into the American judicial system, who is "behind" and who remains "stuck in the sanctuary of its pseudo social model[473]". I would rather, I think, pay taxes than bear the collective shame of Garry Graham's death or John Jackson's unjust conviction.

---

472. "On me tue, on m'assassine...", *L'Humanité*, October 23, 2000, available online: http://www.humanite.presse.fr/popup_print.php3?id_article=233498
473. N. Baverez, "Japon, Allemagne, France, le fossé de la réforme", *op. cit.* (Introd., n. 84), p. 35.

School: better to be rich and stupid than poor and brilliant

In the United States, funding for public elementary and secondary schools is based on a threefold national (federal government), regional (state), and local (district) basis. On average, for every $100 spent, $8 comes from the government, 49 from the state, and 43 from the district[474]. However, these percentages vary substantially from school to school for at least three reasons: 1) the federal government does not provide the same funding to all states; 2) some states are poorer than others and/or more reluctant to invest in their school systems; and 3) there are huge disparities in wealth between districts. With respect to the latter, it can be noted, for example, that local funding for schools is based primarily on property taxes. It doesn't take a rocket scientist to figure out that the property tax will generate significantly more revenue in an affluent residential suburb than in a poor black ghetto. In the end, resource disparities can be substantial not only between states but also within states (*i.e.*, between districts). These disparities become all the more significant when all the actors in the system organize themselves in synergy, to the detriment of the least favored areas: the federal government gives less to poor states, states give less to poor districts, and districts give less to needy schools[475].

To illustrate the above, consider the latest figures published by the National Center for Education Statistics[476]. According to these figures, each student in Mississippi, a Southern state with a large black population

---

474. Jason Hill & Frank Johnson, "Revenues and Expenditures for Public Elementary and Secondary Education: School Year 2002-2003," National Center for Education Statistics, US Department of Education, October 2005, NCES Report 2005-353R, available online: http://nces.ed.gov/pubs2005/2005353.pdf
475. "The Funding Gap 2006," Washington, DC, *The Education Trust*, 2006, available online: http://www2.edtrust.org/NR/rdonlyres/CDEF9403-5A75-437E-93FF-EBF1174181FB/0/FundingGap2006.pdf
476. J. Hill & F. Johnson, "Revenues and Expenditures for Public Elementary and Secondary Education...," *op. cit.* (*supra*, n. 60), table 5.

and 31% of children below the poverty line[477], received $5,792 in funding in 2003. This included the costs of the educational act itself ($3,466; teacher salaries, course materials, etc.) and infrastructure costs ($2,326; buildings, administration, nurses, etc.). Each student in New Jersey, a predominantly white state on the East Coast with 9% of children below the poverty line[478], in the same year, 2003, incurred $12,568 in expenses. This included $7,424 for purely educational activities and $5,144 for infrastructure. Also in 2003, the Sachem County, New York, district, which has 4.3 percent officially poor children, spent $13,289 per student. At the same time, children in La Joya, Texas, received less than $7,000, with a poverty rate of nearly 51 percent[479]. In the face of such disparities, one could argue that the cost of living is higher in wealthier districts and states, which increases the cost of infrastructure and forces teachers to be paid more. Unfortunately, this argument does not hold and the differences between "poor schools" and "rich schools" remain massive, even after accounting for local variations in the cost of living[480]. The inequities are sometimes so stark that some families have taken legal action to assert their rights. In one such case, Judge Margot Botsford in 2004 ruled against the state of Massachusetts on the grounds that it violated the constitutional right of disadvantaged children to a decent education. It is perhaps worth noting that Massachusetts, one of the most virtuous states in education, had already been convicted on the same grounds 11 years earlier[481].

In disadvantaged schools, educational teams are often very creative in raising money for the children. The first line of intervention is usually

---

477. US Census Bureau, Internet Release, 2006, http://pubdb3.census.gov/macro/032006/pov/new46_100125_03.htm
478. *Ibid.*
479. Thomas D. Snyder, Alexandra G. Tan & Charlene M. Hoffman, "Digest of Education Statistics 2005," US Department of Education, National Center for Education Statistics, July 2006, table 89, available online: http://nces.ed.gov/pubsearch/pubsinfo.asp?pubid=2006030
480. "The Funding Gap 2006," *op. cit.* (*supra*, n. 61).
481. Anand Vaishnav, "School Financing Unfair, Judge Rules," *Boston Globe*, April 27, 2004; Anand Vaishnav, "Shifting of State School Aid Eyed," *Boston Globe*, April 28, 2004.

with families. Lists of missing supplies are sent to parents and fairs are organized. At a second level, teachers themselves put their hands in their pockets[482]. According to the National Education Association, this effort is not small. In 2001, it amounted to an average of $450 per teacher[483]. To illustrate this point, consider the case of Steven. Steven is a kindergarten teacher at John Muir, a challenging school in San Francisco. According to figures provided by the independent nonprofit organization greatschools. net[484], Muir has a majority of Hispanic (53%) and black (34%) disadvantaged minority children. Only 3% of the students are white; 75% of the children are poor enough to qualify for free or subsidized lunch. The number of students without basic English skills is 45%, or nearly one in two. Steven's description of his job is as moving as it is harrowing. "I work 16 hours a week in a bar...Last year I spent $3,900 of my own money on my class. That's a lot of money. It's not for anything extravagant. It's things like paper clips and art supplies and paint and the kind of things you would think the district would provide, but they don't. (...) I figured my second job would give me the money I needed to be a good teacher. In other words, I can buy snacks for my kids. For the past 8 years, I have bought the food that carries them through the morning (...) The school does not provide any nutritious snacks for the children[485]." Of course, it is easy to suggest that this nurturing role is the responsibility not of the school, but of the parents. But what if parents are not wealthy enough to provide their offspring with the luxury of a mid-day snack? Paul Vance, superintendent for the city of Washington, apparently decided the issue when he tried, unsuccessfully, to keep his schools open on December 5,

---

482. D.K. Shipler, *The Working Poor...*, *op. cit.* (Introd., n. 68), chap. 9.

483. Daniel Moulthrop, Ninive Clements Calegari & Dave Eggers, *Teachers Have It Easy: the Big Sacrifices and Small Salaries of America's Teachers* (New York: The New Press, 2005), 57.

484. greatschools.net, available online: http://www.greatschools.net/modperl/browse_school/ca/6414/

485. D. Moulthrop, N.C. Calegari & D. Eggers, *Teachers Have It Easy...*, *op. cit.* (*supra*, n. 69) at 57-58.

2002, following heavy snowfall. According to David Shipler[486], Vance's attempt was designed to avoid making life more difficult for poor families by forcing them to choose between the plague and cholera: giving up a day's pay and, in some cases, risking dismissal or leaving sometimes young children at home without proper supervision. Vance also knew that many students in his jurisdiction were poor enough to qualify for subsidized lunches and breakfasts. "He knew - what his critics evidently did not know - that many children would go hungry that morning if the schools closed. Two months later, in the same city, President George W. Bush submitted a budget making it harder for children across the country to qualify for free school meals[487]."

When school fairs and the goodwill of teachers are no longer enough, public educational institutions turn to private companies. Under the guise of patronage and patriotism, they have been investing heavily in American schools for the past 30 years, especially in the poorest neighborhoods. It all really started in 1983, when the companies pounced on a federal report commissioned by Ronald Reagan's Secretary of Education. The report, already mentioned, detailed the catastrophic performance of the American school system[488]. The incompetence and spinelessness of negligent officials had put the nation at risk. It was urgent that the private sector step in to save America[489]. Mark Fowler, chairman of the Federal Communications Commission under President Ronald Reagan, offered his best epigraph to

---

486. D.K. Shipler, *The Working Poor...*, *op. cit.* (Introd., n. 68), p. 252.
487. *Ibid.*
488. National Commission on Excellence in Education, "A Nation at Risk: the Imperatives For Educational Reform" (Washington, DC: US Department of Education, 1983).
489. Nancy J. Perry, "Saving the Schools, How Business Can Help," *Fortune Magazine*, November 7, 1988; D.T. Kearns, "Why I Got Involved," *op. cit.* (chap. I, n. 263); William B. Johnson, "Workforce 2000," *op. cit.* (chap. I, n. 264); Edward B. Fiske, "Impending Job Disaster: Workforce Unqualified to Work," *New York Times*, September 25, 1989; The Secretary's Commission on Achieving Necessary Skills (scans), "Learning a Living: a Blueprint For High Performance," U.S. Department of Labor, April 1992; Milton Friedman [Nobel laureate in economics], "Public Schools: Make Them Private," *Washington Post*, February 19, 1995.

this vision: "The market will take care of the children[490]." We were about to see what we were about to see... Unfortunately, we didn't see much. As Alex Molnar summarizes, "These corporate efforts were not attempts to create high-quality public schools that were better able to meet the demands of the modern economy. They were attempts to turn public schools themselves into industrial profit centers[491]. Before substantiating this point further, it may be interesting to observe that the opening of schools to market forces over the past thirty years has not exactly produced the miracles advertised. The latest figures published by the National Center of Education Statistics show that 36 percent of American 8-year-olds have not mastered basic reading skills. If we refine this figure according to socio-economic status, it appears that the poorest students (receiving free or subsidized meals) are 54% who do not reach the minimum expected expertise. For more affluent students (not receiving free or subsidized meals), the percentage is 33%[492]. In the field of mathematics, 20% of 8-year-old students do not have the skills considered "basic" for their age. Here again, the difference in achievement is glaring between poor (33% below the minimum competency threshold) and affluent (10% below the minimum competency threshold) students[493]. In science, 32% of 8-year-olds do not have what is considered minimal knowledge. These castaways are poor in nearly 7 out of 10 cases[494]. If we extend the analysis to the international arena, the

490. Quoted in A. Molnar, *Giving Kids the Business...*, *op. cit.* (Introd., n. 28), p. xiii.
491. *Ibid*, p. 17.
492. National Assessment of Educational Progress, "The Nation's Report Card, Reading 2005," National Center for Education Statistics, US Department of Education, 2006, NCES Report 2006-451, available online: http://nces.ed.gov/nationsreportcard/pdf/main2005/2006451. pdf
493. National Assessment of Educational Progress, "The Nation's Report Card, Mathematics 2005," National Center for Education Statistics, US Department of Education, 2006, NCES Report 2006-453, available online: http://nces.ed.gov/nationsreportcard/pdf/ main2005/2006453.pdf
494. National Assessment of Educational Progress, "The Nation's Report Card, Science 2005," National Center for Education Statistics, US Department of Education, 2006, NCES Report 2006-466, available online: http://nces.ed.gov/nationsreportcard/pdf/main2005/2006466. pdf

results do not get much better. The most recent study by the Program for International Student Assessment (PISA) shows that 15-year-olds in the United States have a lower overall level of literacy than those in other OECD countries[495]. In mathematics and problem solving, for example, U.S. students rank 24th out of 29. In science, they rank 16th. In reading and reading comprehension, they rank 10th. In all of these subjects, the United States ranks behind the most shamefully centralized and taxed European countries, including Finland, Sweden, Norway and France. In fact, a World Economic Forum report on global competitiveness showed that Uncle Sam's country ranked dead last among developed countries in the difference in the quality of schools available to rich and poor children[496]. In the words of *Washington Post* reporter Gerald Bracey, "This is shameful in a country as wealthy as ours.[497]

Let's close the efficiency parenthesis and return to the problem of funding American public schools. Over the past 30 years, public schools have become a playground for commercial and advertising companies[498]. The intrusion has taken many forms, including sponsorship, exclusive contracts, the purchase of advertising space, and the provision of equipment. Let's consider the example of Channel One. Since its creation in 1990, this company has offered to provide schools with video equipment in exchange for a commitment to subject 90% of students to a 12-minute

---

495. Mariann Lemke, *et al*, "International Outcomes of Learning in Mathematics Literacy and Problem Solving", PISA 2003, results from the US Perspective, US Department of Education, National Center for Education Statistics, December 2004, NCES Report 2005-03, available online: http://nces.ed.gov/pubs2005/2005003.pdf

496. Gerald W. Bracey, "Why Do We Scapegoat The Schools?", *Washington Post*, May 5, 2002.

497. *Ibid.*

498. Susan Linn, *Consuming Kids* (New York: Anchor Books, 2005), chap. 5; Juliet B. Schor, *Born to Buy* (New York: Scribner, 2004), chap. 5; Naomi Klein, *No Logo* (New York: Picador, 2002), chap. 4; Alissa Quart, *Branded: The Buying and Selling of Teenagers* (New York: Basic Books, 2003), chaps. 10 and 14; Alissa Quart, "Welcome to (company name here) HighTM," *New York Times*, 16 July 2003; A. Molnar, *Giving Kids the Business..., op. cit.* (Introd., n. 28), chaps. 1-3; A. Molnar, "The Ninth Annual Report on Schoolhouse Commercialism Trends: 2005-2006," Commercialism in Education Research Unit (CERU), Arizona State University, 2006, report EPSL-0611-220-CERU.

news flash every day, including 2 minutes of advertising. As Joel Babbit, former president of Channel One, points out, "the advertiser has kids who can't go to the bathroom, can't change the channel, can't listen to their moms screaming in the background, and can't play Nintendo[499]. In short, a totally captive audience, sometimes without the parents' knowledge. One of the most famous illustrations of this commitment is the case of two teenagers who walked out of their class and refused to attend the presentation. The principal of the school decided to send the two strong heads to a detention center for the day[500]. Similarly, four Michigan teachers were threatened with dismissal for refusing to interrupt their classes to make room for Channel One[501]. Jim Bradock was shocked when he learned after several months that his daughter was forced to watch the Channel One program every day[502].

According to company figures, Channel One reaches more than seven million children and teenagers every day[503]. This "educational" program is said to have the second largest audience share in the United States, behind the untouchable Super Bowl[504]. Twelve minutes a day represents six days of instruction each year, including one full day of advertising. One study estimated that each day of instruction offered to Channel One cost the American taxpayer $300 million in 1998[505]. Of course, the poorest schools are also the most likely to subscribe to Channel One's offerings. An early study found that the best-funded schools (more than $6,000 per year/child in 1993) took up Channel One's offer in only 1 in 10 cases. In contrast, the least well-funded schools (less than $2,600 per year/child) ratified

---

499. Quoted *in* S. Linn, *Consuming Kids*, *op. cit.* (*supra*, n. 84) at 78.

500. E. Strickland, "Watch or Go To Jail," 2001, Adbusters, 34.

501. A. Molnar, *Giving Kids the Business...*, *op. cit.* (Introd., n. 28), p. 68.

502. J.B. Schor, *Born to Buy*, *op. cit.* (*supra*, n. 84) at 87.

503. Channel One, website, January 2007, http://www.channelone.com/static/about/

504. J.B. Schor, *Born to Buy*, *op. cit.* (*supra*, n. 84) at 86.

505. Max B. Sawicky & Alex Molnar, "The Hidden Cost of Channel One: Estimates For the Fifty States," Education Policy Studies Laboratory (EPSL), Arizona State University, 1998, report CACE-98-02.

the proposed contract 60% of the time. For these disadvantaged schools, the television tool provided by Channel One did not complement the traditional educational offer symbolized by the written word, but rather replaced it[506]. In a very eloquent essay entitled "How to be stupid: lessons from Channel One", Marc Miller, a professor at New York University, explained in 1997 that the information produced by this medium was of no educational interest because it was "even more compressed and superficial than the stuff the networks deliver to us[507]". A study conducted the same year by William Hoynes provided clear support for this thesis by showing that only 20% of the programs presented to schoolchildren each day dealt with substantive social, political or cultural events. The remaining 80 percent was devoted to sports, natural disasters, weather or Channel One self-promotion[508].

Some of the work directly questioned the educational value of Channel One's information. The results were, to say the least, not very impressive. The studies identified a range of effects, from complete emptiness[509] to a slight influence on the recall of recent news[510]. In fact, and this is the problem, what Channel One captives remember most are commercials. A recent study published in the Journal of the American Academy of Pediatrics (APA) showed that after exposure to Channel One programs,

---

506. Michael Morgan, "Channel One in the Public School: Widening the Gap," 1993, research report prepared for UNPLUG, University of Massachusetts at Amherst, Department of communication, available online, http://www.umass.edu/communication/resources/special_reports/channel_one/ch_one_report.shtml
507. Quoted *in* S. Linn, *Consuming Kids, op. cit.* (*supra*, n. 84) at 83.
508. Quoted *in* S. Linn, *ibid.*
509. Nancy N. Knupfer & Peter Hayes, "The Effects of the Channel One Broadcast On Students' Knowledge of Current Events," *in* Anne DeVaney (ed.), *Watching Channel One* (Albany, NY: SUNY Press, 1994), pp. 42-60; Tim Simmons, "TV News in Classroom Ineffective, Study Finds," *News and Observer*, 21 March 1991.
510. Drew Tiene, "Exploring the Effectiveness of the 'Channel One' School," Telecasts, Educational Technology, 1993, 33, pp. 26-42; Erica Weintraub Austin, Yi-Chun Yvonnes Chen, Bruce E. Pinkleton & Jessie Quintero Johnson, "Benefits and Costs of 'Channel One' in a Middle School Setting and the Role of Media-Literacy Training," *Pediatrics*, 2006, 117, pp. 423-433.

children remembered more commercials than news[511]. This is a sort of implementation of the now famous sentence of Patrick Le Lay, president of the largest French commercial television channel, who declared with touching sincerity during an interview that should have gone unnoticed: "What we sell to Coca-Cola is available human brain time[512]. When applied to Channel One's services, this prescription indicates that the so-called educational portion of the program serves primarily to maximize the potential impact, on children's brains, of the commercials being shown. The results are clear. Not only does Channel One sell[513], but it also profoundly shapes children's representations of the world[514], notably by developing their materialistic apprehension of the world[515]. Thus, students subjected to the influence of Channel One are, all other parameters being held equal, more inclined to consider that "money is everything", that "the rich are happier than the poor", that "a nice car is more important than school", that "brand names make a difference". This might be laughable if an impressive body of research had not demonstrated over the past 20 years the negative impact of materialistic values on individual well-being, self-esteem, the quality of social and

---

511. E.W. Austin, *et al*, "Benefits and Costs of 'Channel One' in a Middle School Setting and the Role of Media-Literacy Training," *op. cit.* (*supra*, n. 96).

512. Quoted in *Télérama*, " L'affaire Le Lay ", 11-17 September 2004, p. 8-21.

513. B.S. Greenberg & J.E. Brand, "Television News and Advertising in Schools: 'Channel One' Controversy," *Journal of Communication*, 1993, 43, pp. 143-151; E.W. Austin, *et al*, "Benefits and Costs of 'Channel One' in a Middle School Setting and the Role of Media-Literacy Training," *op. cit.* (*supra*, n. 96); Primedia, "Primedia Reports First Quarter 2005 Results," 2005, available online: www.primedia.com/1Q05earningsfinal.pdf; A. Molnar, *Giving Kids the Business...*, *op. cit.* (Introd., n. 28) at 71.

514. Roy F. Fox, "How Do Kids Respond to Commercials," in *Harvesting Minds: How TV Commercials Control Kids* (Westport, CT: Praeger, 1996).

515. L. Reid, A. Gedissman, "Required TV Program in Schools Encourages Poor Lifestyle Choices," *AAP News*, 2000, available online: www.aap.org/advocacy/reid1100.htm; J.E. Brand & B.S. Greenberg, "Commercials in the Classroom: the Impact of Channel One Advertising," *Journal of Advertising Research*, 1994, 34, pp. 18-21; B.S. Greenberg & J.E. Brand, "Channel One: But What About the Advertising?", *Educational Leadership*, Dec. 1993-Jan. 1994, p. 57.

family interactions, or anxiety levels[516]. The problem seems all the more insidious in the case of Channel One because, as I have already indicated, this program mainly affects the most socially disadvantaged children. Alex Molnar points out that "the students least likely to be able to afford the products featured on Channel One [are] the students most likely to see the ads. This [seems] a perverse situation that [can] only add to the cynicism, frustration, and bitterness of children living in poverty[517]." When I recall Anna's tears[518], I think that this childish resentment is often compounded by the despair of mothers who blame themselves for all the bad things that happen, and experience a lot of anguish because they cannot say yes to children who do not always understand the cause of the rejections they receive. Of course, Channel One's advocates argue strongly that students are subject to advertising outside of school anyway and that 10 minutes more or less each week is not so bad, especially if it means that classrooms can be equipped with efficient audiovisual equipment. The argument seems wise. It is only more fallacious. The fact is that Channel One's ads have the implicit blessing of the education system and teachers, whether we like it or not. All other things being equal, children who watch Channel One are more likely to believe that advertising helps them form "correct" opinions about the nature of the products shown[519]. In fact, the school context leads 85% of students to believe that the content of Channel One programs is "often," "very often," or "consistently" approved by teachers[520].

---

516. For an outstanding review, Tim Kasser, *The High Price of Materialism*, 2002, Cambridge, MA, MIT Press.

517. A. Molnar, *Giving Kids the Business...*, *op. cit.* (Introd., n. 28), p. 72.

518. See, in the first part of this book: "Anna: at the heart of reality".

519. M. Krcmar, "Channel One: the Effect of Commercials in the Classroom - A Natural Experiment," paper presented at the annual meetings of the International Communication Association, Chicago, IL, May 27, 2001.

520. E.W. Austin, *et al*, "Benefits and Costs of 'Channel One' in a Middle School Setting and the Role of Media-Literacy Training," *op. cit.* (*supra*, n. 96).

The market's aspiration to save the public school system is fortunately not limited to Channel One. The patriotic spirit of corporate America knows no bounds. Food and beverage giants like Pepsi and Coke, for example, are in a fierce battle to become the lucky benefactors of failing schools. When they agree to exclusive contracts, they receive a percentage of the sales. It is no doubt out of pure philanthropy that commercial companies are sometimes forced to impose consumption quotas or contractual clauses stipulating that schools must do their best to maximize beverage sales[521]. "Drink, eat, become obese if necessary, it's good for the bottom line." A few years ago, this maxim allowed a Colorado Spring superintendent to make history after one of these memos was leaked: by any means necessary, students had to be encouraged to consume or quotas would not be met and the school would lose money[522]. Our man, who apparently called himself "The Coke Dude," even allowed drinks to be consumed during class to boost sales[523]. In another famous example, a Georgia school principal organized a "Coke Day" in response to a request for proposals from[524]. The school with the most successful promotional plan received $500. On the day of the event, the students arrived wearing T-shirts with the company's logo. In the courtyard, they were photographed in a formation of the letters COCA. Company representatives were invited to speak at the school. Everything was going well, until one student decided to be a hothead. The miscreant showed up wearing a Pepsi-Cola T-shirt. Such an outrage could only end with a proper expulsion. For $500, you have to give up some principles, including those associated with freedom of conscience and expression. *Business is business* in American public schools.

There are dozens of examples of this. One school will rename its gym after a local supermarket. Another will have Pizza Hut offer free pizza to

---

521. S. Linn, *Consuming Kids, op. cit.* (*supra*, n. 84), at 85-87; J.B. Schor, *Born to Buy, op. cit.* (*supra*, n. 84), at 88-91; N. Klein, *No Logo, op. cit.* (*supra*, n. 84), pp. 90-91.
522. S. Linn, *Consuming Kids, op. cit.* (*supra*, n. 84) at 86.
523. J.B. Schor, *Born to Buy, op. cit.* (*supra*, n. 84), at 88-89.
524. N. Klein, *No Logo, op. cit.* (*supra*, n. 84), p. 95.

children who read more than a certain number of books. Another will have her students collect coupons on cereal boxes or soup cans. Another may organize field trips to various sports, pet or toy stores. These trips are more economical than visiting the local zoo, and the absence of an elephant is compensated for by coupons at the end of the visit. There is nothing innocent about these practices. In the case of Pizza Hut, for example, a mother once tried to replace the pizza her daughter had won with another gift. The child refused. The child was not a fan of pizza, but the program had worked so well that this student had come to believe that the pizza was the actual marker of her success and that any other reward was just a half-success fallback[525]. As for outings, a walk to a sporting goods store ended with the words, "There's a little lunch bag here and a coupon to give to your parents to bring back so you can buy all the things we talked about today. So how does that sound to you? You like shopping here, right[526]?" It's easy to imagine the impact words like that can have on a 5, 6, or 7 year old. One parent reported that her daughter's visit to a pet store was "cruel and unusual punishment for the parents. (...) We're going to have to deal with the disillusionment[527]." This is true, but there are worse things, as illustrated by this sample letter from a file provided by a publishing company, which officially has a dual purpose: to teach children how to write a letter and to obtain funds to buy computers[528].

Dear Grandmother,
My school needs more computers for our classrooms. You can help by ordering new magazines or extending your current subscription now.

---

525. A. Molnar, *Giving Kids the Business...*, *op. cit.* (Introd., n. 28), p. 45.
526. S. Linn, *Consuming Kids, op. cit.* (*supra*, n. 84) at 92.
527. Quoted *in* S.Linn, *ibid.*
528. Reported *in* A. Molnar, *Giving Kids the Business...*, *op. cit.* (Introd., n. 28), p. 24.

You'll save money with the school prizes and your magazine orders will allow me to get more practice on the computer. Order before the deadline and I can win the school team t-shirt.
Please help me if you can,
Amy

PS: I love you.

It is easy to imagine the state of mind of a grandmother upon receiving this letter... and the consequences that a refusal to subscribe could have on Amy's feelings. Clearly, the letter conveys the idea that the act of subscribing is an act of love. The implicit message is quite simple: if your grandmother doesn't sign up, she doesn't love you and doesn't care about your future. Not very fair, but definitely very effective.

To be honest, we have to admit that commercial companies do not always aim to make a direct financial profit from their actions. Some approaches are much more insidious, in the sense that they aim to distort children's beliefs, manipulate their values and develop a true brand loyalty phenomenon (the famous "brand loyalty from cradle to grave"). This kind of strategy pushes companies to directly enter the educational program space through the creation of course materials. Nike, for example, created an "innovative education program" in 1998 with the goal of "encouraging students to think about the life of our planet and associate it with the 'stuff' we use every day[529]." In this program, students are given several lessons, one of which involves recycling a used shoe. A detailed lesson plan and teaching tips are provided for teachers to follow. It is no longer the teacher but the company that does the teaching. Unfortunately, behind the noble environmental justification put forward, it is indeed a terrible promotional plan that is hidden. In the idea of children, Nike becomes a citizen

---

529. "Nike, Air to Earth Education kit", available online: http://www.nike.com/nikebiz/nikebiz.jhtml?page=27&cat=ate

company approved by teachers. Thus, as Tamara Schwartz, president of the Center for Public Education Free of Advertising, pointed out at the time of the release of the Kit: "Ostensibly it is an environmental lesson. But you have to ask: why is the logo everywhere? In many ways it's only a Nike ad in the classroom[530]." If the company's own figures are to be believed, since 1998 more than 630,000 children between the ages of 9 and 14 would have been exposed to this advertising[531].

In a recent book, nicely titled "Born *to* Buy," Juliet Schor discusses many of the academic materials published by the commercial sector[532]. Kellog's, for example, has a "breakfast kit" that states that fat content is the only factor to worry about when putting together a morning menu. Other major companies have helped develop a reading kit, the first exercise of which is to recognize the K-Mart, Pizza Hut, M&M's, Jello and Target logos. The Court TV cable network, which reaches 86 million homes[533], has created a forensics kit[534]. The company's official website states that the kit is "a piece to [Court TV's] ongoing commitment to education[535]." From Evan Shapiro, the company's senior vice president of marketing, however, we learn that the program has reached "400,000 students and 1.2 million consumers without ever looking like marketing" for a mere $60,000. If Shapiro is to be believed, the CSI kit has had "a huge impact for Court TV in terms of brand awareness, ratings and revenue[536]." If a child ever asks you what cynicism is, I think you'll be hard-pressed to find a better example than the one that pits the official version of Court TV's

---

530. Quoted in Josh Freit, "Nike in the Classroom," *Willamette Week*, April 15, 1998, available online: http://www.wweek.com/html/nike042298.html

531. "Nike, Air to Earth Education kit," *op. cit.* (*supra*, n. 115).

532. J.B. Schor, *Born to Buy, op. cit.* (*supra*, n. 84), at 91-96; see also A. Molnar, *Giving Kids the Business..., op. cit.* (Introd., n. 28), pp. 32-35.

533. Short TV, http://www.courttv.com/about/index.html

534. "Forensics in the Classroom", an educational kit produced by Court TV, available online: http://www.courttv.com/forensics_curriculum/

535. "Forensics in the Classroom," comments on the educational kit prepared by Court TV, http://www.courttv.com/forensics_curriculum/about.html

536. Quoted *in* Susan Linn, *Consuming Kids, op. cit.* (*supra*, n. 84) at 93.

website, against the off-the-record confession of one of its top executives. Although... The game could be closer than expected if we include in the contest the "study guide" that was provided by the Fox audiovisual company, following the release of the cartoon *Anastasia*[537]. This guide outlined various exercises and possible discussions about the film. For example, it was suggested that teachers could study Anastasia's journey with a map in hand for geography. According to Jeffrey Godsick, Fox's senior vice president of advertising and marketing, the guide was not an illegitimate promotional intrusion into the academic sphere. It was an act of pure patronage, a selfless favor to public schools whose "teachers... are eager for materials that will excite children."[538] It would take a shamefully deranged mind to suspect Fox of having developed the Anastasia kit for mercantile and commercial purposes...

Perhaps it is worth pointing out, in relation to the above, that the lack of integrity in the educational packages produced by commercial firms is not the exception but the rule. In a 1995 study, a consumer association decided to analyze 77 course materials provided by private companies; 80% of these materials were defined as biased, incomplete, and supportive of the advertiser's economic agenda or viewpoint[539]. A Procter & Gamble kit, for example, explained that cutting down trees was good for the environment because it "mimics the way nature gets rid of trees." The same kit also stated that disposable diapers were better for the environment than cloth diapers. The company, the largest U.S. producer of disposable diapers, was forced to withdraw this "educational material" (*sic*) under threat of legal action.

In fact, the doctrinal hype on environmental issues starts early in Uncle Sam's life. Consider, for example, the case of children who were raised in

---

537. Available online: http://www.filmeducation.org/filmlib/Anastasia.pdf
538. Quoted *in* Naomi Klein, *No Logo*, *op. cit.* (*supra*, n. 84), p. 93.
539. "Consumers Union, "Evaluations", Captive kids: a Report on Commercial Pressure on Kids in Schools", Washington, DC, Consumers Union, 1995, available online: http://www. consumersunion.org/other/captivekids/

the mid-1990s and who are now of voting age. Many of these children were exposed to the soothing rhetoric of the big energy lobbies during their school years. The "education" kits of that era, sponsored by the American Coal Foundation, the National Energy Foundation, or the American Gas Association, stubbornly preached to their parish by downplaying the problems posed by fossil fuel use and presenting alternative energy as expensive and unaffordable. The American Coal Foundation's kit is still being distributed to this day. It states, among other things, that scientists still disagree about the greenhouse effect and that "the earth could benefit, rather than suffer, from increased carbon dioxide, which makes plants grow larger[540]." No wonder, after that, that George W. Bush refuses to ratify the Kyoto Protocol without causing a particular stir in his nation's heart.

Of course, given the above, one might wonder why teachers use the course materials provided by commercial companies. One would think that a competent teacher would not need to rely on *Anastasia*'s kit to give his or her students a geography lesson. The life of Marco Polo, for example, offers, no doubt, material that is rich in both academic and imaginative ways. So why Anatasia rather than Marco Polo? For two reasons: one of means, the other of competence. In terms of resources, to study Marco Polo's journey, one needs books, atlases, maps, and/or an Internet connection. Many poor schools do not have all of this. In terms of skills, it takes dedication, motivation, and genius to teach in the midst of poverty. As one teacher interviewed by David Shipler points out, "It's very easy to work with students who have always had A's and B's. They have discipline at home, they have a sense of purpose, and they have a sense of responsibility. They have discipline at home, something is expected of them at home. But I think it takes a master teacher, it takes a sensitive teacher, it takes a concerned teacher - it takes something special, I think, to work with students that nobody else wants[541]." It is quite difficult to reject this state-

---

540. "Power From Coal, American Coal Foundation," Washington, DC, available online: http://www.teachcoal.org/teacherstore/documents/PowefromCoal.pdf, p. 7.
541. D.K. Shipler, *The Working Poor...*, *op. cit.* (Introd., n. 68), p. 240.

ment for anyone who takes the time to visit a disadvantaged school or to read in the words of Shipler[542] or Kozol[543] the daily life of poor schools. In contact with these authors, it is *Germinal* that resurfaces at the dawn of the 21st century. When I was a kid, I wanted to be a researcher, a veterinarian, an astronaut, a doctor, a Saint-Cyrien, an archaeologist, a fireman. From his ghetto school in Akron, Colorado, Don only dreams of paving the streets of his city, because "the pay is good[544]." I think it must take a lot of calamities for a 12-year-old to have only that dream left in his life.

In the schools that answer to the sweet name of "disadvantaged", one encounters all the evils of the superb liberal universe "made in the USA": failing parent(s) - not because of resignation or drunkenness, but because miserable salaries force them to multiply the hours and the jobs -, corrosive environments, lack of educational support, cultural deprivation, material deprivation, hunger, drugs, violence, absenteeism, etc. Pamela, for example, was sent by her teacher to the principal for insubordination[545]. When asked who had custody of her, she was, in all honesty, unable to answer. Her mother, her father, her aunt? Pamela simply did not know who was responsible for her. When the girl was reprimanded for not turning in an assignment, she wrote a long letter to her teacher explaining that she had not been able to spend the weekend at home. Her mother's friend had beaten her and she had run away with Pamela. Pamela found herself in another house with no classes or instruction. As Pamela's teacher said, "They don't have the basics. If you don't have a roof over your head, if you don't know who you're living with - I wouldn't care about English either[546]." It's hard to argue with the sentence. But it is also hard not to notice the strange syntactical structure of the quote. It seems that Pamela is not the only one to have some dislike for the language of Shakespeare.

---

542. *Ibid.* chapter 9.
543. J. Kozol, *Savage Inequalities, op. cit.* (Introd., n. 18).
544. Quoted *in* D.K. Shipler, *The Working Poor...*, *op. cit.* (Introd., n. 68), p. 232.
545. Quoted *in* D.K. Shipler, *ibid*, pp. 238-239.
546. Quoted *in* D.K. Shipler, *ibid*, p. 239.

Real incompetence or fleeting wandering? It is impossible to say. What we can safely say, however, is that not all teachers in America are talented, especially in poor schools. Many recent studies have shown that poor schools concentrate the most novice and least capable educators[547].

The incompetence of some educators sometimes seems so thick that it is beyond comprehension[548]. Allow me, for once, to give a personal example. When I arrived in San Francisco, I began the process of enrolling my stepdaughter Charlotte in a public school. Since the official application deadline had passed, she was assigned to a school that was not yet full: McKinley. According to figures provided by the independent non-profit organization greatschools.net[549], this school has a majority of Hispanic (27%) and black (35%) disadvantaged minority children. Only 12% of the students are white. At McKinley, 59 percent of the children are poor enough to qualify for subsidized or free lunch. Charlotte's teacher, Miss M., clearly had no teaching skills. She spoke to

547. Jay Mathews, "Top Teachers Rare in Poor Schools," *Washington Post*, September 10, 2002, available online: http://www.washingtonpost.com/wp-dyn/articles/A59173-2002Sep9. html; Cynthia D. Prince, "The Challenge of Attracting Good Teachers and Principals to Struggling Schools," Arlington, Virginia, American Association of School Administrators, January 2002, available online: http://www.aasa.org/files/PDFs/Policy/challenges_teachers_principals.pdf; Richard M. Ingersoll, "Why Do High-Poverty Schools Have Difficulty Staffing Their Classrooms with Qualified Teachers?", University of Pennsylvania, report prepared for: The Center for American Progress and the Institute for America's Future, November 2004, available online: http://www.americanprogress.org/kf/ingersoll-final.pdf; Thomas G. Carroll, Kathleen Fulton, Karen Abercrombie & Irene Yoon, "Fifty Years After the Brown V. Board of Education: A Two-Tiered Education System," report prepared for The National Commission on Teaching and America's Feature, Washington, DC, May 2004, available online: http://www.nctaf.org/documents/Brown_Full_Report_Final.pdf; K. Grossman, B. Beaupre & R. Rossi, "Poorest Kids Often Wind Up With the Weakest Teachers," *Chicago Sun-Times*, September 7, 2001; Chris Davis & Matthew Doig, "Poor Schools Can't Keep Good Teachers," *Herald Tribune*, December 13, 2004; "A Shared Responsibility: Staffing All High-Poverty, Low-Performing Schools With Effective Teachers and Administrators. A Framework for Action," Washington, DC, Learning First Alliance, May 2005, available online: http://www. learningfirst.org/publications/staffing/
548. Michael Crowley, "That's Outrageous: Expel These Teachers," *Reader's Digest*, September 2005.
549. Available online: http://www.greatschools.net/cgi-bin/ca/other/6407

her 5-year-old students in the morning with her back to them and wrote her instructions on a board. None of the children were listening and none, of course, could read. This did not seem to bother the teacher. One evening, when I was picking up Charlotte, I could read this sentence on the board: "*Remember, their will be no school tomorrow.* Miss M. obviously didn't know the difference between the possessive adjective "their" and the adverb "there". On another occasion, I overheard a conversation between our teacher and the mother of a student. The mother asked how much 5% off a $19 book was. Miss M. could not answer and was only "saved" by the kind intervention of a colleague. Charlotte eventually switched schools when a spot opened up at her local school. Concerning the appalling incompetence of Miss M., I thought for a long time that it was an anecdotal epiphenomenon. I was wrong. Incompetent teachers are legion in America.

The first comprehensive study was conducted in Illinois by reporters from the *Chicago Sun-Times*[550]. The results showed that between July 1998 and April 2001, 1 in 10 teachers failed tests designed to measure educators' basic skills in English, math or grammar. The figure is even more staggering because the tests are a simple measure of illiteracy, according to Tom Loveless, director of the Center for the Study of Education Policy at the renowned Brookings Institution[551]. Normally erudite 14- and 15-year-olds usually pass[552]. The fact that incompetent teachers are, according to *Chicago Sun-Times* figures, five times more likely to be in the poorest schools will surprise no one. Research by the *Herald Tribune*

550. R. Rossi, B. Beaupre & K. Grossman, "5,243 Illinois Teachers Failed Key Exams," *Chicago Sun-Times*, September 6, 2001.

551. Quoted *in* R. Rossi, B. Beaupre & K. Grossman, *ibid.*

552. Ana Mendiata, "Kids Take the Test, Say It's Too Easy," *Chicago Sun-Times*, September 6, 2001; R. Rossi, B. Beaupre & K. Grossman, "5,243 Illinois Teachers Failed Key Exams," *op. cit.* (*supra*, n. 136); M. Crowley, "That's Outrageous: Expel These Teachers," *op. cit.* (*supra*, n. 134); Jerome Dancis, "Do the Math: Easy Test for Teachers Will Hurt Students," *Washington Post*, December 4, 2003.

found that what was true in Chicago was also true in Florida[553]. In that state, 500,000 students found themselves facing teachers who had failed their qualifying tests in 2004. The record holder of the presentations was still teaching, despite 59 unsuccessful attempts. More than 1,400 teachers had 10 or more failed attempts. In desperation, some applicants were even granted a de facto certification waiver. Again, unqualified educators were concentrated primarily in poor schools[554]. In light of these findings, David Shipler's account of his time in several disadvantaged schools takes on an unexpectedly general value[555]. What appeared to be a motley collection of scattered observations becomes the expression of a mass truth. In other words, the examples reported by Shipler can no longer be seen as a list of singular epiphenomena. They reflect a sadly ordinary truth. The mediocrity of some teachers is no longer an anachronistic entertainment. It becomes the embodied expression of a unanimous symptom. Among the most proven stigmas of this symptom, we find, for example, the case of this teacher asking an 8 year old child to describe three effects of a snowstorm. In her response, our student mentioned "*a hard time getting* through *the snow*". The teacher took her best pen and crossed out "*throw*" and wrote "*threw*". She obviously didn't know the difference between the past tense of "throw" ("jeta", "*threw*") and the prepositional phrase "*through*".

During a math exercise, another teacher became interested in the following problem: Jack buys a pony for $50. One week later, he sells it for $60. Two weeks later, he buys it back for $70. After a week, he sells it again for $80. How much did Jack make or lose? As a solution, the teacher offered the following explanation: - 50 + 60 - 70 + 80, for a total gain of $20. Suspecting a mistake, a student suggested a different solution. On the board, she wrote next to 60 "wins 10", next to 70 "loses 10", and next

---

553. Chris Davis & Matthew Doig, "Teachers Who Fail," *Herald Tribune*, December 12, 2004.
554. C. Davis & M. Doig, "Poor Schools Can't Keep Good Teachers," *op. cit.* (*supra*, n. 133).
555. D.K. Shipler, *The Working Poor...*, *op. cit.* (Introd., n. 68), chap. 9.

to 80 "wins 10", for a total win of $10. Overwhelmed by this logic, the teacher quickly gave up trying to understand the origin of the hiatus[556]. The students never got the solution. Apparently, the teacher had neither the skill nor the will to get to the bottom of the problem. Fortunately, some educators are more persistent. Take Miss D., for example, and consider the lesson she gave her students on "How to identify the subject of a sentence." Selected excerpts.

> Miss D. (after a long litany of unsuccessful attempts): "Have you listened to the new Gloria Estefan CD?"
> Student: "CD?"
> Miss D.: "No. Who are they talking to?"
> Student: "You."
> Miss D.: "Right."
> Miss D. (offering another example): "These reporters have been interviewing the mayor all day."
> Student: "These reporters."
> Miss D.: "Right. Damion, can you tell us what the simple subject is?"
> Damion: "The Mayor."
> Miss D.: "No. Stan?"
> Stan: "Reporters." [If it's not the mayor, it can only be the reporters!]
> Miss D.: "Because reporters, that's what we focus on."

---

556. The problem should however seem trivial to any mathematics teacher worthy of the name. I asked the question to three friends, one a statistician, the other a doctor in neuroscience, the last a teacher. None of them stumbled for more than a minute on the problem. When we consider the student's solution, it appears that by buying 70, Jack does not lose 10. Our man first buys 50, then sells 60. So he gains 10 on the first transaction. He then buys 70, but this purchase is unrelated to the resale price obtained in the first transaction. This point is easily understood by imagining that Jack buys a different pony the second time (which is the same thing from a logical point of view). In this second purchase, Jack buys 70 and sells 80. Again, he gains 10. Total: 10 + 10 = 20.

As David Shipler points out, "with such appalling explanations, it's not surprising that most kids don't get"[557]. In Miss B.'s defense, however, there is a genuine pedagogical desire. Not all teachers have this elegance, as shown by the case of the science teacher, who did not teach or do homework and whose role was apparently limited to plugging in the TV so that the students could connect their Nintendo[558].

In the face of the above observations, two rhetorics are possible. The first, which is in the minority, suggests that public schools need more and more fairly distributed resources to carry out their mission[559]. The second, which is dominant, asserts that the resources are sufficient but poorly used because of the propensity of government institutions to manage taxpayers' money in an irresponsible, calamitous and expensive manner[560]. Conceptually, this second position speaks directly to the liberal myth that there is no public prerogative whose efficiency and effectiveness cannot be improved by the market. Privatize and the moribund education system will rise from the ashes like the mythological Phoenix. This is the thesis defended by Milton Friedman, winner of the 1976 Nobel Prize in Economics[561]. In an article published by the *Washington Post* in 1995, this researcher first tells us that the performance of public schools deteriorated considerably between 1955 and 1995 because of the development of unions and an increasing tendency towards administrative centralization (between 1955 and 1995, the number of districts in the United States fell from 55,000 to 15,000, according to the article). Second, Friedman explains that the world has undergone two major revolutions in the space of a few decades, one technological, facilitating trade, the other political, opening up borders. These two revolutions have, says our Nobel Prize winner, increased the inequalities between rich and poor in the developed

---

557. D.K. Shipler, *The Working Poor...*, *op. cit.* (Introd., n. 68), p. 243.
558. *Ibid*, p. 240.
559. D. Moulthrop, N.C. Calegari & D. Eggers, *Teachers Have It Easy...*, *op. cit.* (*supra*, n. 69).
560. John E. Chubb & Terry Moe, *Politics, Market and America's Schools* (Washington, DC: Brookings Institution, 1990).
561. M. Friedman, "Public Schools...," *op. cit.* (*supra*, n. 75).

countries. This tendency would, in the long run, represent a threat to social peace. The school system, through the education of the masses, would be the only viable antidote to this threat. Unfortunately, at this stage of the discourse, Friedman fails to explain how education could help reduce socio-economic inequalities. This omission is, in essence, annoying (or should I say *revealing*?). Indeed, as we have seen elsewhere, the technological revolution feeds mainly not on excellence, but on low-skilled, low-paying jobs[562]. In fact, increasing the number of higher education graduates does not reduce the unemployment rate, but increases the qualifications of the unemployed[563]. But let us accept Friedman's thesis out of concern and see where it leads us.

After affirming his faith in education, our economist turns geneticist and disciple of Burt[564] to assert that "innate intelligence plays a major role in determining the opportunities available to individuals. However, [intelligence] is by no means the only human quality that is important, as many examples demonstrate. Unfortunately, our current educational system does little to enable individuals with low or high IQs to make the most of their qualities." For Friedman, "the only way to achieve major improvements in our educational system is through privatization to the point where a substantial fraction of all educational services would be delivered to individuals by private companies.... Nothing else will provide the competition to public schools that will force them to improve in order to retain their clientele.... We know from the experience of all other industries how imaginative and competitive free enterprise can be, what new products and services can be introduced, how oriented it is to satisfying its consumers - that is what we need for education." To build his school of the future, Friedman proposes the widespread use of "*vouchers*," a term that could be translated as "coupons." Under this framework, each student would be given a voucher representing

---

562. See, in the first part of this book: "Causality: a structural failure".
563. A. Molnar, *Giving Kids the Business...*, *op. cit.* (Introd., n. 28), p. 6.
564. See, in the first part of this book: "Hugo: cursed from father to son".

an amount that is both less than what the government spends on each student and enough to cover the costs of a for-profit private school offering a high-quality education. Everyone would benefit: children, parents, taxpayers and businesses. For the sake of consistency, however, it is regrettable that Friedman omits any mention of the past. The privatization of the school system advocated by our great economist was attempted, on a large scale, in the early 1970s. The official terminology at the time was "performance contract". The fiasco was total[565]. In a 1993 article in the *Baltimore Sun*, William Salganik summarized the experience as follows: "More than 100 schools around the country tried performance contracts during the 1970s and '71. Soon all you needed to know about performance contracts was this: first, a federal evaluation showed that performance contracts did not work any better than traditional programs; second, there was evidence of contractor tampering," such as this institution "teaching some of the standardized tests used to assess progress and determine payments.[566]

The *New York Times was* one of the first to publicize the extent of the debacle in 1972, in a particularly hard-hitting article that reported the findings of an independent study. According to one of the authors of this study: "There is great wisdom... in determining in which basket we should not put our eggs.... It is better to stop now than to wait until hopes and expenditures have massively exploded[567]." Unfortunately, memory fades quickly in the face of the ravages of time and the onslaught of special interests. Twenty years after the unprecedented disaster of the "performance contracts", the frenzy of free competition rose from the ashes. The results were again mixed, to say the least. Several studies of large programs in

---

565. A. Molnar, *Giving Kids the Business...*, *op. cit.* (Introd., n. 28), chapters 4 and 5.
566. William Salganik, "The Coming Scandal," *The Baltimore Sun*, December 11, 1993, quoted *in* A. Molnar, *Giving Kids the Business...*, *op. cit.* (Introd., n. 28), p. 78.
567. J. Rosenthal, "Learning Plan Test Is Called a Failure," *New York Times*, February 1, 1972, quoted *in* A. Molnar, *Giving Kids the Business...*, *op. cit.* (Introd., n. 28), p. 78.

Milwaukee[568], Washington[569], or New York[570] failed to find a significant effect of voucher policy on student achievement. In a 2002 book, Howell and Peterson argued for a significant effect in New York City, but only for the black population[571]. To explain this result, the authors suggested that vouchers acted not by stimulating free competition, but by allowing black children to escape the particularly depressing and dilapidated schools in their disadvantaged neighborhoods. It should be noted that Howell and Peterson's positive results were re-analyzed and challenged in a later study[572]. This is a far cry from the stellar expectations of Friedman and the market advocates.

Faced with the recurring rhetoric of public ineptitude, some districts opted for a radical measure: turning over school management to the private sector. Bad move, as the kids like to say. Not only did the private sector do no better than the bureaucratic bureaucrats of public institutions, it did worse. Framed by the laws of the "sacrosanct market," the schools spent more without getting better results. The example of Education Alternative Inc (EAI) is quite revealing in this respect: huge salaries for the directors, significant gains on the stock market thanks in particular to stock options, accounting malpractice, increased administrative costs, declining academic results, the replacement of qualified teaching assistants with good salaries ($12/hour) and social benefits (health insurance, vacations) by poorly paid assistants ($7/hour), without qualifications and without

---

568. Russ Kava, "Milwaukee Parental Choice Program," Wisconsin Legislative Fiscal Bureau, *Informational Paper*, 29, January 2007, available online: http://www.legis.state.wi.us/lfb/Informationalpapers/29.pdf; A. Molnar, *Giving Kids the Business...*, *op. cit.* (Introd., n. 28), pp. 121-124.

569. William G. Howell & Paul E. Peterson, *The Education Gap: Vouchers and Urban Schools* (Washington, DC: Brookings Institution Press, 2002).

570. Alan B. Krueger & Pei Zhu, "Another Look at the New York City School Voucher Experiment," Princeton University, Education Research Section, Working Paper, April 2003, available online: http://www.ers.princeton.edu/workingpapers/1_ers.pdf

571. W.G. Howell & P.E. Peterson, *The Education Gap...*, *op. cit.* (*supra*, n. 155).

572. A.B. Krueger & P. Zhu, "Another Look at the New York City School Voucher Experiment," *op. cit.* (*supra*, n. 156).

social benefits, etc.[573]. As Alex Molnar summarizes, what the experience of privatizing public schools via Education Alternative Inc. proves is that it is always possible to make an already bad situation even worse[574]. In light of this, perhaps Milton Friedman and his cronies might consider for a moment that children are neither cars nor sausages. At the risk of appearing irredeemably stupid to all these great minds permeated with certainties, I claim to find plausible the thesis of the inapplicability of the rules of free enterprise in the fields of public health (I will come back to this later), justice (I have already spoken about this) and education. It seems obvious to me that the liberal myth of "doing better with less" is more a media chimera than an organic reality. In line with this idea, we could quote a report published in 1992 by the very official "Office of Management and Budget". Although it is old, this report is particularly interesting in that it was produced at the request of the Bush administration (father) at the end of the large-scale privatization of the economy that began under Reagan. The result of the report, according to the *New York Times,* is that "after years of trying to transfer government prerogatives to private companies, the White House now recognizes that contractors are wasting vast sums of money.... [This report represents] the most incisive government critique yet of a central precept of the Reagan-Bush era: the idea that private companies can do the federal government's job better and for less money[575]." The evidence for this conclusion is actually quite clear if one accepts that the private sector is draining a significant portion of its resources to feed the appetite of its executives and shareholders. The state has no CEO to pay, no shareholders to fatten, and no stock market price to support. On the other hand, in a sausage factory, it may well be that the replacement of skilled workers who are properly paid (e.g., $12/hr, plus benefits) with low-paid (e.g., $7/hr, without benefits) novice

---

573. For a documented discussion, A. Molnar, *Giving Kids the Business...*, *op. cit.* (Introd., n. 28), pp. 96-115.

574. *Ibid,* p. 107.

575. K. Schneider, "US Cites Waste in Its Contracts," *New York Times*, December 2, 1992.

laborers will yield large financial margins without altering the operation of the company in terms of performance and efficiency. In a school, this kind of short-sighted accounting manipulation can only have major deleterious effects. Indeed, there is a clearly proven causal link between the competence of the educational team and the academic results of the children[576]. The first part of this equation cannot be touched without seriously altering the second. Therefore, the blind application of liberal economic therapies to the school field seems at least risky and uncertain.

In short, the idea that a demanding and rigorous private sector would, given the same resources, do better than a faint-hearted public sector is wrong, at least in the educational field. That being said, it remains clear that high quality private schools have substantially better educational records than the mass of public institutions[577]. However, the funding structure of these schools caters only to the most affluent families. Ben and Courtney, for example, experienced this cruelly when they had to withdraw their daughter from her private school. The cost of sending the two younger children to kindergarten was unaffordable at $22,500 per child per year[578]. Similarly, when Caroline wanted to take Charlotte out of McKinley and

---

576. J.P. Shonkoff & D.A. Phillips (eds.), *From Neurons to Neighborhoods...*, *op. cit.* (chap. I, n. 121), chap. 13 ("Promoting Healthy Development Through Intervention"); M.E. Lamb, "Nonparental Child Care: Context, Quality, Correlates," 1998, in Handbook of Child Psychology, vol. 4 : W. Damon, I.E. Sigel & K.A. Renninger (eds.), *Child Psychology in Practice* (New York: John Wiley & Sons, 5th ed.), pp. 73-134; D. Moulthrop, N.C. Calegari & D. Eggers, *Teachers Have It Easy...*, *op. cit.* (*supra*, n. 69), pp. 7-8 and section IV; Katy Haycock, "Good Teaching Matters... A Lot," *Thinking K-16*, 1998, 3, pp. 3-14, published by The Education Trust, available online: http://www2.edtrust.org/NR/rdonlyres/0279CB4F-B729-4260-AB6E-359FD3C374A7/0/k16_summer98.pdf; Linda Darling-Hammond, "Doing What Matters Most: Investing in Quality Teaching," report prepared for The National Commission on Teaching and America's Feature, Washington, DC, November 1997, available online: http://www.nctaf.org/documents/DoingWhatMattersMost.pdf
577. "Private Schools: A Brief Portrait", National Center for Education Statistics, US Department of Education, NCES Report 2002-013, 2002, available online: http://nces.ed.gov/pubs2002/2002013.pdf
578. Susan Berfield, "Thirty & Broke: The Real Price of a College Education Today," *Business Week*, Special Report, November 14, 2005, available online: http://www.businessweek.com/magazine/content/05_46/b3959107.htm

enroll her in the Lycée International Franco-Américain in San Francisco, she was charged $18,000 for tuition. In addition, there was a $2,600 fee for the after school program. For 16-year-old Mark, the cost of enrollment would have been $26,000[579]. These amounts were significantly higher than those for the La Pérouse high school that Caroline also visited ($14,000 and $16,500 for Charlotte and Marc respectively[580]). In fact, according to data from the National Center of Education Statistics, La Pérouse High School is quite close to national norms. Indeed, tuition averages $11,000 per year at non-religious private schools[581]. This estimate is slightly lower than that produced by the National Association of Independent Schools (NAIS), which federates 1,200 schools and suggests a median fee of $15,012 for all its members[582]. By comparison, public school children in Utah are funded at $4,838 per year. Those in Mississippi receive $5,792[583].

Given the costs involved, it is not surprising that private schooling accounts for only 11% of all students enrolled[584]. Similarly, it is not surprising that the socio-economic status of these 11% of students is quite high[585]. On this point, the data show, for example, that the number of schools with no students eligible for subsidized meals was 1.2 percent and 50.5 percent for public and private schools, respectively, in 2002. At the same time, the proportion of black and Hispanic ethnic minority students was 32 percent in public schools and 18 percent in private schools in

---

579. French American International School and International High School, San Francisco, available online, http://www.frenchamericansf.org/pk12/

580. Lycée Français La Pérouse, San Francisco, available online, http://www.lelycee.org/

581. T.D. Snyder, A.G. Tan & C.M. Hoffman, "Digest of Education Statistics 2005," *op. cit.* (*supra*, n. 65), table 59, available online: http://nces.ed.gov/pubsearch/pubsinfo.asp?pubid=2006030

582. National Association of Independent Schools, 2005-2006 data, available online: http://www.nais.org/files/PDFs/NAIS%20MEMBERS%20NO%20SALARIES.pdf

583. J. Hill & F. Johnson, "Revenues and Expenditures for Public Elementary and Secondary Education...," *op. cit.* (*supra*, n. 60), table 5.

584. T.D. Snyder, A.G. Tan & C.M. Hoffman, "Digest of Education Statistics 2005," *op. cit.* (*supra*, n. 65), at 1.

585. "Private Schools: A Brief Portrait," *op. cit.* (*supra*, n. 163), table 6.

2002[586]. It is reasonable to assume that if only the most prestigious private schools were taken into account, these differences would be even greater.

Of course, spending \$15,000, \$20,000, or even \$30,000 a year to place one's children in a private educational institution may seem all the more irrational given that affluent families often live in affluent districts with quality public schools. This apparent folly becomes clearer, however, when one considers the highly competitive nature of the college selection process in the United States. For parents who want to send their children to the most reputable institutions, private school is a wise investment. In fact, it is as if America has not a two-tiered but a three-tiered school system. At the bottom of the pyramid are poor, poorly funded public schools that lead to academic failure and desertion. At the top level, there are well-off public schools. These schools open the doors to second-choice and/or short-cycle universities ("community college", 2 years) to the middle classes. Finally, at the top level, there is a private system that is as expensive as it is efficient. This system opens the doors to prestigious universities such as Yale, Harvard, Columbia, or Stanford. Analyses by the official National Center for Education Statistics show, not surprisingly, that the curriculum offered by private institutions is, in terms of excellence, variety and content, better adapted to the recruitment requirements of the major universities[587]. To be on the safe side, many private schools and/or concerned parents also recruit private tutors whose role is twofold: first, to prepare the student for quantitative knowledge tests; second, to help the child shape his or her CV according to the recruitments sought (participation in community service, sports activities, etc.). These tutors charge between \$100 and \$1,000 per hour for their services[588]. In the end, the results are quite convincing. In a perfectly homogeneous world, private students should have the same weight in secondary and higher education, i.e. 11%. In many prestigious universities, however, the actual percentage is often between 40 and 50

---

586. *Ibid*, Figure 3.
587. *Ibid.* at 21-25.
588. *A. Quart*, Branded: The Buying and Selling of Teenagers, op. cit. *(supra, n. 84), chap. 10.*

percent. To take just a few examples recently reported by the *Wall Street Journal*, the private representation rate is 51% at Georgetown, 49% at Bowdoin, 48% at the University of Pennsylvania, 46% at Yale, 43% at Columbia, 36% at Princeton, 34% at Dartmouth, 33% at Stanford, etc.[589].

Of course, one could argue that 50% or 60% of the enrolment is still a very honourable score for the public sector. This allegation would be all the more inappropriate given that the students of the major American universities are distinguished as much by their academic background as by their socio-cultural origin. A study published in 2003 by Carnavale and Rose showed that 75% of the 170,000 students enrolled in the 146 most selective universities in the United States came from the wealthiest 25% of the population[590]. Only 3 percent of those elected came from the lowest 25 percent of families. For the poorest 50 percent of households, the representation rate was 9 percent. Across all universities, families in the wealthiest quartile of the population provided more than 42 percent of the membership, compared to less than 10 percent for the least advantaged quartile. The most direct interpretation of these figures assumes that students with the highest socioeconomic status are also those with the best academic skills. This is hardly debatable when one considers that these students have been exposed, from an early age, to a richer "cultural bath," more diverse learning opportunities, better schools, and more sophisticated extracurricular guidance[591]. What is questionable from my perspective is that this long list of advantages is compounded by a financial factor. According to a 2001 report entitled "Access Denied" by a U.S. Congressional committee, more than 53 percent of poor, "highly

589. Nancy Keates, "Opting Out of Private School," *Wall Street Journal*, September 15, 2006, available online: http://online.wsj.com/public/article/SB115828002076463790-RIumPH-d9endi7yzGpaXIMcBSKX4_20070914.html?mod=rss_free
590. Anthony P. Carnevale & Stephen J. Rose, *Socioeconomic Status, Race/Ethnicity, and Selective College Admission* (New York: The Century Foundation, March 2003), available online: http://www.tcf.org/Publications/Education/carnevale_rose.pdf
591. See, in the first part of this book: "Hugo: cursed from father to son".

qualified" students forego a traditional four-year university education[592]. The figure is only 33 percent for students from affluent homes. In a second report released in 2002, "Empty Promises: The Myth of College Access in America," the same committee concluded that "financial barriers to a college education have risen sharply due to changes in federal, state, and institutional policy and priorities, resulting in a shortage of student aid... and rising tuition. As a result, students from low- and moderate-income families who graduate from high school fully prepared to attend college face daunting financial barriers, with major consequences for these students and the nation[593]." These barriers, moreover, do not only affect the enrollment process. They remain, as a study by the National Center of Education Statistics shows, largely in place throughout the education cycle[594]. For example, a student in the top quartile in terms of proficiency but in the bottom quartile in terms of prosperity will have only a 29 percent chance of graduating. A student with similar proficiency characteristics, but from an affluent family (upper quartile) will be successful 74% of the time. An affluent (upper quartile) but low-skill (lower quartile) student will graduate 30% of the time. This last figure is troubling, in that it indicates that one is slightly more likely to earn a college degree in the United States if one is rich and dumb than if one is poor and bright.

To understand the above figures, one must realize that higher education is incredibly expensive in America. For public universities, tuition averages $5,000 per year (2004 figures). For private institutions, it is $19,000[595]. Beyond the initial four years, if a student wishes to enroll in medical school,

---

592. "Access Denied: Restoring the Nation's Commitment to Equal Opportunity," Report by the Advisory Committee On Student Financial Assistance, Washington, DC, February 2001, Figure 14, available online: http://www.ed.gov/about/bdscomm/list/acsfa/access_denied.pdf
593. "Empty Promises, the Myth of College Access in America," report by the Advisory Committee On Student Financial Assistance, Washington, DC, June 2002, p. v, available online: http://www.ed.gov/about/bdscomm/list/acsfa/emptypromises.pdf
594. M.A. Fox, B.A. Connolly & T.D. Snyder, "Youth Indicators 2005..." *op. cit. (supra*, n. 12), table 21.
595. T.D. Snyder, A.G. Tan & C.M. Hoffman, "Digest of Education Statistics 2005," *op. cit. (supra*, n. 65), table 313.

the average annual cost for a place at a public university is $13,000. For a private university, the cost will be $31,000[596]. Thus, a publicly trained physician will have spent $72,000 on tuition alone by the time he or she graduates. If they leave the private sector, they will have to pay $200,000. Of course, financial aid is available. However, most of these are in the form of loans. The main source of direct aid, the Pell Grant, is capped at $4,050 per year, which is about one-third of the expenses incurred by students at public universities (tuition, housing, food)[597]. In 2003, recipients of this program received, on average, less than $2,469[598]. This amount represents about half the cost of tuition and one-fifth of the estimated total cost of a year of public university education[599]. Including all available aid, students spend an average of $2,200 and $11,600 per year on tuition at public and private institutions respectively[600]. Adding room and board and supplies to the above amounts, the average annual cost is $8,800 (public) and $19,400 (private)[601]. For the sake of readability, it may be worthwhile to refer these amounts to the threshold incomes of the most affluent and most indigent households. After deducting all actual aid, an affluent family (top quartile) wishing to send one of its children to a public university would have to spend 11 percent of its annual income. For a poor family (bottom quartile), the burden will approach 50%[602]. Faced with such financial pressure, it is no wonder that half of disadvantaged students give up on their college plans. For those who choose to go anyway, studying means working part-

---

596. *Ibid*, table 315.

597. *Trends in Student Aid* (Washington, DC: College Board, 2005), p. 17, available online: http://collegeboard.com/prod_downloads/press/cost05/trends_aid_05.pdf

598. *Ibid*, p. 10.

599. T.D. Snyder, A.G. Tan & C.M. Hoffman, "Digest of Education Statistics 2005," *op. cit.* (*supra*, n. 65), table 313.

600. *Trends in College Pricing* (Washington, DC: College Board, 2005), Figures 8a and 8c, available online: http://collegeboard.com/prod_downloads/press/cost05/trends_college_pricing_05.pdf

601. *Ibid*, figures 8b and 8d.

602. *Ibid*, Figure 9a.

time (evenings, weekends, vacations) and taking on a lot of debt[603] : 34% of American students report working a "food" job between 10 and 20 hours a week; 31% report working more than 20 hours[604]. After 5 years, 50% of students from poor families (bottom quartile) have still not graduated, compared to 25% of students from affluent families (top quartile)[605]. 62% of public school graduates end up with debt. The proportion is over 80% in the private sector[606]. Upon graduation, the median loan is $15,500 for public and over $20,000 for private[607]. This median represents about 50% of the annual starting salary of a young graduate[608]. It does not include the weight of credit card use. This use generates a median debt equal to $1,000. For over 25% of students, the bill exceeds $3,000[609].

In short, the U.S. school and university systems severely penalize the poorest children. They end up in the poorest and least well-funded schools. When the sacrosanct market does address the problem, it is always out of sheer commercialism. For business, the child is not, as Rabelais wrote, "a fire to be lit. He is "a cow to be milked". Under the rule of the market, CEOs are fattened, competent educators are dismissed and students are left with unqualified guards. There is nothing illogical or reprehensible about this. Profit is, after all, the main (only?) raison d'être of the market economy. This reason for being is not, however, that of the school. Therefore, there is, as the educationalists say, a discrepancy between the logic of the game (to educate) and the logic of the player (to make money). Of course, one

---

603. S. Berfield, "Thirty & Broke: The Real Price of a College Education Today," *op. cit.* (*supra*, n. 164).

604. *Undergraduate Students and Credit Cards in 2004*, Braintree, MA, Nellie Mae, May 2005, table 10, available online: http://www.nelliemae.com/library/ccstudy_2005.pdf

605. T.D. Snyder, A.G. Tan & C.M. Hoffman, "Digest of Education Statistics 2005," *op. cit.* (*supra*, n. 65), table 310.

606. Trends in Student Aid, op. cit. (supra, *n. 183) at 12*.

607. *Ibid*, Figure 5.

608. T.D. Snyder, A.G. Tan & C.M. Hoffman, "Digest of Education Statistics 2005," *op. cit.* (*supra*, n. 65), Figure 25.

609. Undergraduate Students and Credit Cards in 2004, op. cit. (supra, *n. 190)*, *Tables 6 and 7a.*

can always suggest that it is by optimizing its educational work that the company will eventually get rich. This may be a good calculation for large private schools with large entrance fees. For these institutions, the market is clearly the master of its own destiny. It defines the desired services and calculates its costs by integrating a profit margin. For the other institutions, the equation is different, if not the opposite: the State grants a budget to each child and the market obtains its margin by cutting costs. The facts show that this budgetary slashing invariably takes place at the expense of educational quality. One can of course choose to honor the obscure beauty of the model at the expense of objective reality. One can... but that does not prevent the facts from being stubborn.

When you leave the school world and look at the university world, nothing really gets better. Indeed, the astronomical cost of higher education places an enormous burden on the shoulders of modest and poor families. In the land of opportunity, the wealthiest (top quartile) households are 25 times more likely than the poorest (bottom quartile) households to have their children attend a prestigious university. At the same time, students from good families with indigent outcomes have a slightly higher probability of graduating than students from modest backgrounds but with brilliant intellectual makeup. As Linda Darling-Hamond and Laura Post point out in the preamble to a remarkably well-documented work, "Few Americans realize that the U.S. education system is one of the most unequal in the industrialized world, and students routinely receive vastly different lear-ning opportunities depending on their social status[610]. When I was a kid, my parents didn't have much money. The much maligned public school paid to educate me. It spent as much money on my education as it did on the son of a good family who lived in the most upscale parts of my city. The public school took me, with the help of public taxes, from kindergarten

---

610. Linda Darling-Hamond & Laura Post, "Inequalities in Teaching and Schooling: Sup-porting High Quality Teaching and Leadership in Low Income Schools," *in* Richard Kahlen-berg (ed.), *A Notion at Risk: Preserving Public Education As an Engine for Social Mobility* (New York: The Century Foundation Press), pp. 127-167, citation p. 127.

to a doctorate. I had to work, but the school institution never challenged me. Not every teacher I met had the same pedagogical value. Not all had the same drive. None of them, however, was intellectually inept and none of them lacked the minimum material means necessary to do their work. I prefer, I think, this statist solidarity orchestrated by the hand of taxation, to the rugged individualism of a system that, in Kozol's words, denies poor children the very means to compete[611]. That being said, it would seem that for some years now, the schools of France have deserted their original ambition to follow the path of America. The "market", advertising, and brands are increasingly penetrating our classrooms, with the benevolent collaboration of the legislator[612]. Teaching is disintegrating under the influence of a flabby and disqualifying pedagogism[613]. Are these developments the fruit of an unfortunate incompetence or the product of a compelling design? For Jean-Paul Brighelli, the question is clear[614]. In a superb book, this professor of literature, a graduate of the Ecole Normale Supérieure, brilliantly shows that the educational system has recently been reorganized to produce "a cheap workforce, put in competition with an exotic sub-proletariat, (...) trained for a precise task, and above all stripped of the global culture that used to allow them to analyze the system, to represent themselves in it - and, *in fine,* to criticize it. (...) Our society has understood that it is of the utmost importance to produce the acculturated personnel that the market needs. (...) The dream of the industrialist is the ilote, the slave without conscience of the ancient societies, the idiot of the modern societies. The industrial society works to refine it[615]". From this point of view, America still generously surpasses "old Europe". Let us bet, however, that market forces will quickly work to reduce our annoying "backwardness".

---

611. J. Kozol, *Savage Inequalities, op. cit.* (Introd., n. 18), p. 83.

612. Viviane Mahler, *Souriez, vous êtes ciblés. La grande manipulation des consommateurs,* Paris, Albin Michel, 2007, in particular p. 250-263.

613. Jean-Paul Brighelli, *La Fabrique du crétin,* Paris, Gallimard (Folio Documents), 2006.

614. *Ibid.*

615. *Ibid,* pp. 21, 22 and 37.

Health: pay or die

In a February 24, 2007 speech, U.S. President George W. Bush said that "America has the best health care system in the world, because it puts doctors and patients in control, encourages new technologies and finds new ways to improve quality[616]. A few years earlier, in February 2000, Bill Clinton made a similar speech, assuring his fellow citizens that they did indeed have "the best health care system in the world[617]." The idea seems so indisputable, in fact, that it seems beyond refutation. A 2002 exchange on CNN's "Crossfire" illustrates this point superbly[618]. A Canadian listener challenged conservative journalist Robert Novak with these unkind words: "I can't imagine being a senior citizen in your country and not being able to pay for a much needed drug. If I lived in the United States, I would probably be dead by now. For such a wealthy country, you should be ashamed of yourselves for not offering the elderly extensive medical coverage." Novak's response was brief but dense: "Marg, like most Canadians, you are misinformed and wrong. The US has the longest life expectancy of any country in the world, including Canada. That's the truth." Unfortunately, it is one thing to call Lady Truth to the table and another to give her the respect she deserves. At most, Mr. Novak can be given the benefit of peremptory and blind incompetence. To this man who claims to be a friend of truth and to all those who still doubt the barbarity of competitive systems guided only by the call of profit, I would like to dedicate the few lines below. Not only is the American health care system not the best in the world, but in many ways it is perfectly mediocre, barbaric and unworthy of a civilized nation.

To avoid any quantitative misunderstanding, let's start with some figures from official and academic girons. No OECD country spends as

---

616. George W. Bush, Radio Address, February 24, 2007, available online: http://www.white-house.gov/news/releases/2007/02/20070224.html
617. Quoted *in* D.L. Barlett & J.B. Steele, *Critical Condition, op. cit.* (Introd., n. 21).
618. CNN Crossfire, June 19, 2002, transcript available online: http://premium.asia.cnn.com/TRANSCRIPTS/0206/19/cf.00.html

much as America on its health care system[619]. In 2004, the United States spent 15.3% of its GDP on health care. This compares with 10.9% for Germany, 10.5% for France, 9.1% for Sweden, 8.9% for Denmark, and 8.0% for Japan. Expressed in absolute terms, this means that health care spending in the United States averaged $6,102 per capita in 2004. This is roughly double the amount paid by European countries such as Germany ($3,005), France ($3,159), Sweden ($2,825), or Denmark ($2,881). This is nearly three times the expenditure of Japan ($2,249) and ten times that of Turkey ($580). Despite this financial primacy, America is at the bottom of the OECD list for life expectancy (22nd)[620] and infant mortality rate (23rd)[621]. Regarding the first parameter, the deficit is, for example, 2.2 years with France, 2.9 years with Sweden, 4.4 years with Japan, 1.2 years with Germany, and 2.5 years with Canada (with all due respect to Robert Novak). As for infant mortality, there are 6.9 deaths per 1,000 children in the United States, compared to 5.3 in Canada, 4.2 in Germany, 4 in France, and 3 in Japan.

The picture becomes even darker when ethnicity is taken into account. While the infant mortality rate in the United States is 5.8/1,000 for children of white mothers, it is 14.6/1,000 for children of black mothers[622]. While there are many possible explanations for these differences in life expectancy or infant mortality, it seems clear that the highly unequal structure of the U.S. health care system is largely responsible. As Lawrence Mishel and his colleagues point out in a landmark book on the state of America, "many in the United States enjoy a first-rate health care system while others have none. Compared to the United States,

---

619. OECD, 2004 figures, available online: http://ocde.p4.siteinternet.com/publications/doifiles/012006061T02.xls

620. OECD, 2000 figures, available online: http://www.oecd.org/dataoecd/7/42/35530071.xls

621. OECD, 2003 figures, available online: http://www.oecd.org/dataoecd/7/41/35530083.xls

622. Center for Disease Control and Prevention, "Infant Mortality Rates...," *op. cit.* (Introd., n. 81), table 23, http://www.cdc.gov/nchs/data/hus/tables/2001/01hus023.pdf

other countries are more concerned with the health and well-being of their people through more universal coverage and more complete health systems[623]." This observation is consistent with the findings of a World Health Organization (WHO) report[624]. "This report states that the different degrees of efficiency with which health systems organize and finance themselves, and respond to the needs of their populations, explain much of the widening gap in mortality rates between rich and poor, within and between countries, around the world"[625].

The least we can say is that America is a sad paragon of this observation. According to the WHO, America ranks 37th, between Costa Rica and Slovenia, for the overall quality of its health care system[626]. On the sole variable of equity, the United States ranks 54th, just behind Bangladesh, the Maldives and the Republic of Korea, and just ahead of Iraq, Oman and Chad[627]. With a modicum of mischief, one might even believe that the WHO chose its definition of inequity with the United States in mind. In the words of the organization, "a well-funded system provides financial protection for all. A health care system in which individuals or households are sometimes pushed into poverty through the purchase of necessary care, or are forced to go without care because of cost, is unfair[628]." Consistent with this definition, it appears that in the United States, citizens must often "choose between risking financial ruin and risking their lives[629]." Each year in America, 750,000 families (or two million people) are reportedly driven to bankruptcy by medical debt[630].

---

623. The State of Working America 2006-2007, op. cit. *(Introd., n. 13), p. 340.*

624. World Health Organization, *The World Health Report 2000, Health Systems: Improving Performances*, Geneva, Switzerland, available online: http://www.who.int/whr/2000/en/whr00_en.pdf

625. *Ibid*, p. xii

626. *Ibid*, Appendices, Table 10.

627. *Ibid*, Appendices, Table 7.

628. *Ibid*, p. 35.

629. D.L. Barlett & J.B. Steele, *Critical Condition, op. cit.* (Introd., n. 21), p. 3.

630. D.U. Himmelstein, E. Warren, D. Thorne & S. Woolhandler, *MarketWatch..., op. cit.* (Introd., n. 73).

At the same time, millions of individuals - insured and uninsured - would be unable to obtain the care they need for financial reasons[631]. For 20,000 of these unfortunate people, the game would end abruptly at the death box[632]. Twenty thousand deaths a year for the crime of indigence! That means one jumbo jet crashing every week. It also means six times the number of victims of the September 11, 2001 attacks. From a concrete point of view, the source of these unnecessary deaths can, for example, be apprehended through the question of the management of breast cancer in women. This cancer occurs with greater frequency in white women than in black women. Yet it is more often fatal in black women than in white women. This inconsistency did not exist in 1970[633]. It emerged with the gradual application, since the "Reagan years," of market rules to the health care system (privatization, competition, cost cutting, etc.).

The case of Lisa Friedman is instructive in this regard. When this woman felt a nodule in her breast in 2001, she asked her insurer for the right to have a mammogram. She was denied this right. Luckily, Lisa was a doctor and she was able to challenge this decision to force her insurer to authorize the examination. The examination revealed a cancer with several metastases[634]. Lisa was treated surgically. There is no need to ask what would have happened if this patient had not been a physician and had not had the skill to successfully challenge her insurer's original rejection. The answer can be summed up in a few simple words: "four planks of fir". This is what happens to many uninsured and underinsured patients. Consistent with this assertion, a recent study unequivocally demonstrated that breast

---

631. David U. Himmelstein & Steffie Woolhandler, "Care Denied: US Residents Who Are Unable to Obtain Needed Medical Services," *American Journal of Public Health*, 1995, 85, pp. 341-344.

632. S. Brownlee, "The Overtreated American," in *The Real State of the Union, op. cit.* (Introd., n. 8), pp. 129-138, see p. 129; D.L. Barlett & J.B. Steele, *Critical Condition, op. cit.* (Introd., n. 21), p. 3.

633. Center for Disease Control (CDC), "Comparing Breast Cancer by Race and Ethnicity," available online: http://www.cdc.gov/cancer/breast/statistics/race.htm

634. Nancy Gibbs & Amanda Bower, "What Insiders Know About Our Health-Care System That the Rest of Us Need to Learn," *Time*, May 1, 2006.

cancer kills more in the black population than in the white population, not for genetic factors, but for socioeconomic reasons of access to care. Compared to white women, black women are more likely to be detected late, less likely to receive radiation therapy, less likely to have surgery, and ultimately more likely to die from their cancer[635]. As Otis Brawley, an internationally recognized expert on cancer pathology and co-director of the prestigious Winship Cancer Institute at Emory University, points out, "It's a sad thing that race influences someone's chances of getting proper medical care. In the United States, it's ugly to have cancer; it's worse to be poor and have cancer; it's even worse to be poor, black and have cancer[636]."

Perhaps the message from Bush, Clinton and Novak is really only that America has the best health care system in the world... *for those who can pay*. Woe betide the others, first and foremost the uninsured, as Susan Sered and Rushika Fernandopule call them[637]. Thus, according to these researchers, "the current American system in which health coverage is linked to employment is creating a caste of the chronically ill, the infirm and the marginally employed (...). Unemployed or marginally employed because of poor health, members of this new "untouchable caste" are denied consistent access to the health care system[638]. One of the most directly visible traits of members of this caste undoubtedly refers to their teeth. Loretta, for example, a mother married to a self-employed bricklayer, has seen her teeth rot away one after the other. When she met Sered and Fernandopule, Loretta was working part-time in a university laboratory. This temporary job offered no medical coverage. The family's income was between $1,000 and $2,500 per month. This was too much to qualify for

---

635. Cathy J. Bradley, Charles W. Given & Caralee Roberts, "Race, Socioeconomic Status, and Breast Cancer Treatment and Survival," *Journal of the National Cancer Institute*, 2002, 94, 490-496.
636. Otis W. Brawley, "Disaggregating the Effects of Race and Poverty on Breast Cancer Outcomes," *Journal of the National Cancer Institute*, 2002, 94, pp. 471-473.
637. S.S. Sered & R. Fernandopulle, *Uninsured in America...*, *op. cit.* (Introd., n. 21), pp. 14-17 and pp. 163-169.
638. *Ibid*, p. 15

social programs, but not enough to purchase private insurance. In Loretta's own words, "I had such bad toothaches that I literally pulled my own teeth out. They break after a while and you just grab them and they come out on their own. So it's a relief to just get them out of there. The hole closes itself anyway. Afterwards, it's so much better[639]."

Unlike Loretta, Caroline was on Medicaid. Unfortunately, this program does not cover dental surgery in a majority of states[640]. Caroline had the toothless face of the poor caste. She looked much older than her age and symbolized, as David Shipler writes in a terrible sentence, "the forgotten history of American prosperity[641]." Caroline worked for Wallmart and, by her manager's own admission, she was serious, eager to learn, and hardworking. Yet this woman saw every potential promotion as a definite turn-off. "The people who were promoted had something Caroline didn't have. They had teeth[642]." It is difficult, though no boss will ever openly admit it, to place a client in front of the ugly face of destitution. In fact, as Shipler deciphers with superb lucidity, Caroline was caught in a terrible spiral. If she had not been poor, she would have had teeth. If she had had teeth, she might not have remained poor. In the world of poverty, the space between cause and effect is often very difficult to arrange. Yet Caroline was not lacking in courage. She had even had her last healthy teeth pulled in hopes of getting Medicaid to fund braces. The denture she got turned out to be poorly designed and unusable. Caroline was offered a repair, but at a cost ($250) that she could not afford[643].

When I told Marie about this in 2006, she didn't believe me. Marie had just arrived in San Francisco and was still very much in love with her childhood dream of living in America. One morning, we went to visit Northern California. In Fort Bragg, at a motel, Marie approached

---

639. *Ibid*, pp. xvi-xvii, see also pp. 165-169.
640. *Ibid*, p. 166.
641. D.K. Shipler, *The Working Poor...*, *op. cit.* (Introd., n. 68), p. 51.
642. *Ibid*, p. 52.
643. *Ibid*.

the receptionist. Clearly overwhelmed by the English offered to her, the receptionist called out to another woman who was working on a computer a little further away. When this woman stood up and began to speak, Marie imperceptibly recoiled from the devastated face of a woman who had no age, no teeth and no smile left. The face of extreme poverty. A face that the American myth takes great care not only to erase, but also - and above all - to ignore. That Europeans are blind to this fact is basically understandable, since their representations depend so much on external and indirect mediation.

What is more unexpected is undoubtedly that Americans themselves are so blind to the failings of their own socio-economic system[644]. This blindness borders on mass denial, not to say collective anosognosia. In the words of Barlett and Steele, the American imagination feeds on the implausible myth that "all citizens have access to the best quality of care if they really need it[645] ". A report from the Institute of Medicine also under-scores this belief by showing that a majority of Americans believe that "people who don't have insurance get the care they need[646]." Barlett and Steele's survey work concludes, "In some cases this is true..., [for] winners of some kind of disease lottery.... However, the overwhelming majority of people, especially the working poor and middle-class families - including those with insurance - can only receive this [best quality] care if they make drastic sacrifices. They must be willing to lose everything[647]." The Institute of Medicine concludes, "The key findings of the report are that uninsured working-age Americans [ages 18 to 65] are more likely to: receive inade-quate medical care and receive it too late; get sicker and die sooner; and receive poorer care while in the hospital, even for acute situations such as a car accident.... People without health insurance often live without proper

---

644. Institute of Medicine, "Coverage Matters: Insurance and Health Care," *op. cit.* (chap. I, n. 227).
645. D.L. Barlett & J.B. Steele, *Critical Condition*, *op. cit.* (Introd., n. 21), p. 14.
646. Institute of Medicine, "Coverage Matters: Insurance and Health Care," *op. cit.* (chap. I, n. 227), "Report in Brief," p. 2.
647. D.L. Barlett & J.B. Steele, *Critical Condition*, *op. cit.* (Introd., n. 21), pp. 14-15.

care. For example, it is more common for the uninsured : do not receive cancer screenings, which delays diagnosis and leads to premature deaths; do not receive timely recommended care for chronic conditions, such as eye and leg exams to prevent blindness and amputations in people with diabetes ; Lack regular access to medications to control their conditions such as high blood pressure or HIV infection; Receive fewer diagnostic tests and treatment after a traumatic injury or heart attack, resulting in an increased risk of death, even in the hospital[648]."

These results have been confirmed by many other studies and there seems to be little doubt about their validity[649]. America, the world's leading economic power, is allowing those of its children who cannot afford private insurance or pay for their care to suffer, sometimes to death. This may seem unreal, implausible and ignominious, but it is an objective fact that cannot be ignored.

In the United States, there are officially 46.6 million people without health insurance[650]. This represents more than 18% of the population, excluding people over 65[651] (who have "universal" coverage through the Medicare program). Breaking this down further, it appears that the uninsured are

648. Institute of Medicine, *Care Without Coverage: Too Little, Too Late*, Committee on the Consequences of Uninsurance, Board on Health Care Services (Washington, DC: National Academy Press, 2002); quote from "Report in Brief," pp. 1-2, available online: http://books. nap.edu/html/care_without/reportbrief.pdf

649. See, for example, H.R. Burstin, S.R. Lipsitz & T.A. Brennan, "Socioeconomic Status and Risk for Substandard Medical Care," *Journal of the American Medical Association*, 1992, 268, pp. 2383-2387; J. Hadley, "Sicker and Poorer: the Consequences of Being Uninsured," *Medical Care Research and Review*, 2003, 60 (2 Suppl.), pp. 3S-75S; J. Hadley, "Insurance Coverage, Medical Care Use, and Short-Term Health Changes Following an Unintentional Injury or the Onset of a Chronic Condition," *Journal of the American Medical Association*, 2007, 297, pp. 1073-1084; S.M. Asch, *et al*, "Who Is at Greatest Risk for Receiving Poor-Quality Health Care?", *New England Journal of Medicine*, 2006, 354, pp. 1147-1156.

650. C. DeNavas-Walt, B.D. Proctor & C.H. Lee, *Income, Poverty, and Health Insurance Coverage, op. cit.* (Introd., n. 22), Report P60-231, table C-1, available online: http://www.census. gov/prod/2006pubs/p60-231.pdf

651. "Who Are the Uninsured? A Consistent Profile across National Surveys," Kaiser Commission on Medicaid and the Uninsured, *op. cit.* (Introd., n. 54), available online: http://www. kff.org/uninsured/upload/7553.pdf

mainly adults between 18 and 65 (83%). Children represent "only" 17% of those excluded (the criteria for inclusion in social programs - Medicaid, SCHIP - are more permissive for children than for adults). However, this 17% includes a large number of "false negatives", i.e. children who escape assistance mechanisms because their parents do not think they are eligible and/or are powerless to carry out the required administrative procedures (it would seem that "old Europe" does not have a monopoly on bureaucracy). The majority of the uninsured come from disadvantaged households with incomes below twice the poverty line (between 52% and 59% depending on the study)[652]. More than 70% of uninsured adults are employed, and 60% of these unfortunate individuals work for companies that do not offer health coverage to their employees; the remaining 40% of individuals generally do not enroll because they are not eligible for the programs offered (seniority, part-time, etc.) or cannot afford this "luxury. Contrary to a persistent myth, the uninsured are not young, healthy scatterbrains with a taste for Russian roulette[653].

To illustrate this point, consider the case of Gina, as reported by Susan Sered and Rushika Fernandopulle[654]. After working for 10 years as a clerk at the Home Depot, this woman decided to train for a better job. She chose to study hairdressing, which she did for 14 months with a $15,000 credit ($7,000 for tuition and $8,000 for living expenses). Upon graduation, Gina found a job at a low-cost shop. The pay was "by the slice". Working 9 hours a day, Gina was able to earn an average of $900 a month. When there were no customers, Gina stayed there and got nothing. Her company offered health coverage, at a cost to Gina of $200 per month. This insurance included substantial co-payments and a $1,000 per year deductible (*i.e.,* the insurance would not pay out until Gina paid $1,000).

---

652. *Ibid.*

653. Institute of Medicine, "Coverage Matters: Insurance and Health Care," *op. cit.* (chap. I, n. 227), especially p. 2.

654. S.S. Sered & R. Fernandopulle, *Uninsured in America...*, *op. cit.* (Introd., n. 21), pp. 40-44.

Of course, Gina was unable to take advantage of this offer. She could have hoped to take advantage of her husband's insurance. Her husband worked for a distribution chain for $6.25 an hour. Unfortunately, he didn't have health coverage either. His company was careful to keep him just below the hourly rate that would give him access to the health insurance plan. A common strategy in America. One day, Gina fell ill. After accumulating a debt of nearly $10,000 in various tests, our patient learned that she had a gallbladder problem and needed to see a surgeon. However, the surgeon refused to see her until she paid $200 up front. Gina was unable to raise the money. After several months, she still had not seen a surgeon. She was trying to live as normally as possible despite significant episodic pain and the risk of potentially serious - even lethal - complications should her gallbladder rupture.

Gina's example is unfortunately not unusual. Uninsured patients are very often forced to pay a sum of money in advance or risk being refused an appointment with their doctor. Even if they pay, the indigent are not sure to be seen. Many doctors refuse to see uninsured patients at all. Other practitioners "blacklist" those covered by social systems such as Medicare or Medicaid on the grounds that reimbursement is too low[655]. This excluded cohort is usually left with the emergency room as the only place to seek care[656]. These services have a legal obligation to receive patients, insured or not, to stabilize their condition and to treat any life-threatening condition. However, there is no obligation on the part of emergency services to provide follow-up or prevention (e.g., to prevent a recurrence)[657]. In

---

655. Angela Galloway, "Uninsured Have Little Hope of Getting Specialized Care," *Seattle Post-Intelligencer*, January 2, 2006; D.K. Shipler, *The Working Poor...*, *op. cit.* (Introd., n. 68), p. 296; S.S. Sered & R. Fernandopulle, *Uninsured in America...*, *op. cit.* (Introd., n. 21), p. 166.

656. D.K. Shipler, *The Working Poor...*, *op. cit.* (Introd., n. 68), p. 37; S.S. Sered & R. Fernandopulle, *Uninsured in America...*, *op. cit.* (Introd., n. 21), pp. 12 and 202; M.R. Rank, *One Nation Underprivileged...*, *op. cit.* (Introd., n. 10), p. 113.

657. S.S. Sered & R. Fernandopulle, *Uninsured in America...*, *op. cit.* (Introd., n. 21), pp. 17-18.

practice, hospitals have a formidable deterrent to minimizing access to emergency platforms: presenting undesirables with outrageously generous bills. A given procedure may thus be billed between 4 and 10 times more expensively to an uninsured person than to a person with coverage[658]. For a heart bypass, for example, an insurer will be charged between $55,000 and $60,000. A patient without coverage will be charged between $123,000 and $177,000[659]. For a cyst removal, the fee may range from $6,900 to $74,396[660]. For an appendectomy, the rates will be $2,500 and $14,000 respectively[661]. If the patient cannot pay the bill, he or she will be pursued with formidable aggression. In some cases, failure to pay a medical bill may even result in imprisonment[662]. In fact, hospitals frequently turn over their debts to collection agencies that are paid on a percentage basis. Sometimes, patient debts are simply resold at a rate of 10 or 20 cents per dollar[663]. The calculation is not necessarily stupid. By multiplying the price of care by four or five and reselling the debts to specialized agencies for 10 or 20 cents on the dollar, hospitals are certain to receive at least the "insurer" rate for their services. The onus is on the purchasing organizations to recoup their costs through sometimes aggressive practices[664]. As Barlett and Steele point out, "In the end, many have their salaries garnished, or are forced into bankruptcy. Some lose their homes"[665]. This is what happened, for example, to Jack and Donna when she received a $57,000 bill for colon surgery (including post-surgical complications)[666].

---

658. "Outsourcing Your Heart," *op. cit.* (Introd., n. 76), pp. 44-47; D.L. Barlett & J.B. Steele, *Critical Condition, op. cit.* (Introd., n. 21), pp. 15-24.

659. "Outsourcing Your Heart," *op. cit.* (Introd., n. 76).

660. D.L. Barlett & J.B. Steele, *Critical Condition, op. cit.* (Introd., n. 21), p. 18.

661. S.S. Sered & R. Fernandopulle, *Uninsured in America..., op. cit.* (Introd., n. 21), p. 12.

662. L. Lagnado, "Hospitals Try Extreme Measures to Collect Their Overdue Debts," *Wall Street Journal*, October 30, 2003.

663. S.S. Sered & R. Fernandopulle, *Uninsured in America..., op. cit.* (Introd., n. 21), p. 13.

664. D.L. Barlett & J.B. Steele, *Critical Condition, op. cit.* (Introd., n. 21), pp. 19-24.

665. *Ibid.* at 3 and 22.

666. *Ibid,* p. 22.

A 2006 study published in the *Seattle Post-Intelligencer* by Angela Galloway sums up the situation of the uninsured in America quite well. In the words of the paper, "If you're working, poor and uninsured in King County, an emergency room doctor will put a cast on your broken leg. But, after the hospital, will probably throw you out[667] - with a bottle of narcotics and a prescription for an orthopedist who can make sure your leg heals properly but whom you will probably never see. Even as the percentage of uninsured grows among King County residents, fewer and fewer local specialists are willing to treat uninsured patients.... It may be virtually impossible to obtain care for uninsured patients in fields such as orthopedics, gastroenterology, mental health, dermatology and neuro-logy.... There are some specialties where there is virtually zero access. [For example], Wereta, a 42 year old caregiver...has a lump in her abdomen. It doesn't look cancerous, but the lump needs to be removed.... But Wereta has stopped her search for a willing specialist (...). Wereta says she already owes $15,000 for lab tests, and her husband hasn't worked in a year due to a work-related injury. "My husband doesn't work, and because of that I'm scared. I don't want my kids to be stressed or in pain, and I don't have anyone to pay my bills (...), I'm just going to pray"[668].

As I read Wereta's words, I think of Mr. Baverez's words about France being "stuck in the sanctuary of its pseudo social model[669]". I sincerely believe that I prefer this type of blockage to the fluidity of a model that leaves Wereta untended and unexamined. A matter of perspective, no doubt. But let's close that parenthesis here and get back to the point. In addition to the almost 47 million uninsured mentioned above, there are another 50 million or so individuals who are so-called underinsured[670]. These people do have insurance, but it is so restrictive that it leaves its

---

667. The original quote includes a pun between "*cast*" and "*cast out.*

668. A. Galloway, "Uninsured Have Little Hope of Getting Specialized Care," *op. cit.* (*supra*, n. 241).

669. N. Baverez, "Japon, Allemagne, France, le fossé de la réforme", *op. cit.* (Introd., n. 84).

670. D.L. Barlett & J.B. Steele, *Critical Condition*, *op. cit.* (Introd., n. 21), pp. 26-27; S.S. Sered & R. Fernandopulle, *Uninsured in America...*, *op. cit.* (Introd., n. 21), p. 201.

holders largely helpless in the face of illness. In fact, insurers have all sorts of restrictive clauses relating to the absence of coverage for pre-existing conditions, deductibles (the insurer only contributes after the first $500 or $1,000), expenditure ceilings (the patient is no longer covered beyond $250,000 or $500,000), the existence of co-payments (the patient keeps 20% of the costs), or the nature of the conditions concerned (exclusion of psychiatric illnesses, dental problems, etc.). For a quarter of families with insurance, the annual bill reaches $2,000 or more[671]. Gaynelle Harris, for example, a department store cashier, was left with $10,000 in "residual" debt following a hysterectomy. This debt was the beginning of an irreversible slide that ended with a personal bankruptcy judgment[672]. Another patient's fate was sealed by a $13,000 bill following a broken leg with knee ligament damage[673]. Suzanne Gibbons' story is similar. Following a stroke and heart condition, the 58-year-old nurse was left with tens of thousands of dollars in debt not covered by her insurance. The near-sexagenarian lost her home and was declared personally bankrupt in 2001[674]. Lynette's case is equally damning. Despite what she thought was solid insurance coverage, she continues to pay for her husband's extensive cancer treatments in the form of a payroll deduction of one-third of her income before he died[675]. Another patient had lung surgery before suffering a heart attack. The medical costs were covered by his insurance, but he had to change jobs because his previous job was no longer compatible with his physical limitations. His new insurance refused to cover him for a "pre-existing condition" that required expensive chronic treatments. Bankruptcy

---

671. "Underinsured in America: Is Health Coverage Adequate?", *op. cit.* (chap. I, n. 221), available online: http://www.kff.org/uninsured/upload/Underinsured-in-America-Is-Health-Coverage-Adequate-Fact-Sheet.pdf
672. Heath Foster, "Hard Work, Hard Times: One Setback Can Send a Middle-Class Family Reeling," *Seattle Post-Intelligencer*, March 15, 2005.
673. D.U. Himmelstein, E. Warren, D. Thorne & S. Woolhandler, *MarketWatch...*, *op. cit.* (Introd., n. 73).
674. Bonnie Miller Rubin, "Medical Bills Pave Way to Poorhouse...," *op. cit.* (Introd., n. 72).
675. Kerry Howley, "I Can't Afford to Get Sick," *Reader's Digest*, April 2006, available online: http://www.rd.com/content/the-cost-of-health-care-in-america/

ensued. Unfortunately, history does not tell us what happened to our unfortunate patient[676].

The litany of examples above could go on and on. According to a recently published study by Harvard University researchers, 750,000 families are pushed into financial bankruptcy each year because they cannot pay their medical bills. These families include 2 million individuals and hold, on average, $11,854 in medical debt at the time of their bankruptcy. This may not seem like much at first glance, but it still represents $230 in monthly repayments for ten years, at a rate, not very high for the United States[677], of 20%. In fact, $230 is 25 per cent of the income of a minimum wage earner; $230 can be enough to sink many middle class families with already strained budgets. As Steffie Woolhandler, co-author of the above study, points out, $11,854 "is a lot of money to pay if your income has been reduced because you are too sick to work[678]. It is also, one might add, a terrifying sword of Damocles waiting to descend blindly on its victims at the slightest deviation in their lives. Indeed, it is often less the debt itself that is problematic than its potentially cumulative effect. It is not always easy to wait until the end of the first loan to fall ill again, break a leg, or have a car breakdown. This additive risk is undoubtedly the most worrying message of the study published by the Harvard team, through the gradual impoverishment it underlies. In this study, the subjects concerned "were mainly middle class (...). They were typical Americans who got sick"[679]. For these ordinary people, a simple illness turned into a relentless slide that nothing could stop. The process is basically quite simple: a person gets sick, they can't work temporarily, their income plummets (if they are lucky enough to keep any), debts pile up, access to care is reduced, health deteriorates, court orders come down, the courts rule, the house is fore-

---

676. D.U. Himmelstein, E. Warren, D. Thorne & S. Woolhandler, *MarketWatch...*, *op. cit.* (Introd., n. 73).
677. See in the first part of this book: "Anna: at the heart of reality".
678. Bonnie Miller Rubin, "Medical Bills Pave Way to Poorhouse...," *op. cit.* (Introd., n. 72).
679. D.U. Himmelstein, E. Warren, D. Thorne & S. Woolhandler, *MarketWatch...*, *op. cit.* (Introd., n. 73).

closed, and there is nothing left to hold on to or stop the spiral. In some cases, the individual cannot return to work, either because of incapacity or simply because the company has fired him (as happened to Anna[680] or Denise[681]). The individual loses his or her coverage, and when he or she is fortunate enough to regain coverage, the company generally refuses to cover the pre-existing conditions. It is difficult to identify a way out of this vicious circle.

In short, for tens of millions of uninsured or underinsured individuals, the U.S. health care system is far from being "the best in the world. Of course, one could argue that this shortcoming is less a matter of the technological competence of hospitals than of the procedures for accessing care. In other words, the American health care system is certainly unequal in terms of accessibility, but it is also unequal in terms of efficiency. In form, this principle fits quite well with the concept of technological excellence that we generally associate with the "United States" brand. In substance, however, it does not correspond to any quantitatively identifiable reality. As Barlett and Steele point out at the end of their remarkable survey on the subject, the American health care system does include pockets of extreme competence, but these "benefit no more than 2 or 3 percent of the population, and the wealthiest citizens of other nations who come [to the United States] for highly specialized treatment. Overall, and except for these pockets of excellence, the system is second-rate when it comes to meeting the day-to-day medical needs of the broader population[682]."

When one goes beyond fiction to fact, it appears that American hospitals have an unfortunate tendency to be not only inefficient, but also dangerous. A first line of evidence on this point is based on two comprehensive studies published in 2003 and 2006 in the prestigious *New England Journal of*

---

680. See in the first part of this book: "Anna: at the heart of reality".
681. See in the first part of this book: "Anna: in the heart of reality"; S.S. Sered & R. Fernandopulle, *Uninsured in America...*, *op. cit.* (Introd., n. 21), pp. 159-162.
682. D.L. Barlett & J.B. Steele, *Critical Condition*, *op. cit.* (Introd., n. 21), pp. 12-13.

Medicine[683]. According to these studies, when we compare, for different pathologies, the nomenclature of recommended care and examinations with the table of care and examinations actually performed, the gap reaches an average of 55%. Significant differences are indeed observed according to patients' economic status, but in the words of the authors of the most recent study, "the differences between socio-demographic subgroups in the quality of medical care are small compared to the gap for each subgroup between the observed and desirable quality of medical care[684]". In other words, the poor are less well cared for than the rich, but both the rich and the poor are largely less well cared for than they should be. To take some concrete examples, this means that: only 45% of myocardial infarction patients receive beta-blockers immediately after admission to the hospital (these drugs very substantially improve - by up to 25% - the vital prognosis); only 24% of diabetic patients have their glycated hemoglobin measured at least every 6 months (this measurement is essential to assess the appropriateness of the treatment and to ensure that it is adapted if necessary); only 48% of patients suffering from recurrent dysuria (painful emission of urine) have their urine analysed bacteriologically (this urine culture is essential to identify an infection)[685].

It is not surprising, then, that the American health care system is the site of an impressive number of blunders of all kinds. The magnitude of these blunders has become so alarming that the term "epidemic" was recently used by Robert Wachter and Kaveh Shojania in a widely read

---

683. E.A. McGlynn, *et al*, "The Quality of Health Care Delivered to Adults in the United States," *New England Journal of Medicine*, 2003, 348, pp. 2635-2645; S.M. Asch, *et al*, "Who Is at Greatest Risk for Receiving Poor-Quality Health Care?" *op. cit. (supra*, n. 235).

684. S.M. Asch, *et al*, "Who Is at Greatest Risk for Receiving Poor-Quality Health Care?", *op. cit. (supra*, n. 235), at 1147.

685. E.A. McGlynn, *et al*, "The Quality of Health Care Delivered to Adults in the United States," *op. cit. (supra*, n. 269); for the information presented here, see additional data associated with the paper, available online, http://www.rand.org/pubs/working_papers/2006/RAND_WR174-1.pdf

book[686]. Each year, medical errors are estimated to cause between 50,000 and 100,000 deaths in the United States[687]! The most alarmist studies even put the number of victims at over 200,000[688]. Of course, some errors are gross and directly attributable to the deficiencies of the health care team: amputations of the wrong limb, brain resections in the wrong hemisphere, mastectomy of the valid breast, materials forgotten inside the patient, organ transplants in the presence of a blood incompatibility between the donor and the recipient, erroneous dosages during drug infusions, etc. These errors are usually the ones that make the headlines and trigger the boisterous laughter of medical students. However, they are neither the most frequent nor the most revealing. Other blunders, less spectacular but just as dramatic, lurk at the very heart of the system. These blunders are "remarkable" in the sense that they are the direct result of the culture of profit, of the accounting approach to medical acts and of the annexation by insurance companies of the power to make therapeutic decisions. By trying to apply the rules of the market economy to health care, America has created the most expensive, inefficient, dangerous and barbaric health care system in the civilized world. As Barlett and Steele summarize with their customary acuity, "the market is a devastating failure[689]." Perhaps it is worth noting that this conviction is neither singular nor atypical. It is consistent with the experience of millions of patients and the conclusion of several leading scientific studies, including one published in 1999 by Himmelstein and colleagues in the *Journal of the American Medical Association* (JAMA). At the conclusion of this study, the authors state that "the experiment in market medicine is a failure. The profit motive is compromising quality of care, the number of uninsured is growing, those

---

686. *Robert Wachter and Kaveh Shojania,* Internal Bleeding: the Truth Behind America's Terrifying Epidemic of Medical Mistakes, *New York, Rugged Land, 2004.*

687. Institute of Medicine, *To Err Is Human: Building a Safer Health System* (Washington: National Academy Press, 2000), Report in Brief, available online at http://books.nap.edu/html/to_err_is_human/reportbrief.pdf

688. D.L. Barlett & J.B. Steele, *Critical Condition, op. cit.* (Introd., n. 21), pp. 55-56.

689. *Ibid,* p. 248.

with insurance are increasingly dissatisfied, bureaucracy is proliferating, and costs are again rising rapidly[690]." The violence of these words is all the more significant because they appear in a scientific setting with a generally cautious and polite vocabulary. The following paragraphs illustrate more concretely the failure of market forces in the medical field.

In the beginning was the myth. The essence of the myth is expressed in a few simple words by Ronald Reagan in his inaugural address to the nation on January 20, 1981: "In the present crisis, government is not the solution to our problem. Government is the problem[691]. This sentence was applied with surgical rigour to the field of health care. The credo was very simple[692]: public systems are corrupt, expensive and inefficient. To reduce the cost of care and optimize its quality, all that is needed is to *unleash free market forces*. Through severe competition between hospitals and health maintenance organizations (HMOs), the greatest number of people will have access to an efficient health care system. As we have seen above, the results have hardly matched the original expectations. This does not, of course, stop our liberal friends from staunchly supporting their potion. If the method has failed, these market advocates tell us, it is because the process of liberalizing the health care system was neither drastic enough nor deep enough.

This message has found a strong ally in the almost unhealthy hatred Americans have for anything that could remotely be called "socialism. The inhabitants of the New World instinctively associate the word with the Soviet model, with liberticidal constraint, with long lines, with scarcity, with crass incompetence, with misery. I have often been struck by the visceral distrust that Americans have of the Canadian, Swedish or French health care systems, which are described as "socialist" and where one

690. D.U. Himmelstein, S. Woolhandler, I. Hellander & S.M. Wolfe, "Quality of Care in Investor-Owned vs. Not-for-Profit HMOs," *JAMA*, 1999, 282, pp. 159-163, citation p. 163.
691. Ronald Reagan, "First Inaugural Address," January 20, 1981, available online: http://www.reaganfoundation.org/reagan/speeches/first.asp
692. Sam Allalouf, "Letting Market Forces Help Govern Provision of Health Care," *New York Times*, February 9, 1981.

would wait months to be forced to see an incompetent specialist in a clinic unworthy of a third world country. This myth is largely maintained by exalted liberals, as shown, for example, in an article published before the 2004 presidential elections in the *USA Today* newspaper by Michael F. Cannon, then director of health policy studies at the Cato Institute. The article states that "the last thing patients need is for the government to inject more socialism into their health care system in the name of expanded coverage.... Ronald Reagan demonstrated that free markets are superior to socialism. So why do we continue to tolerate socialism in our health care system[693]?" I think a summary answer to this question might be that this reviled "socialism" allows the poorest to access decent care and members of the middle class - insured or not - to be treated without risking personal bankruptcy. Another, more fundamental, justification might point out that the financial logic of insurers, pharmaceutical groups and hospitals rarely dovetails with the therapeutic needs of the patient[694]. In a mutualized system without profit motive, the latter are central. Conversely, in a private for-profit system, they become auxiliary. In this case, there is a de facto subordination of care to profit, and patient safety is often sacrificed on the altar of profitability.

Since the Reagan years, this trend has only been reinforced in the United States, notably through the rapid conversion of the health care system from a predominantly *"non-profit"* orientation to a predominantly *"for profit"* orientation. Between 1981 and 1997, the number of individuals dependent on for-profit structures increased from 12% to 62%[695]. This

---

693. Michael F. Cannon, "Free Market Is the Answer," *USA Today*, June 16, 2004, available online: http://www.usatoday.com/news/opinion/editorials/2004-06-14-oppose_x.htm

694. D.L. Barlett & J.B. Steele, *Critical Condition*, *op. cit.* (Introd., n. 21); R. Kuttner, "Must Good HMOs Go Bad?", Part ¹, *op. cit.* (Introd., n. 27); R. Kuttner, *ibid*, Part ², *op. cit.* (Introd., n. 27); D.U. Himmelstein, S. Woolhandler, I. Hellander & S.M. Wolfe, "Quality of Care in Investor-Owned vs. Not-for-Profit HMOs," *op. cit.* (*supra*, n. 276).

695. D.L. Barlett & J.B. Steele, *Critical Condition*, *op. cit.* (Introd., n. 21), pp. 88-94; R. Kuttner, "Must Good HMOs Go Bad?", Part ¹, *op. cit.* (Introd., n. 27), p. 1558; Kaiser Family Foundation, "For-Profit Health Care Companies: Trends and Issues," 1998, Fact Sheet, 1359, available online: http://www.kff.org/kaiserpolls/1359-facts.cfm

inevitable transition has left only one true cuckold: the patient. As Robert Kuttner writes in a remarkable article in the prestigious *New England Journal of Medicine*, "At some point, there is a clear conflict of interest between the provider's desire to save money and the patient's need for good care. At that point, money is saved, not by maximizing quality but by cutting back on services, shifting the costs of care to the patient's family or physician, and sometimes increasing suffering[696]." In other words, the market does not (as trumpeted) rationalize care on the basis of optimality, it rationalizes it on the basis of cost. Most studies have thus confirmed that "privately owned HMOs deliver a lower quality of care than nonprofit [HMOs][697]." For example, according to work published in 1999[698], patients with myocardial infarction were 10% less likely to receive beta-blockers when they belonged to a for-profit HMO (these drugs, as I have already said, very substantially improve the patient's vital prognosis). For women between 50 and 69 years of age, the likelihood of getting a mammogram dropped. According to the authors of the study, if all women between the ages of 50 and 69 had been subjected to mammography with the same frequency, regardless of the purpose (profit or not) of their care organization, nearly 6,000 lives could have been saved.

In order to better understand the excesses of the market, it is perhaps interesting to take a few concrete examples. Let's start with the pharmaceutical companies through the "misfortune" of Jennifer Rufer[699]. This woman was 22 years old when she went to her gynecologist for bleeding and abdominal pain. A test revealed an elevated pregnancy hormone marker. Jennifer was not pregnant. The marker identified could also be linked to a rare form of cancer. The test was repeated several times. Aggressive chemotherapy followed. The tests continued to show abnormal

---

696. R. Kuttner, "Must Good HMOs Go Bad?", Part 1, *op. cit.* (Introd., n. 27), p. 1559.
697. D.U. Himmelstein, S. Woolhandler, I. Hellander & S.M. Wolfe, "Quality of Care in Investor-Owned vs. Not-for-Profit HMOs," *op. cit.* (*supra*, n. 276), at 159.
698. *Ibid.*
699. Reported by D.L. Barlett & J.B. Steele, *Critical Condition, op. cit.* (Introd., n. 21), pp. 61-63.

results. A hysterectomy was performed. When "nodules" were found in the lungs, the doctors thought it was a metastasis. A portion of the right lung was amputated. Just as Jennifer was preparing for the worst, the good news came: she had never had cancer! All forty tests she had undergone were "false positives. The terrible thing was that Abbott, the company that marketed the offending tests, was aware that these "false positives" could occur and that the test results could lead to unnecessary cancer treatments. Prior to Jennifer's case, more than 40 reports had been sent to Abbott in this regard. Despite a legal obligation to refer to these reports, the lab remained silent. The Rufers received $16 million in compensation. Little consolation, it seems, for a young woman who will never have children and will have to live the rest of her life with a largely amputated right lung. Douglas Axen and Kenneth Kurtz met a similar fate in a slightly different field[700]. Kenneth Kurtz, for example, was 73 years old and had an irregular heartbeat when his cardiologist prescribed Cordarone in February 1997. Within a few weeks, our man lost his sight and was declared blind in June 1997. On that same date, the Wyeth-Ayerst laboratory, which marketed Cordarone, issued a warning that the drug could cause vision loss. The same warning had been issued several years earlier in Canada. A court ruled against the laboratory on the grounds that the choice to delay issuing a warning in the United States was motivated by a commercial concern to preserve sales. It is difficult to be clearer.

After the pharmaceutical companies, let's take a look at the wonderful world of HMOs. Let's start with the story of the unfortunate Basil Pappas[701]. Upon waking up one morning, this man had severe difficulty moving his limbs. Doctors at the local hospital diagnosed a spinal infection and arranged for the patient to be transferred to a nearby facility for a delicate operation. Unfortunately, just before the patient was scheduled to leave, a problem arose: the facility Basil Pappas was going to was not under

---

700. Reported by D.L. Barlett & J.B. Steele, *ibid*, pp. 43-44.
701. Lisa Sanders, "When Your HMO Says 'No Way,'" *Business Week*, May 19, 1997.

contract with his insurance company. It took three hours before a transfer to a competent hospital was approved. With an immediate transfer, it is not impossible to think that Pappas' chances of escaping the wheelchair would have been increased. As the reporter who covered this event points out, "Although extreme, Pappas' case illustrates the complications that arise when a company's managed care policy is at odds with a physician's order. Critical or potentially life-saving treatments can be deferred because the HMO does not approve the provider, as in Pappas' case, or because the plan's administrators feel the procedure is too costly[702]."

In their merciless fight against profiteers of all kinds, the HMOs have an absolute weapon: the *"guidelines"* (or "guidelines"). These define, for a given pathology, the length of hospitalization required or the type of examination to be performed. As these guidelines aim to control costs, they are by nature restrictive and, according to many doctors, even dangerous for the health and vital prognosis of patients[703]. I must admit that it is sometimes difficult to choose between laughter and dismay at certain guidelines, such as the one issued a few years ago by a leader in the field of guidelines, which stipulated that cataract surgery should only be performed on one eye in the elderly, on the grounds that it is not essential to see with both eyes[704]. Consternation apparently prevailed and the idea was shelved. The same outrage arose at the same company's idea of sending mothers and their infants home on the day of delivery. The federal government and several states passed laws to prevent this practice[705]. Each mother was

---

702. *Ibid.*

703. R. Rutledge, "An Analysis of 25 Milliman & Robertson Guidelines for Surgery," *Annals of Surgery*, 1998, 228, pp. 579-587; J.W. Meredith, R. Burney, S. Burton, R. Annechiarico & J. Wallace, "Milliman & Robertson Length of Stay Guidelines Are Not Appropriate For Trauma Patients: A Comparison With the NTDB," paper presented at the 59th Annual Meetings of the American Association For the Surgery of Trauma, Marriott Copley Place Hotel, Boston, Massachusetts, September 16-18, 1999, abstract published in *The Journal of Trauma*, 1999, 47, p. 208; D.L. Barlett & J.B. Steele, *Critical Condition, op. cit.* (Introd., n. 21), pp. 161-170.

704. Quoted *in* D.L. Barlett & J.B. Steele, *Critical Condition, op. cit.* (Introd., n. 21), p. 164.

705. *Ibid.*

now entitled to two days of hospitalization for a delivery. After this time, negotiations are required, and they are not always easy.

Caroline knows a thing or two about this, having given birth in San Francisco in September 2005[706]. Following the delivery of her daughter, this 35-year-old woman experienced severe headaches and neck pain. The doctor asked for an extension of her stay. He obtained one night. Caroline's roommate left after 24 hours to avoid putting herself in financial jeopardy due to a high level of co-payment (these early departures are known to significantly threaten the child's prognosis[707]). Following her first extension, Caroline was discharged, although her condition remained precarious. The insurer refused to issue a new stay. He had also refused a request for a scan, requested by the doctor, who suspected cervical damage following the delivery procedure. During the three weeks following her discharge, Caroline suffered from intense migraine and neck pain. From her three visits to the emergency room, she brought back only $150 in co-payments, soothing words and enough painkillers to knock out a horse (painkillers apparently better suited to induce intense vomiting than to relieve Caroline's migraines). During her last visit to the emergency room, Caroline also complained of severe stomach pains. The resident on duty explained to her that these pains were normal, given the proximity of the delivery. Caroline did not see a gynecologist or midwife. In November, she still had vaginal bleeding. During her "end of pregnancy" visit, the midwife noted that everything was normal. However, on December 20, 3 months after her delivery, Caroline was still bleeding. She had a severe stomachache and called her health care provider to make a gynecological appointment. The administrative officer who took the call had no medical qualifications. However, he deemed the case "non-urgent" and Caroline obtained an appointment first for March with her regular doctor, and then at great

---

706. Caroline is the companion of the author of this book.
707. J.D. Malkin, S. Garber, M.S. Broder & E. Keeler, "Infant Mortality and Early Postpartum Discharge," *Obstetrics and Gynecology*, 2000, 96, 183-188.

length for the end of January - but with a practitioner she did not know. Concerned about her condition, Caroline called back on the morning of December 23 and explicitly asked to speak to a doctor. When she refused, a midwife called her back in the afternoon. The midwife told her that bleeding was "normal" until six months after the delivery. The appointment initially set for the end of January was maintained. Just after New Year's Eve, Caroline collapsed. She was taken to an emergency room and operated on. During the delivery, some placenta had been "forgotten" by the medical team, causing a major infection. Caroline was lucky. She recovered perfectly from her mishap and did not suffer any long-term deficits.

Herschel Pybas did not have that privilege[708]. The 83-year-old had been admitted to a Texas hospital after a series of serious problems (anemia, kidney failure, heart problems). He had suffered several strokes in previous years. When his condition improved, he was transferred to a nursing home. His condition continued to improve slowly. After two weeks, his HMO decided, based on its guidelines, that it was time to send the patient home. The doctor objected and Pybas gained a week. The insurer then reformulated his discharge request. The doctor vigorously disagreed, but he had to comply. He signed the transfer order, however, only in exchange for a formal assurance that the patient would receive the same care at home as he had received during his placement. This did not happen. The patient, normally on oxygen, was deprived of this support both during his ambulance ride and at home. Pybas had a "rough night," as his relatives put it. When the doctor was informed in the morning, he ordered the family to call an ambulance and take Pybas to the emergency room. Pybas arrived in a state of extreme fatigue, and although his condition improved slightly at first, the original exhaustion could never be made up. Pybas died in the

---

708. Reported in B. Rice, "A Jury Holds an HMO Accountable," *Medical Economics* 2005; 82: 55-57.

following days. His widow filed a lawsuit, after which both parties agreed on an undisclosed amount of financial compensation.

In his misfortune, Pybas had some luck: he got the advice and attention of a doctor. This is not always the case. Indeed, incredible as it may seem, it is commonplace for life-threatening decisions to be made by telephone operators who have no medical knowledge[709]. These operators screen incoming calls, ask you a number of pre-determined questions, enter your answers into the computer and... ultimately decide whether or not you deserve to speak to a caregiver. In a pilot program, which caused a scandal and was effectively shut down in 2002, Kaiser Permanente, the largest HMO in California, even implemented a financial bonus system in three call centers in the state to encourage its operators to be frugal[710]. The bonus, worth up to 10% of base salary, was given to employees who met three of four goals: 1) administer routine calls in less than 3 minutes 45 seconds; 2) make or request an appointment for less than 35% of callers; 3) transfer for in-depth assessment less than 50% (60% at night and on weekends) of calls to the on-call nurses; and 4) spend at least 75% of the daily volume of time handling calls. In the words of Dr. Linda Peeno, who is known for speaking out against these practices after putting them to music as medical director of a large HMO, all of this "virtually ensures that you will not get a proper assessment and you certainly won't have access to anyone who would be able to assess you properly. It's a recipe for not minimal care but no care at all[711]."

A small example of application from Barlett and Steele[712]. Margaret Utterback had just experienced severe abdominal pain when she called her clinic at 8:15 a.m. on January 26, 1996. Her call was automatically transferred to a call center at Kaiser, her insurance company. After a

---

709. D.L. Barlett & J.B. Steele, *Critical Condition*, *op. cit.* (Introd., n. 21), pp. 182-189.
710. C. Ornstein, "Kaiser Clerks Paid More for Helping Less," *Los Angeles Times*, May 17, 2002.
711. Quoted *in* C. Ornstein, *ibid.*
712. Reported by D.L. Barlett & J.B. Steele, *Critical Condition*, *op. cit.* (Introd., n. 21), pp. 155-158.

long, fruitless wait, Margaret hung up. At 9:45 a.m., she tried again in the presence of her daughter. She got a caller, explained her symptoms and asked for an appointment. She was told that her doctor had no room in his schedule that day. Utterback insisted and asked to be put in touch directly with her doctor. She was denied this privilege and asked to call back at 3:00 p.m. to request an emergency appointment for that evening. Utterback nevertheless called back at 10:15 a.m., secretly hoping to find a more accommodating ear. The person who took the call offered to send an email to Utterback's doctor. Utterback was asked to wait for him to get back to her. At 1:45 p.m., Utterback called again. She explained her condition to several callers before getting a voice mail. She called again and was again transferred from one operator to another until someone finally gave her an appointment for 4:15 p.m. Utterback didn't wait and, accompanied by her daughter, showed up at the clinic at 2:45. She was not examined until 4:30. The doctor had no trouble diagnosing an abdominal aneurysm. It took another hour to arrange for the patient's transfer to a hospital that could receive her. At 5:31 p.m., just after arriving at a competent emergency department, 9 hours after her first phone call, Utterback's abdominal aorta ruptured. He was pronounced dead the next morning at 5:45 a.m. The insurer was ordered to pay a fine of $1.1 million. While this figure may seem high, it is probably very reasonable compared to the amount of money saved through restrictive access mechanisms. With a modicum of liberality, one could say that this type of "collateral damage" represents a worthwhile investment. It may be interesting to note here that what has just been said about telephone operators has also been applied, in a different but similar form, to doctors themselves. It has thus been shown that certain doctors, and in particular the *gatekeepers* who administer patients' care protocols, were offered significant financial bonuses when they succeeded in meeting a certain number of objectives in terms of prescribing examinations, hospitalizations or redirecting patients to specialized practitioners[713]. For doctors who are insensitive to this carrot, the stick is of course always at hand, in the form of termination of their contract with the healthcare network. Beware of those who prescribe more than the authorized standard in liberal lands.

Of course, the rationing of health care in the United States is not always so "transparent. Some abuses are more subtle because they are embedded in the very heart of the system. Thus, in its constant quest to contain costs, the market has led to a drastic reduction in hospital capacity[714]. In the decade from 1993 to 2003 alone, America lost 703 hospitals and nearly 200,000 beds[715]. At the same time, emergency department use exploded by 26%, from 90 to 114 million visits. It is not uncommon for patients to be confined to the emergency department for 48 hours before being transferred to an appropriate care unit (e.g., neurology, cardiology, etc.). In this context, the tendency to limit the volume of hospitalizations as much as possible is understandable. Patients sometimes pay with their lives. This is what happened to Annie Jackson[716]. When this 60-year-old woman felt a pain in her chest, she dressed decently to make a good impression on the doctors and went to the hospital. She was given an electrocardiogram and a blood troponin test (a protein that increases in concentration during a heart attack). Both tests were abnormal, but not enough to clearly indicate a heart attack. The cardiology department was crowded and had already

---

713. J.F. Sullivan, "Officials Scrutinizing Doctor Bonuses in Managed Care Plans," *New York Times*, September 21, 1995; R. Kuttner, "Must Good HMOs Go Bad?", Part ¹, *op. cit.* (Introd., n. 27).

714. Institute of Medicine, *Hospital-Based Emergency Care: At the Breaking Point* (Washington: The National Academies Press, 2006); R. Wachter and K. Shojania, *Internal Bleeding...*, *op. cit.* (*supra*, n. 272), p. 405, note 31; D.L. Barlett & J.B. Steele, *Critical Condition*, *op. cit.* (Introd., n. 21), pp. 45-51.

715. Institute of Medicine, "The Future of the Emergency Care in the United States Health System," Report Brief, 2006, available online: http://www.iom.edu/Object.File/Master/35/014/Emergency%20Care.pdf; Institute of Medicine, "The Future of the Emergency Care: Key Finding and Recommendations," Fact Sheet, 2006, available online: http://www.iom.edu/Object.File/Master/35/040/Emergency%20Care%20Findings%20and%20Recs.pdf

716. Reported *in* R. Wachter and K. Shojania, *Internal Bleeding...*, *op. cit.* (*supra*, n. 272), pp. 99-103.

seen several patients from the emergency room. The doctor chose to discharge Annie Jackson. She died the next morning. She was found by her family curled up on the floor of her bathroom. "The expression on her face - suffering and surprise - reflected in the mirror above the sink was probably the last image she saw in her life[717]. In the words of the two physicians who analyzed this case after the fact in a book on "Medical Errors," the electrocardiogram and blood test, "although 'nonspecific,' were both clearly abnormal and therefore warranted admission, regardless of the degree of engorgement in the cardiac unit[718]." According to these physicians, it is possible that Annie Jackson was sent home all the more easily because she was black. Indeed, it has been shown that physicians in the United States are quicker to hospitalize white patients than black patients when faced with a strictly identical clinical picture[719]. "Depending on whether you are rich or poor...", La Fontaine might have written in a contemporary version of his famous fable[720].

It is clear that hospital capacity is not the only collateral victim of market forces. All areas are exposed to the accounting fury of the liberal zealots. It does not matter what the health logic is, as long as appearances remain intact and profit is at the end of the road. Of course, the cost of patient care must be controlled, but should that be the only control? As I have already said, it is dangerous to superimpose, under the pretext of semantic proximity, the concepts of rationalization and rationing. Rationalization is, in the words of the *Petit Larousse*, "to make a production process more efficient and less costly[721]". In other words, it is "doing better with less". At the same time, to ration is "to distribute in measured quantities[722]". This

---

717. R. Wachter and K. Shojania, *Internal Bleeding...*, *op. cit.* (*supra*, n. 272), at 102.
718. *Ibid.*
719. K.A. Schulman, J.A. Berlin & W. Harless, "The Effect of Race and Sex on Physicians' Recommendation for Cardiac Catheterization," *New England Journal of Medicine*, 1999, 340, pp. 618-626; R. Wachter & K. Shojania, *Internal Bleeding...*, *op. cit.* (*supra*, n. 272), p. 103.
720. Jean de La Fontaine, *Fables*, "The Animals Sick of the Plague".
721. *Petit Larousse Illustré*, Paris, Librairie Larousse, 1973.
722. *Ibid*

approach certainly makes it possible to "do better with less", but only in the financial domain. In fact, if one wanted to give this adage a plenary form, one would probably have to say "make more profit with less care". Obviously, this rephrasing significantly detracts from the charm of the original equation. Indeed, there is nothing honourable about accumulating large profits on the graves of unfortunate patients. For those who are doubtful, I suggest that you consider the following examples.

Despite its (self)declared genius, the market often lacks imagination. When called upon to make savings, it always starts by slashing the workforce and the payroll. Several studies have denounced the reduction in the number of nurses to a critical level[723]. For example, according to a remarkably well-documented article in the *Chicago Tribune*, "nursing services have been deliberately cut even in financially buoyant hospitals - the result of staffing reductions being used to preserve historic profit margins. In the U.S., "overwhelmed and inadequately trained nurses kill and injure thousands of patients each year as hospitals sacrifice safety for a better bottom line[724]." In response to the magnitude of the problem, several states have even legislated (or are considering legislation) to mandate a minimum number of nurses per patient, especially in sensitive units such as critical care[725]. California was the first to act in 1999 (effective July 2003)[726]. A study published in 2002 by Linda Aiken and her colleagues in the prestigious *Journal of the American Medical Association* (JAMA)

---

723. M.J. Berens, "Nursing Mistakes Kill, Injure Thousands," *Chicago Tribune*, September 10, 2000; S.G. Stolberg, "Patient Deaths Tied to Lack of Nurses," *New York Times*, August 8, 2002; Henry J. Kaiser Family Foundation, "Survey of Physicians and Nurses," 1999, available online: http://www.kff.org/kaiserpolls/1503-index.cfm; J. Shindul-Rothschild, D. Berry & E. Long-Middleton, "Where Have the Nurses Gone? Final Results of Our Patient Care Survey," *American Journal of Nursing*, 1996, 96, pp. 25-39; A. Trafford, "Second Opinion: Less Care for Patients," *Washington Post*, August 20, 2002.
724. M.J. Berens, "Nursing Mistakes Kill, Injure Thousands," *op. cit.* (*supra*, n. 309).
725
726. L.H. Aiken, *et al*, "Hospital Nurse Staffing and Patient Mortality, Nurse Burnout and Job Dissatisfaction," *JAMA*, 2002, 288, pp. 1987-1993.

validated the relevance of this choice[727]. Indeed, it was shown that the risk of a patient dying within 30 days of admission increased by 7% each time the number of patients per nurse increased by one.

In addition to nurses, hospitals have also attacked service workers, including cleaning staff[728]. In one high-profile case, more than 100 patients who contracted serious post-operative infections due to poor sanitary conditions sued the hospital where they were treated[729]. At least 16 deaths occurred, according to the lawyer handling the case. In another hospital in the same chain, faulty sterilizers were kept running for weeks without the surgeons' knowledge, operating on several hundred patients with contaminated instruments[730]. The director of the department of surgery resigned with a bang to mark his disapproval. In another facility, also under the control of the same chain, a more subtle approach was taken to maximize profits. Doctors subjected patients who had no need for them to heart surgeries that were as profitable as they were dangerous and disabling[731]. Although this is an extreme case, it appears that the problem of overtreatment and overmedication is becoming increasingly acute in the United States, especially for the wealthiest and/or most heavily insured patients[732]. There are two reasons for this. One, which can be admitted, is due to the hypervigilance of physicians and their fear of being sued. The other, less honourable reason is the tug-of-war between the various players in the health care system. While insurers are trying to limit the care offered to their members and the extent of reimbursements

---

727. *Ibid.*

728. D.L. Barlett & J.B. Steele, *Critical Condition, op. cit.* (Introd., n. 21), p. 116.

729. M. Davis, "Whistleblower Wants Tenet to Come Clean," July 25, 2003, TheStreet.com, available online: http://www.thestreet.com/stocks/melissadavid/10103544.html; D.L. Barlett & J.B. Steele, *Critical Condition, op. cit.* (Introd., n. 21), pp. 99-109.

730. *Ibid.*

731. *Ibid.*

732. N. Gibbs & A. Bower, "What Insiders Know About Our Health-Care System That the Rest of Us Need to Learn," *op. cit.* (*supra*, n. 220); S. Brownlee, "The Overtreated American," in *The Real State of the Union, op. cit.* (Introd., n. 8), pp. 129-138; D.L. Barlett & J.B. Steele, *Critical Condition, op. cit.* (Introd., n. 21), pp. 195-233.

granted, hospitals and pharmaceutical groups are trying as much as possible to "push" consumption in order to boost their profits and amortize increasingly expensive investments. It is a remarkable schizophrenia that prevents millions of Americans from having access to necessary care when hundreds of thousands of others are being force-fed unnecessary (and in some cases dangerous) tests, drugs and treatments.

This is the sorry state of the "best health care system in the world": denial of care, preventable deaths, untreated illnesses, unnecessary suffering, serial bankruptcies, an epidemic of errors, all for profit. The preamble of a law article published by John Humbach in 2001, sums up for me the horror of a system as brutal as it is abject. "A child is seriously ill. She will not live much longer if action is not taken promptly. However, her parents' HMO has refused to approve the treatment she needs. According to her doctor, the treatment has a good chance of working. It could extend her life by a few months or even years. The treatment is, however, expensive, more than her parents can afford. Moreover, the initial cost is just the beginning. As long as the child lives, she will need expensive care. That's a burden the HMO doesn't want to bear. As a result, in a few days - perhaps less - [the child] will go into a coma and - soon after - she will die[733]." Let me be dubious about the extent of such barbarity and the supposed miracles of an omniscient market. Regarding this last point, it may be interesting to point out, to add to the irony, that no country in the world supports such a massive and costly bureaucracy in health care as America. According to a study published in 2003 in the *New England Journal of Medicine*[734], the administration of the health care system consumes $1,059 per year per capita in the United States, compared to $307 in Canada! Between 1969 and 1999, the percentage of staff dedicated to administrative tasks increased from 18.2% to 27.3% in the United States. Canada only increased from

---

733. J.A. Humbach, "Criminal Prosecution for HMO Treatment Denial," *Health Matrix*, 2001, 11, pp. 147-187, citation p. 147.
734. S. Woolhandler, T. Campbell & D.U. Himmelstein, "Costs of Health Care Administration...," *op. cit.* (Introd., n. 27), 349, pp. 768-775.

16.0% to 19.1% between 1971 and 1996. Within the U.S., the cost of care and the burden of administrative costs are greater in market-based (*for-profit*) hospitals than in not-for-profit institutions[735]. More and more Americans, especially older ones, are being forced to cross the Canadian border to obtain medications[736]. Many others are going to Thailand, India or Malaysia for surgery[737]. For the unlucky ones with serious pathologies and exhausted finances, there are still the fairs[738]. Buy my nice hot doughnuts and this brave little girl will get a nice new kidney. For a hot dog or a t-shirt, you will offer prostheses to this road accident victim. Once again, I have a hard time measuring, at the end of this chapter, the backwardness of the pseudo social system of our old Europe. I also find it difficult to understand how leading politicians can persist in selling us again and again these liberal potions that have given America the worst health care system in the industrialized world. Just yesterday, France's new Prime Minister, Mr. Fillon, spoke on the radio about how he wanted "health care not only to be considered a burden. When we look at other countries around us, we see that health is an economic sector in its own right that drives the production of wealth and employment. Well, in our country too, health must be looked at from this angle[739]. Perhaps Mr. Fillon should be told that just because other countries have done it doesn't mean they have done it successfully. America shows how the subordination of the health care system to the primacy of the economy is positive for business, but disastrous for human health.

735. S. Woolhandler & D.U. Himmelstein, "Costs of Care and Administration at For-Profit and Other Hospitals in the United States," *New England Journal of Medicine* 1997; 336: 769-774.

736. D.L. Barlett & J.B. Steele, *Critical Condition*, *op. cit.* (Introd., n. 21), pp. 35-45.

737. "Outsourcing Your Heart," *op. cit.* (Introd., n. 76), pp. 44-47.

738. D.L. Barlett & J.B. Steele, *Critical Condition*, *op. cit.* (Introd., n. 21), pp. 9-11.

739. François Fillon, *in* "L'interview de Jean-Pierre Elkabbach", May 23, 2007 at 8:20 am, Europe 1.

To conclude

Since its origins, America has been a mythical land. For many of us, this nation is synonymous with dreams, envy, opulence, freedom, equity, and justice. As the song says, "over there, if you have the strength and the faith, gold is at your fingertips (...). Here, everything is set in stone, and you can't change anything, everything depends on your birth, and I wasn't born well (...). There, everything you deserve is yours[740]. When I was a child, "Pic-Pic", the butcher in my neighborhood, would accompany his thickest steaks with a loud "that's not America, my good lady! When a journalist tries to sell us an uncertain (or even calamitous) idea, he often explains that "American researchers have shown that...". When a declining singer wants to regain his artistic virginity, he resolutely announces that his new album will be (or has been) recorded "in the United States". When a publisher wants to boost sales, he proudly reports that "in the United States, such a book sold more than 170,000 copies in three months and made the *New York Times* bestseller list". Et cetera, et cetera, et cetera. One could multiply these examples ad infinitum, so much has the American dream penetrated our culture and our imaginations.

Of course, there is no denying that America is a noble and great country. This nation is exemplary for its democratic values. It is rich in contagious vigor. It has, on several occasions, saved Europe from overwhelming

---

740. Jean-Jacques Goldman, "Là-bas", in *Entre Gris Clair et Gris Foncé*, 1987.

barbarism. All this cannot be disputed. However, all the students in our high schools know that it is a long mathematical path from application to bijection. To say that America is noble and great does not mean that everything in America is noble and great. We must be careful not to believe that this country resembles our fantasies, the Hollywood series or the colorful anecdotes of our childhood.

Over the past thirty years, America has undergone profound changes. It is high time that we adapt our knowledge to this reality. Indeed, the ignorance that inhabits us carries with it two major embarrassments. First, it exposes us to the darkest manipulations by allowing the first miscreant to say anything without risk of being contradicted. Secondly, it leads us to consider as plausible, not to say desirable, policies that we would bitterly reject if we knew their true nature. Hidden behind the American myth, liberalism moves forward in hidden steps. It imposes itself without deliberation, strengthened by a clement a priori and an unquestionable guardian. Who would dare deny a word whose very root carries a promise of freedom? Who could reject a model that guarantees wealth and opulence to everyone "according to their efforts"? For that is what it is all about. Since I was old enough to read more than my first name, I have been hearing the same nonsense about the United States. In the United States, there is no unemployment. In the United States, those who work get rich. In the United States, only the lazy are poor. In the U.S., the poor are poor only in relative measure; they own houses, cars, televisions... In the U.S., the tax rate is derisory. In the United States, deserving students receive scholarships to pay for their education. In the U.S., those who really need it are cared for free through religious and private charity systems. In the United States, everything is bigger, better, stronger, more modern.

Conclusion: let's stop behaving like fearful backward people "stuck in the sanctuary of their pseudo social model". Let's do as they do in the United States, and the dusty old Europe will rise from its ashes. For a long time I believed this nonsense and for a long time I vociferated to the liberal Cassandras. Eight years in America have exhausted my illusions. The theory is beautiful, but the reality is brackish. I believe it was necessary to bear witness to this. I wanted to do it for Anna, for those poor people who see liberalism as a salvation, for those middle classes drifting under the wind of the sacrosanct market, for those children that the odious "socialist" model of old Europe still protects a little from the horrors of life. Of course, Europe has its shortcomings, its weaknesses, its indignities. However, it also has a humanist dimension that honors and transcends it. Bringing this humanism to life in the "globalist" era no doubt requires reforms and adaptations. It is not my place to discuss this here. However, it is up to me to emphasize how much the American liberal model is the antithesis of the founding values of my "old Europe". This model is barbaric, undignified, unjust and inequitable. Its successes, its achievements, its feats of arms are like the chansons de gestes of the old days: chimeras at the orders of their powerful sponsors. In the game of misconceptions, let's just remember, to conclude, some of the most perfidious ones.

No, liberalism does not bring financial prosperity to the many. Of all the so-called developed countries, America has the highest poverty rate[741]. Since 1980 and the advent of the great liberal night, the percentage of poor (income below the poverty line) has not changed significantly in the United States. However, the percentage of "very poor" (income below half the poverty line) has exploded. The very poor represented 43% of the total number of poor in 2005, up from 28% in 1976. Today, 5.5 percent of the

---

741. T.M. Smeeding, L. Rainwater & G. Burtless, "United States Poverty in a Cross-National Context," *op. cit.* (Introd., n. 44); David Jesuit & Timothy M. Smeeding, "Poverty Levels in the Developed World," *Luxembourg Income Study, Working Paper Series*, 2002, No. 321, Maxwell School of Citizenship and Public Affairs, Syracuse University, Syracuse, NY; *United Nations Development Programme, op. cit.* (Introd., n. 56); *The State of Working America 2006-2007, op. cit.* (Introd., n. 13), chap. 8.

U.S. population, or 16 million people, live in extreme poverty[742]. Of these 16 million souls, 6 million are children[743] !

The situation of the middle class has also deteriorated massively since the Reagan years[744]. Under the influence of the market, wage earners have seen their access to health insurance, a decent pension and reliable unemployment coverage drastically undermined. Whereas a skilled worker's salary was enough to keep an American household in the middle class in 1970, it now takes two incomes to achieve the same result[745]. Since the late 1970s, inequality between the rich and the "not-so-rich" has grown massively in the United States[746]. In three decades, the modest and middle classes have suffered a massive erosion of their resources, while the wealthiest few percent of Americans have seen their fortunes explode. To date, America is by far the most unequal developed country in terms of wealth distribution[747]: the wealthiest one percent of Americans hold 2.3 times more wealth than the bottom 80 percent of Americans[748].

---

742. US Census Bureau, Internet Release, 2006, http://www.census.gov/hhes/www/poverty/histpov/hstpov22.html; *The State of Working America 2006-2007*, *op. cit.* (Introd., n. 13), see Figure 6D.

743. US Census Bureau, Internet Release, 2006, http://pubdb3.census.gov/macro/032006/pov/new01_50_01.htm

744. M. Lind, "Are We Still a Middle Class Nation?" in *The Real State of the Union, op. cit.* (Introd., n. 8), pp. 15-26; T. Draut, *Strapped...*, *op. cit.* (Introd., n. 9); Elizabeth Warren & Amelia Warren Tyagi, *The Two Income Trap, op. cit.* (Introd., n. 10); M. Conlin & A. Bernstein, "Working... and Poor," *op. cit.* (chap. I, n. 39).

745. Elizabeth Warren & Amelia Warren Tyagi, *The Two Income Trap, op. cit.* (Introd., n. 10).

746. T. Piketty & E. Saez, "The Evolution of Top Incomes: a Historical and International Perspective," *op. cit.* (chap. I, n. 232); T. Piketty & E. Saez, "Income Inequality in the United States, 1913-1998," *op. cit.* (chap. I, n. 229); "Effective Federal Tax Rates", 1979-1997, The Congress of the United States, Congressional Budget Office, 2001; P. Krugman, "For Richer", *op. cit.* (Introd., n. 61); *The State of Working America 2006-2007, op. cit.* (Introd., n. 13), chaps. 1, 3, 5; M.R. Rank, *One Nation Underprivileged...*, *op. cit.* (Introd., n. 10), pp. 157-163; T. Draut, *Strapped...*, *op. cit.* (Introd., n. 9), pp. 21-22.

747. *The State of Working America 2006-2007*, *op. cit.* (Introd., n. 13), chap. 8, see, in particular, table 8.16.

748. *The State of Working America 2006-2007*, *op. cit.* (Introd., n. 13), chap. 5, see, in particular, table 5.3.

No, the "market" is not doing better than the public sector with the same resources. In 1992, the Bush administration commissioned a report from the official Office of Management and Budget to assess the effects of the broad privatization of the economy that began under Reagan. It concluded: "After years of efforts to transfer government prerogatives to private companies, the White House now recognizes that contractors are wasting vast amounts of money.... [This report represents] the most incisive government critique yet of a central precept of the Reagan-Bush era: the idea that private companies can do the federal government's job better and for less money[749]." One example is the privatization movements in health care and education. These have proved to be disastrous: huge salaries for managers, stock market manipulation, accounting malpractice, increased administrative burdens, reduced efficiency, dismissal of competent professionals and recruitment (in the best of cases) of poorly paid, unqualified staff. In the health and education sectors, the private sector has not done any better than the public sector. On the contrary, in contrast to the liberal rhetoric, the latter has proved to be less costly "in use" for better operational results[750].

No, lower taxes do not mean more individual wealth. In the final analysis, funding must be found for the judicial, educational, health or pension systems. This funding can come from the community or the consumer. Because they contribute so little to put their children through college or to get chemotherapy, many Europeans - and especially the French - tend to forget the exorbitant cost of these services and consider that Americans are fortunate to have such thrifty rulers. This reasoning is as partial as it is primitive. The reason Americans pay less tax than Europeans is that the scope of taxation is much narrower in the United States than in Europe. Of all the developed countries, America has the least generous

---

749. K. Schneider, "US Cites Waste in Its Contracts," *New York Times*, December 2, 1992.
750. On education: A. Molnar, *Giving Kids the Business...*, *op. cit.* (Introd., n. 28); for health: D.L. Barlett & J.B. Steele, *Critical Condition*, *op. cit.* (Introd., n. 21).

To conclude

social system[751]. In Uncle Sam's case, the state does not finance health insurance (except partially for pensioners and the most needy), maternity leave, childcare, sick leave or a judicial investigation (except, in theory, for the most needy). On Uncle Sam's side, unemployment insurance is reduced to a minimum (only 35% of the unemployed are compensated, for a maximum of 26 weeks at an average of 47% of the original salary[752]). On Uncle Sam's side, public financing of pensions borders on anorexia (the "social security" system only replaces an average of 39 per cent of the income of those who retire at age 65, a percentage that should fall to 30 per cent by 2030[753]). On Uncle Sam's side, university tuition fees are astronomical not only in the private sector ($19,000/year on average; ~ 14,650 euros) but also in the public sector ($5,000/year on average; ~ 3,850 euros)[754].

In the end, I'm not sure that middle and lower class Americans are benefiting from the tax frugality of their leaders. Perhaps some of my compatriots should check their calculators before expressing their disgust with taxes. Contrary to what I often hear, based on various anecdotes, taxes do not only serve to fatten the lazy at the expense of the active. It supports all of us, the sick, schoolchildren, students, pregnant women, pensioners, the disabled, etc. I believe that we should keep some distance from these stories of abuse, which are certainly terribly striking for the

---

751. V.-M. Ritakallio, "Trends of Poverty and Income Inequality in Cross-National Comparisons," *op. cit.*; M.R. Rank, *One Nation Underprivileged...*, *op. cit.* (Introd., n. 10), pp. 60-62; J. Iceland, *Poverty in America...*, *op. cit.* (Introd., n. 9), p. 65; *The State of Working America 2006-2007*, *op. cit.* (Introd., n. 13), chap. 8.

752. US General Accounting Office, "Unemployment Insurance: Role of Safety Net for Low-Wage Workers Is Limited," GAO-01-181, December 2000; Maurice Emsellem, *et al*, "Failing the Unemployed," Economic Policy Institute, Center on Budget and Policy Priorities, 2002.

753. A.H. Munnell & P. Perun, "An Update on Private Pensions", *op. cit.* (chap. I, n. 208); A.H. Munnell & A. Sunden, "Private Pensions: Coverage and Benefit Trends," *op. cit.* (chap. I, n. 211); Social Security Online, Benefit Calculators, http://www.ssa.gov/OACT/quickcalc/index.html

754. T.D. Snyder, A.G. Tan & C.M. Hoffman, "Digest of Education Statistics 2005," *op. cit.* (chap. II, n. 65), table 313.

Mad in U.S.A.: The ravages of the American model

mind, but whose message is basically unrepresentative of the general use of taxes. If we were to give up the latter, the bill would eventually be much heavier for those of us who are not part of the most privileged classes. Obviously, this deterioration would not only be financial, it would also have a human dimension. Indeed, the taxing parsimony so dear to the liberal zealots masks a terrible brutality. In America, people die and suffer because they do not have enough money to access the health care system[755]. In America, people die and suffer because they cannot afford a competent lawyer[756]. In America, newborns die from being black instead of white[757]. In America, women die from being black instead of white[758]. In America, men toil for poverty wages that do not even allow them to lift their families out of poverty[759].

No, the poor are not depraved slackers who are resistant to effort. Even in times of strong growth, the U.S. market does not create enough jobs for all potential applicants[760]. When the unemployment rate threatens to fall below 4-5%, the central bank takes monetary action to "slow down the economy," which in ordinary language means maintaining an incompressible pool of structural unemployed[761]. 25% of jobs pay wages too low

---

755. S.S. Sered & R. Fernandopulle, *Uninsured in America...*, *op. cit.* (Introd., n. 21); D.L. Barlett & J.B. Steele, *Critical Condition*, *op. cit.* (Introd., n. 21).
756. *D.R. Dow*, Executed On a Technicality..., op. cit. *(Introd., n. 20); J. Reiman,* The Rich Get Richer and the Poor Get Prison..., op. cit. *(Introd., n. 19)*.
757. Center for Disease Control and Prevention, "Infant Mortality Rates...," *op. cit.* (Introd., n. 81), table 23.
758. Cathy J. Bradley, Charles W. Given & Caralee Roberts, Race, Socioeconomic Status, and Breast Cancer Treatment and Survival, *Journal of the National Cancer Institute*, 2002, 94, 490-496.
759. An example is St. Anna, which I have had occasion to discuss in detail; see also D.K. Shipler, *The Working Poor...*, *op. cit.* (Introd., n. 68); B. Shulman, *The Betrayal of Work...*, *op. cit.* (Introd., n. 10); B. Ehrenreich, *Nickel and Dimed*, *op. cit.* (Introd., n. 67).
760. Tomothy Bartik, "Poverty Jobs and Subsidized Employment," *Challenge*, 2002, 45, pp. 100-111; T. Bartik, *Jobs For the Poor...*, *op. cit.* (chap. I, n. 254).
761. M.R. Rank, *One Nation Underprivileged...*, *op. cit.* (Introd., n. 10), pp. 152-156; Louis Uchitelle, "Companies Try Dipping Deeper Into the Labor Pool," *New York Times*, March 26, 2000.

to lift a family of four out of poverty[762]. Five million full-time workers live below the poverty line[763]. One in four Americans earns less than 65% of the national median wage (the ratio is one in ten in France or Germany)[764].

In such a picture, the question is not whether there will be poor people, but who will be poor, because it is inevitable that some will be poor. When the market offers only limited access to excellent, decently paid jobs, it does not matter what the individual characteristics of the players are, the percentage of castaways is written into the structure of the game. If every child in America had the intelligence and pugnacity of the greatest tomorrow, poverty would not disappear. There would still be a shortage of jobs (the market would see to that if necessary) and poverty wages would still be the lot of 25 percent of workers. The Bureau of Labor Statistics (BLS) projects that 47% of available jobs in 2014 will be "unskilled. Only 26% of all jobs will require a college degree[765]. Of the 30 activities that are expected to grow the most until 2014, 37% do not require a degree and are associated with "very low wages" according to the BLS terminology. The question that arises is, therefore, relatively simple: is it acceptable to leave this cohort of poor people, inherent to the very nature of the liberal system, to rot on the side of the road by alleging its moral indignity?

No, equal opportunity does not exist without strong state interventionism. America has the lowest inter-generational social mobility of all developed countries[766]. In the United States, the magnitude of the estimated relationship (correlation) between the incomes of a father and

---

762. M. Conlin & A. Bernstein, "Working... and Poor," *op. cit.* (chap. I, n. 39); B. Shulman, *The Betrayal of Work...*, *op. cit.* (Introd., n. 10); *The State of Working America 2006-2007*, *op. cit.* (Introd., n. 13), chap. 3, table 3.7.
763. Bureau of Labor Statistics, "The Profile of the Working Poor 2003," Report 983, 2005.
764. T.M. Smeeding, L. Rainwater & G. Burtless, "United States Poverty in a Cross-National Context," *op. cit.* (Introd., n. 44), Figure 2.
765. Daniel E. Hecker, "Employment Outlook 2004-2014," *Monthly Labor Review*, Bureau of Labor Statistics, 2005, see table 6.
766. The State of Working America 2006-2007, op. cit. *(Introd., n. 13), see chap. 2.*

his son has doubled since the great liberal night of the Reagan years. It now stands at around 0.60. This means that if the father is among the poorest 5% of the population, then the probability that his son will one day belong to the wealthiest half of the population is only 11%. The probability that the son will be among the poorest 20 percent is over 50 percent. The probability that he will reach the richest 20 percent stagnates below 2 percent[767]. These results are related to the extreme shortcomings of the American education system. The decentralization of school funding means that America spends less money on educating poor children than it does on more affluent children[768]. The poorest schools also concentrate the least competent teachers[769]. It is not surprising, then, that only 3 percent of students enrolled in the 146 top-performing U.S. universities come from the bottom 25 percent of families[770].

Modern neurophysiology has shown that if the brain does not receive the stimulation it needs to build itself at the right moment, it builds itself

---

767. G.R. Solon, "Intergenerational Income Mobility in the United States," 1992, *op. cit.* (chap. I, n. 102), 82, pp. 393-408; G.R. Solon, "Intergenerational Income Mobility in the United States," 1989, *op. cit.* (chap. I, n. 102).

768. "The Funding Gap 2006," *op. cit.* (chap. II, n. 61); J. Kozol, *Savage Inequalities, op. cit.* (Introd., n. 18); D.K. Shipler, *The Working Poor..., op. cit.* (Introd., n. 68), chap. 9.

769. J. Mathews, "Top Teachers Rare in Poor Schools," *op. cit.* (chap. II, n. 133); Cynthia D. Prince, "The Challenge of Attracting Good Teachers and Principals to Struggling Schools," American Association of School Administrators, Arlington, Virginia, January 2002; Richard M. Ingersoll, "Why Do High-Poverty Schools Have Difficulty Staffing Their Classrooms with Qualified Teachers?", University of Pennsylvania, report prepared for: The Center for American Progress and the Institute for America's Future, November 2004; Thomas G. Carroll, Kathleen Fulton, Karen Abercrombie, & Irene Yoon, "Fifty Years After the Brown V. Board of Education: A Two-Tiered Education System," report prepared for: The National Commission on Teaching and America's Feature, May 2004, Washington, DC; K. Grossman, B. Beaupre, & R. Rossi, "Poorest Kids Often Wind Up With the Weakest Teachers," *Chicago Sun-Times*, September 7, 2001; Chris Davis & Matthew Doig, "Poor Schools Can't Keep Good Teachers," *op. cit.* (chap. II, n. 133); "A Shared Responsibility...," *op. cit.*

770. *A.P. Carnevale & S.J. Rose,* Socioeconomic Status, Race/Ethnicity, and Selective College Admission, op. cit. *(chap. II, n. 176).*

To conclude

badly[771]. However, the situation of deprivation is often accompanied by a form of cognitive under-stimulation. As Guao and Harris write in a fine study, "poverty has a large negative effect on cognitive stimulation, and cognitive stimulation has a large positive effect on intellectual development;... most of the effect of poverty on intellectual development operates through this pathway[772]. When disadvantaged children are adopted between the ages of 4 and 6 by wealthy families, their intellectual performance (IQ) skyrockets[773]. The greater the socio-economic level of the adopting family, the greater the gain. Similarly, the life trajectory of poor children enrolled in high-quality kindergarten between the ages of 3 and 4 is profoundly altered (these "experimental" children are placed back in their native environment at age 5). As adults, 35 years after the end of the experiment, these children show greater academic success, lower unemployment, higher earnings, and lower delinquency[774].

Knowing that poverty severely compromises the development of the individual, how can one claim that a poor child has had the same opportunities as his or her well-to-do neighbor? How can we claim without blinking that we believe in "equality of opportunity, but not in equality of destiny, because it depends largely on the efforts that each person is willing to make[775]"? If this were the case, how can we explain the fact

---

771. For a review: J.P. Shonkoff & D.A. Phillips (eds.), *From Neurons to Neighborhoods...*, *op. cit.* (chap. I, n. 121), chap. 8; Bruce D. Perry, "Childhood Experience and the Expression of Genetic Potential...," *op. cit.* (chap. I, n. 133); for a more specific illustration, see Hubel and Wiesel's seminal work on the development of the visual system: D.H. Hubel & T.N. Wiesel, "The Period of Susceptibility to the Physiological Effects of Unilateral Eye Closure in Kittens," *op. cit.* (chap. I, n. 135); D.H. Hubel & T.N. Wiesel, "Single-Cell Responses in Striate Cortex of Kittens Deprived of Vision in One Eye," *op. cit.* (chap. I, n. 135).
772. G. Guo & K.M. Harris, "The Mechanisms Mediating the Effects of Poverty on Children Intellectual Development," *op. cit.* (chap. I, n. 138).
773. Michel Duyme, Annick-Camille Dumaret & Stanislaw Tomkiewicz, "How Can We Boost IQs of 'dull children'? A Late Adoption Study," *op. cit.* (chap. I, n. 154).
774. L.J. Schweinhart, "The High/Scope Perry Preschool Study Through Age 40: summary, conclusions and frequently asked questions," *op. cit.*
775. Henry de Castries, interview given to the newspaper *Les Echos*, quoted in *Marianne*, September 16-22, 2006, p. 7.

that intergenerational mobility, and therefore equality of opportunity, is substantially lower in the United States than in European countries with a high level of social interventionism, such as Sweden or Finland[776]? When the socio-economic inequalities of birth are not balanced, even partially, by the community, the poorest find themselves in a situation of almost insurmountable handicap. Their bankruptcy is then, not inevitable (miracles do exist), but highly probable.

No, the U.S. unemployment figures are not necessarily flattering. First of all, it should be remembered that the incarceration rate in the United States is staggering, especially among disadvantaged minorities (725 per 100,000 of the total population; 2,500 per 100,000 of the black population; by comparison, it is 91 in France, 96 in Germany, 66 in Finland and 58 in Japan[777]). This prison frenzy removes large numbers of declared candidates for unemployment from the market. As Bruce Western and Katherine Beckett have shown, when this parameter is taken into account, it appears that American workers suffer a higher unemployment rate than their European counterparts[778].

If one were to overlook the problem of incarceration, could one say that unemployment is lower in the United States than in Western Europe? On the surface, yes. In practice, no. This inconsistency is due to a double logical and semantic hiatus. Indeed, all the children in our schools know that one cannot compare carrots and cabbages quantitatively. But when we talk about employment in Europe and the United States, we are not

---

776. B. Mazumder, "Revised Estimates of Intergenerational Income Mobility in the United States," *op. cit.* (chap. I, n. 97), p. 4; G.R. Solon, "Cross Country Differences in Earnings Mobility," *op. cit.* (chap. I, n. 97), 16, pp. 59-66; *The State of Working America 2006-2007, op. cit.* (Introd., n. 13), chap. 2, figure 2G.

777. OECD, Factbook 2007, "Economic, Environmental and Social Statistics...," *op. cit.* (chap. II, n. 26); Human Right Watch, "Race and Incarceration in the United States," *op. cit.* (chap. II, n. 27); B. Western & K. Beckett, "How Unregulated Is the US Labor Market?", *op. cit. (supra,* n. 27), pp. 1030-1060.

778. B. Western & K. Beckett, "How Unregulated Is the U.S. Labor Market? (*supra,* n. 27), p. 1052.

To conclude

talking about the same thing at all. Anna has two jobs and one child[779]. She works 7 days a week for a total of 46 hours and a salary of $1,070 (825 euros). She has no health insurance. She has no paid leave and no maternity leave. When she gets sick, she gets nothing and risks being fired without notice (this has happened to her). She does receive some assistance (tax credit, meal ticket), but these do not allow her, even when added to her salary, to exceed the poverty line.

Of course, it may be acceptable for millions of men and women working full time to be confined below the poverty line, without health insurance, without paid leave, without sick pay. It may be acceptable that an employee is fired without notice because he or she is sick, or has had the effrontery to complain, or because the boss has found "cheaper work elsewhere. We can. However, we can also say that the richest country on the planet could provide those who work with a decent standard of living, social protection, health insurance, paid maternity leave, etc. When the 13,000 richest families in the United States have an annual income equal to that of the 20 million poorest families, when the rich have become "super-rich" and the poor "super-poor" in three decades, when the tax rate for the wealthiest 0.01% of taxpayers has dropped from 70% to 35% in the same period, when 5% of households own 60% of the national wealth, when Mr. Welch receives his last year's paycheck from the U.S. government, and when the U.S. government has no money to spend on the economy. Welch receives 10,000 years of Anna's salary for his last year at the head of General Electric[780], one might think that there must be some room for manoeuvre.

No, the different agents in the market are not dealing on a "level playing field. To repeat: the U.S. market does not create enough jobs for

---

779. See, within the first section: "Anna: at the heart of reality".
780. P. Krugman, "For Richer," *op. cit.* (Introd., n. 61); T. Piketty & E. Saez, "How Progressive Is the US Federal Tax System…", *op. cit.* (chap. I, n. 236), 21, pp. 3-24; *The State of Working America 2006-2007, op. cit.* (Introd., n. 13), chap. 5.

all potential applicants[781]. When the unemployment rate drops too low, the central bank intervenes[782]. When an individual has accumulated 5 years of welfare, he is permanently excluded from the system[783]. When an employee goes on strike, his company can legally replace him with another employee, and this is permanent[784]. When a group of employees tries to create a union, companies do not hesitate to exert, often successfully, intense pressure (legal or not) to break the attempt (harassment, threats, suspension, dismissal, relocation, etc.)[785]. Faced with such a picture, how could the game be fair? Employees who do not possess any rare or valuable skills (and they are the majority) are necessarily in an extremely weak position. The company has the right to impose its conditions, even if they are revolting[786]. Anna has to work, she has to feed her son, she has to pay her rent, even if it means giving in to the unacceptable. If she refuses, another Anna will take the job. In the final analysis, only the state can balance the relationship by bringing some humanity to the sacrosanct law of supply and demand.

*

* *

---

781. Tomothy Bartik, "Poverty Jobs and Subsidized Employment," *Challenge*, 2002, 45, pp. 100-111; T. Bartik, *Jobs For the Poor...*, *op. cit.* (chap. I, n. 254).

782. M.R. Rank, *One Nation Underprivileged...*, *op. cit.* (Introd., n. 10), pp. 152-156; Louis Uchitelle, Companies "Try Dipping Deeper Into the Labor Pool," *New York Times*, March 26, 2000.

783. S.S. Sered & R. Fernandopulle, *Uninsured in America...*, *op. cit.* (Introd., n. 21), pp. 52-56; A. Weil & K. Finegold, *Welfare Reform...*, *op. cit.* (chap. I, n. 19), Introduction.

784. Lance Compa, "Unfair Advantage," *op. cit.* (chap. I, n. 307).

785. Lance Compa, "Unfair Advantage," *op. cit.* (chap. I, n. 307); Kate Bronfenbrenner, "Uneasy Terrain," *op. cit.* (chap. I, n. 307); Chirag Metha & Nick Theodore, "Undermining the Right to Organize," *op. cit.* (chap. I, n. 307); Robert J. Flanagan, "Has Management Strangled US Unions?", *op. cit.* (chap. I, n. 307); American Federation of Labor and Congress of Industrial Organizations (AFL-CIO), "The Silent War," *op. cit.* (chap. I, n. 305).

786. For a demonstration by example, B. Ehrenreich, *Nickel and Dimed*, *op. cit.* (Introd., n. 67).

To conclude

At the end of this book, it seems important to me to question the true nature of our values. Is this American model, without mercy or compassion, compatible with our history and culture? What kind of society do we want to build? What kind of world do we want to leave to our children tomorrow? Uncle Sam is proposing a path of growing divorce between an extraordinarily privileged opulent elite and a hard-working mass that is becoming poorer every day. The richest prosper beyond reason. The poorest collapse into extreme destitution. The middle classes drift slowly but inevitably towards their decline. Millions of people work hard, full time or more, but cannot rise above the poverty line. Millions of unfortunate people suffer and die from not having access to the most basic health care. Millions of children grow up in undignified conditions, denied even the right to a decent education. Men (sometimes innocent) are sentenced to death because they cannot afford to pay for their defense. Old men are reduced to selling Coca-Cola cans found in the garbage to scrap merchants for food. Nowhere in the industrialized world are those born poor more likely to remain so. The ultimate sign of these drifts: the time has come for class ghettos. The enclaves of extreme poverty, generally located on the outskirts of cities[787], were already known. In recent years, communities of extreme wealth have appeared, complete with fences, surveillance cameras, guard dogs and private security guards[788].

This path laid out by post-Reagan America is immoral, unjust and degrading. It is based on a set of constantly reaffirmed but odiously false assumptions: "anyone who really wants to work can", "everyone is treated according to his or her merit", "liberalism brings material well-being to the majority", etc., etc. In truth, the American liberal system reinforces poverty, it impoverishes the middle classes, it degrades the living conditions of the majority, it does not provide - far from it - enough work for

---

787. P. Jargowsky, *Poverty and Places, op. cit.* (chap. I, n. 70).
788. *S. Low,* Behind the Gates: Life Security and the Pursuit of Happiness in Fortress America *(New York: Routledge, 2003); E. Blakely & M.G. Snyder,* Fortress America: Gated communities in the United States, *Washington, DC, Brookings Institution Press, 1997.*

all, it takes away from millions of children any hope for the future, it functions for the main benefit of a wealthy elite, it places profit before life and the economy before people. A short while ago, while I was in a cab on my way to the San Francisco airport, a US senator whose name I have lost, tried to justify this last choice on a local radio station. The premise was quite simple: if the economy is doing well, then people will be doing well. We must therefore put the well-being, not of man, but of the economy, at the center of our concerns. This is a fine equation, but it lacks an important term: equity. Indeed, the link postulated by our learned senator can only be realized if the benefits of growth are distributed in a more or less homogeneous way over all economic actors. When the surpluses are diverted from the majority to a well-born elite, nothing goes right. This is precisely what is happening in America. Since the end of the last recession in November 2001[789], America has experienced relatively robust growth (averaging around 3 per cent per year)[790]. Yet the poverty rate has risen from 11.7 percent to 12.6 percent[791]. Between 2001 and 2004 - the latest figures compiled - the top 20% of households saw their wealth increase by 2% while the bottom 20% of households gave up 9%[792]. In 2001, the wealthiest one percent of Americans had 173 times the median wealth. By 2004, the factor had risen to 190[793]. The healthy economy benefits mostly the most affluent in a liberal country.

Of course, it is easy to look the other way and say "it's not true" and that the most fragile among us are just assisted, drunken, amoral miscreants. In the same way, it is easy to explain that dissenting voices are necessarily the work of "sidereal morons", as I have heard, for example, about Viviane

---

789. US Census Bureau, Internet Release, http://www.census.gov/hhes/www/poverty/hist-pov/recessn.html

790. OECD, Countries Statistical Profiles, 2007, USA, Internet Release, http://stats.oecd.org/WBOS/Default.aspx

791. US Census Bureau, Internet Release, http://www.census.gov/hhes/www/poverty/pover-ty05/pov05fig04.pdf

792. The State of Working America 2006-2007, op. cit. *(Introd., n. 13), chap. 5, table 5.4.*

793. The State of Working America 2006-2007, op. cit. *(Introd., n. 13), chap. 5, figure 5B.*

To conclude

Forrester, Bernard Maris or Philippe Simonot, all authors of iconoclastic works on the economy and its errors[794]. It is also convenient to absolve oneself of any responsibility by proclaiming oneself "Christian", hand on heart, like George Bush Junior ostentatiously draped in the practice of a faith whose words and essence he has obviously not understood. Wasn't it Jesus himself who bitterly denounced "the hypocrites [who] like to camp out in the synagogues and crossroads to pray, so that they may be seen" (Matthew 6:5)[795]? They are "those who claim to be righteous before men, but God knows [their] hearts" (Luke 16:14). This conservative and liberal America, which goes so far as to display its faith on its currency ("*In God we trust*"), should perhaps remember the sayings of a religion that it claims so prominently in the media. "Be compassionate, as your Father is compassionate" (Luke 6:36). "Whatever you want people to do for you, do it for them" (Matthew 7:12). "Is there a poor man among your brothers in any of the cities of your land which the LORD your God has given you? You shall not harden your heart nor close your hand to your poor brother, but you shall open your hand to him and give him what he lacks" (Deuteronomy 15:7-8). "Whoever mocks the poor offends his creator, whoever laughs at the poor will not go unpunished" (Proverbs 17:5), "Whoever shuts his ear to the cry of the weak will also cry out, and no one will answer him" (Proverbs 21:13). "You shall not exploit your neighbor or rob him (...). You shall love your neighbor as yourself" (Leviticus 19:13 and 18). This last law is even the most important of all, it is the law that transcends all the commandments, it is "the Law in its fullness" (Romans 13:10). Woe to those who turn away from it and "neglect the most serious matters of the Law, justice, mercy and good faith" (Matthew 23:23). We could probably continue this game of quotations for a long time. The ones

---

794. Viviane Forrester, *L'Horreur économique*, Paris, Fayard, 1996; Philippe Simonot, *L'Erreur économique*, Paris, Denoël, 2004; Bernard Maris, *Lettre ouverte aux gourous de l'économie qui nous prennent pour des imbéciles (Open letter to the economic gurus who take us for fools)*, Paris, Albin Michel, 1999.

795. For this and the following quotations: Bible de Jérusalem, Desclée de Brouwer, Paris, Éditions du Cerf, 1973.

in this paragraph, however, are enough, I believe, to underline how far the proclaimed faith of conservative America is from its ways of life.

For those that religion leaves cold, there is still morality. Is it humanly possible to accept this economic barbarism? I hear people say that we have no choice, that globalization forces us. I may be a donkey, but it does not seem to me that this factor can account for the fact that the richest country on the planet is the one that, when compared to other developed nations, has the highest percentage of poor people, the highest infant mortality rate, the poorest social welfare system and the lowest life expectancy. Globalization is also hitting Europe and Japan. This does not prevent these countries from maintaining, by political choice, a broad and humanistic social system. It does not seem to me that Sweden, Norway or Finland, countries renowned for their vigorous collective generosity - and their lush taxes - are on the verge of economic chaos. As Paul Krugman points out, the choice is there. In the words of the renowned economist's *New York Times* article, "Many observers seem determined to blame global markets for a host of economic and social dysfunctions in their countries, even though the evidence points indisputably to primarily domestic - and often political - causes.... Many on the right use the rhetoric of globalization to defend the idea that the economy can no longer be expected to fulfill any social obligation (...). [Yet] none of the constraints on the U.S. economy and social policies come from abroad. We have the resources to take far better care of our poor and unfortunate than we do; if our policies have become increasingly narrow, that is a political choice, not something imposed on us by an anonymous force. We cannot escape responsibility for our actions by claiming that the global market has forced us to do this or that[796].

Before concluding definitively, let's try for a moment to plunge into the future and imagine the incredulity of our children in the face of this American economic system that we are so fond of citing as an example.

---

796. Paul Krugman, "We Are Not the World," *New York Times*, February 13, 1997.

To conclude

Will our descendants understand that, in the midst of extraordinary prosperity, we could have allowed men to rot from extreme poverty in filthy and threatening ghettos? Will our descendants understand that we have refused, on financial grounds, to care for our fellow human beings, sometimes at the risk of letting them die? Will our descendants forgive us for having offered so much wealth to so few and so much misery to so many? Those who have difficulty answering these questions should look back at our history and remember, for example, the barbarity of the enslavement of women and the slavery of blacks. In 1860, men could not ignore the ignominy of these practices. Yet, they were often justified with incredible cynicism. The greatest minds of the time offered their pen to the exercise without shame. Thus, for example, Paul Broca, founding father of the theory of cerebral localizations and of modern neurology, declared in 1859 that there was "a remarkable relationship between the development of intelligence and the volume of the brain (...). On the average, the mass of the brain is greater in adults than in old men, in men than in women, in eminent men than in mediocre men, and in superior races than in inferior races[797]. For Carl Vogt, another eminent neuroanatomist of the middle of the nineteenth century, "by its rounded apex and its less developed posterior lobe, the brain of the Negro resembles that of our children, and by the protuberance of the parietal lobe that of our women (...). The adult Negro proceeds, in regard to his intellectual faculties, from the nature of the child, the woman, and the senile white man[798]." Abraham Lincoln himself ventured to denounce, a few years before the outbreak of the Civil War, the "equality of Negroes". "Nonsense [our man said]! How long, in the government of a God great enough to create and conduct the universe, shall there be dishonest men to sell, and fools to swallow, such a piece of low demagogy[799]?" Are we better than these men when we evoke the economic reality or the inescapable weight of an anonymous

---

797. Quoted *in* G. Bechtel, *Délires racistes et savants fous*, Paris, Plon, 2002, p. 19.
798. C. Cerf & V. Navasky, The Experts Speak, New York, Villard, 1998, p. 22.
799. *Ibid.*

Mad in U.S.A.: The ravages of the American model

globalization to justify the intolerable drifts of a liberal system whose extreme violence we know?

In short, the American economic system that we adore so much is infinitely harsh. Behind the mythical "new world" lie, for millions of men and women, the evils of cruelty, injustice, precariousness, inequality, cynicism and atavism. Our "old Europe", so decried for its allegedly obsolete and sterile social systems, would be well advised, before deserting its founding values, to measure precisely the nature of the model it covets. Fraternity, equity, humanism, compassion, sharing, these words certainly have a cost, but they are what makes us worthy of our humanity. May Europe not lose itself on the altar of liberal madness. May it also remember its history and the sufferings it has gone through for more than 2000 years. Age is sometimes a sign, not of vile senility, but of wise plenitude.